King of the Mountain

Presented to St. Laurence
Seminary, by the author,
in memory of the late
Rev. Dr. John Murray
Atwood.

B.J. Chandler
(Student, SLU, 1950-53)
Kingsville, Texas
October 11, 1989

Courtesy of LIFE Picture Service, photo by Michael Stern

Salvatore Giuliano   **1922–1950**

King of the Mountain

*The
Life and Death
of
Giuliano the Bandit*

Billy Jaynes Chandler

NORTHERN ILLINOIS UNIVERSITY PRESS

DeKalb, Illinois   1988

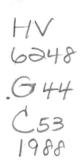
© 1988 by Northern Illinois University Press
Published by the Northern Illinois University Press, DeKalb, Illinois 60115
Manufactured in the United States of America
Design by Julia L. Fauci

Library of Congress Cataloging-in-Publication Data

Chandler, Billy Jaynes.
    King of the mountain : the life and death of Giuliano the Bandit /
Billy Jaynes Chandler.
    p.   cm.
    Bibliography: p.
    ISBN 0-87580-140-4
    1. Giuliano, Salvatore, 1922–1950.   2. Brigands and robbers—
Italy—Biography.   I. Title.
HV6248.G44C53 1988
364.1'55—dc19   88-5322
[B]   CIP

To the memory of the Reverend Doctor John Murray Atwood,
patron, teacher, and friend

Contents

Preface

BY THE TIME in 1980 that I first visited Montelepre, the Sicilian town which is the setting of this true story, it gave the appearance of being much farther away from Salvatore Giuliano's time than the three decades that actually had passed since his death. His mountain still looked the same, one assumes, but the town had changed much. It was no longer as isolated. Palermo, Sicily's capital, was less than an hour away by paved, though still winding, road. Where once the town had looked as if time had stood still for centuries, apartment buildings of three, four, and five stories sat on its periphery and modern homes dotted the lower slopes of the mountains around. By 1984, a motor hotel had opened between Montelepre and its sister town of Giardinello—something that would have been appreciated greatly by the journalists who flocked to Montelepre in the late 1940s to seek Giuliano out for an interview or just learn more about him. Now, one had to be in the town's old center to clearly imagine him creeping down in darkness from Sagana Mountain to direct a few rounds at the *carabiniere* barracks or slipping into the house on Via Castrense di Bello to see his mother, not to mention holding off an army with his tiny independence army atop Monte d'Oro. By 1980, too, the surviving members of Giuliano's outlaw band had all been released from prison, although not many years had passed since 1964, when the last arrest of one of their number had taken place.

Giuliano's remains no longer lay in the modest burial niche in which they were first placed in 1950 but in a marble coffin in the ornate Giuliano family chapel on the cemetery's main walkway. Of gothic lines, it was erected in 1952 at considerable cost after a design furnished by the firebrand Swedish journalist, Maria Cyliakus, who long cherished memories of her night with Giuliano. The elder Salvatore, Giuliano's father, had joined his son there in 1955, as had Mamma

Giuliano in 1971. The tomb, the town's only tourist attraction still drew a steady trickle of visitors. Although most were from Sicily or mainland Italy, not a few came from farther away. Included in the guestbook were the names of a good many Americans of Sicilian descent, some of Giuliano's cousins among them.

After leaving Giuliano's burial place, the visitor had to walk only a few steps to enter the Pisciotta family chapel. It housed the remains of Giuliano's friend, Gaspare, and, constructed later than the Giuliano chapel, was visibly more costly, as if its builders had intended to outdo the Giulianos. Atop his marble coffin—as if there were no cause for shame—sat a large and handsome photograph of Gaspare, who of all men Giuliano loved the most.

This book tells Giuliano's story and sometimes Gaspare's, too. I have written it as a work of scholarship, but I hope that it will serve also the general reader who wants a truthful account of Giuliano. Some traditional rural bandits particularly deserve serious study, not only for the attention that they claimed but also for what their lives reveal about their societies. They stand out in a class of their own in the worldwide history of banditry. Lampião of backlands Brazil in the 1920s and 1930s and Jesse James of the post-Civil War American West quickly come to mind, and so does Sicily's Salvatore Giuliano.

On Giuliano, in English, the only book that has been available is Gavin Maxwell's *Bandit,* which is long out of print. The several books on him in Italian are, in the main, either polemical or concessions to popular fancy. The few that are neither deal with only limited aspects of his story. It is my aim then to present herein a trustworthy, documented, reasonably complete, and dispassionate rendering of Giuliano's life. My development of the story is naturally chronological, except when larger events impinged upon it. These crucial matters—the Sicilian independence movement, the Mafia, the agrarian–peasant conflict over control of the soil, and the political struggle between the right and the left—are introduced at appropriate points. For those readers who are interested not only in Giuliano but in his land, too, the story in this way furnishes a unique perspective on Sicily, one from the underside, during the seven critical years that followed the Allied landings in the summer of 1943.

I have not attempted to set Giuliano's story within an all-encompassing theory about banditry or peasant societies. I prefer to let the story speak for itself. There is, I think, a considerable amount of meaning in it—about Sicilians and, most certainly, about bandits—but if all readers do not discover the same meanings in it, there should seem to be no cause for alarm. Such differences in interpreting historical events, especially controversial ones, appear to be inherent in the nature of human life. Indeed, if this work were unambiguously clear in its meaning, one might rightly suspect that the author had chosen his evidence with excessive care and structured it so as to produce the meaning he sought. For those readers whose interests in bandits go beyond this particular story, however, in the last chapter I have included a discussion of some of the matters that relate to the formulation of theory about bandits.

When I was writing this work, I read Mario Puzo's *The Sicilian,* the 1984 novel that was inspired by Giuliano's story. I enjoyed reading the book, but I found the real Giuliano often missing in it. I admire the imaginative powers of good novelists, but in Giuliano's case, in which the truth is both fascinating and strange, I would have liked to see the novel built more solidly upon it.

My debts to Sicilians and other Italians who helped me in my search for information about Giuliano, or who simply befriended me, are many. Especially, I want to mention the personnel in the national libraries in Florence, Rome, and Naples, the regional library in Palermo, the Library of Modern and Contemporary History in Rome, and the Central State Archives, also in Rome, in which I did much of the basic research for this study; my dozen or so roommates and their families and friends who in a Catania hospital in 1980 helped me, taught me, cheered me up, and entertained me to no end, most of all Signora Moschello who as she cared for her young son Vito in the bed next to mine adopted me as her own; several citizens of Castelvetrano and Montelepre who talked with me of Giuliano and the mysteries that still surrounded his story, but especially Giuseppe Sciortino and Mariannina Giuliano Sciortino, his nephew and sister respectively, who dealt with me and my persistent questioning with patience and friendliness.

I am much in debt, in addition, to those who read and criticized one version or another of this work while I was struggling to bring it to light: Richard Drake of the University of Montana; Denis Mack Smith and Christopher Duggan of All Souls College, Oxford; the university press readers who carried out their indispensable tasks behind the curtain of anonymity; and Mary Lincoln, director of Northern Illinois

University Press. They, in turn, encouraged me to try to make my flawed drafts into a worthwhile book. If, even yet, I have not met their expectations, responsibility for the failure does not fall on them.

Two persons, in addition, were indispensable to me. Karen Abdel-hadi of Colleyville, Texas, expeditiously and expertly typed more than one draft of the manuscript. Anita Murray, the Department of History secretary at Texas A&I University, typed portions of the last one and graciously performed many other tasks.

King of the Mountain

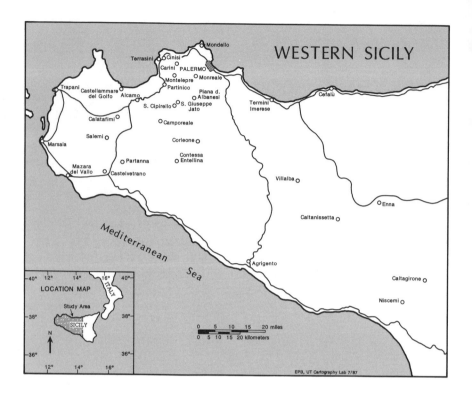

CHAPTER ONE

The Beginning of the Legend

YOUNG FRANK MANNINO HAD AGREED to join the independence army some time ago, and now he was told to report for duty. The word came by way of one of the town's barbers, Giuseppe Iacona, who relayed the order from the rebel chieftain in the mountains. Iacona, who was back in his native town of Montelepre after a long stay in America, led Frank and some forty other recruits to the cemetery just beyond the town's last houses. There, after the exchange of a secret password with an emissary from the command, they proceeded to an abandoned house on a slope of Sagana Mountain. It was well into the night when they heard footsteps and saw two men with lanterns approaching. They saw a third figure behind the two, a young man with a silver insignia on his leather jacket and a tommy-gun slung across his back. He was Colonel Salvatore Giuliano, the western region commander of the Army for Sicilian Independence.

On that night in late 1945 Giuliano explained why they had been summoned. The hour had come, he declared, to separate their beloved island from Italy, "to liberate it from the condition of inferiority" in which it had been held for so long. But the goal was not independence alone; the real aim was no less than annexation to the United States of America. Then, Sicilians would be able to travel freely to America, to work there and live there, for it would be their country, too. Soon, the 23-year-old colonel told his expectant band of recruits, they would all be smoking Lucky Strikes.

This incident, reported here as Mannino remembered it from his penitentiary cell more than a decade and a half later, occurred during the course of one of the major episodes in Giuliano's career.[1] By the time Mannino talked of it to a journalist, Giuliano was long since dead, but the story of his life was still a swirling controversy. A small-town boy from Mafia country, Giuliano became an outlaw when in

1943 he shot and killed a national policeman who caught him trafficking in the black market. Subsequently both loved and feared by his fellow townsfolk, both a henchman and a rival of mafiosi, a major actor in the tragically comic Sicilian independence movement, a political boss in his own right, courted by establishment politicians and berated by their leftist opposition, and known the world around, Giuliano left a story virtually unparalleled in bandit history. Yet he was only twenty-seven years old when death mysteriously overtook him in 1950.[2]

Reconstructing the true story of Salvatore Giuliano was not an easy task, because many of his acts have remained enveloped in mystery. Such is often the nature of bandit history, but in this case, the tendency was accentuated. He revealed little about the most secretive of his moves, the highly placed politicians who dealt with him told even less, and those high mafiosi who knew him so well said nothing, of course. The unvarnished truth of the most controversial episodes in his life and death may never be known fully by the public. People are still alive who know much of the story, but they do not talk about it except maybe among themselves, either because they were involved in the events or because they fear those who were. The widespread adherence to the rule of *omertà*, which dictates that one does not admit to knowledge of crimes committed by others, still has force. A perusal of Sicilian history over the past century suggests the wisdom of the reticence. Giuliano himself was a tenacious enforcer of the custom.

Fortunately for the historical record, the "King of Montelepre," as he was sometimes called, lived much of his life in public, and public interest in him was intense, both before and after his death. Reporters sought to interview him, occasionally with success. Newspapers avidly followed his exploits. Dozens of trials sought to throw light on the crimes of his surviving associates. In time, his family, some of his companions, and various of the police who pursued him recorded their memories of him. Last, leftist members of a parliamentary commission spent years attempting to expose his links to a network of Mafia figures and conservative politicians. Their zeal grew mainly out of the desire to tarnish their opponents, but the documents and testimony that they brought to light—often exacted with difficulty from men who were trying to cover their tracks or protect the reputations of their political parties—added measurably to the knowledge of him. Today, over four decades after the commencement of Giuliano's outlaw career, it is possible to write a reasonably complete account of him, albeit here and there with judgments based on circumstantial evidence.

Giuliano's outlaw career began in the war-torn Sicily of late summer 1943.[3] In July and August, the British and American armies had moved across from North Africa and, in an increasingly hard-fought campaign of thirty-nine days, driven Hitler's and Mussolini's forces from Sicily. The invaders were welcomed warmly. Sicilians had long since grown tired of Benito Mussolini's fascist rule and, after 1941, had ill understood why they should be fighting their American brothers. After all, Sicilians had emigrated to the United States in such large numbers that those who remained behind regarded that country almost as a second homeland. In 1943, to most of them, the mainland fascists and their German cohorts were invaders, while the British and Americans were the forces of liberation. Especially, this seemed to be true of the American army, which had many Sicilian-Americans in it.

But the times were hard, even desperate. Lawlessness was virtually unchecked as a result of the retreat of the Axis troops and the collapse of the fascist state. Everywhere, it seemed, outlaw bands were being formed and individual acts of criminality committed by the desperate or by those who simply seized the opportunity of the breakdown in law to take advantage of others. The British and Americans moved quickly to reestablish normalcy. The Allied Military Government was set up and steps were taken to rebuild the civil structure with Sicilians who had not had close relations with the fascists. Nonetheless, the Allies had more to do in those days than concern themselves with Sicily's internal order. The defeat of Hitler appeared to be far away then and Sicily a mere way station on the road to that objective.

Lawlessness notwithstanding, the most pressing problem in Sicily by late summer of 1943 was the scarcity of food. Wartime itself had produced shortages but the immediate aftermath of peace worsened the condition. The causes were several. The Germans had taken as much food from Sicily as they could carry in their retreat, and the supplies that remained were drastically reduced by rampant looting. Too, the government offices that might have ensured a rational allocation of available supplies were hardly functioning. The problem was further compounded by the general destruction of war, especially by the widespread damage done to highway and rail transportation. In short, there was no regular distribution of bread, pasta, and other foods, and the threat of severe malnutrition and even starvation was present.

Allied Military Government officials reimposed rationing to avert a catastrophe. To try to make it effective, they had to confront the widespread black market in food, which, having long flourished under fascist controls, already was in place. The black market operated on all levels, from well-organized, generously financed ventures involving warehouses and trucks all the way down to a lone individual carrying a small sack or two of grain on a mule over mountain trails.

Large-scale trafficking was bold and out in the open, so much so that it was clear it enjoyed the tolerance of the newly appointed civilian authorities. That they also shared in the profits was popularly assumed, for such had usually been the story of public administration in Sicily. Small-scale trafficking was oftentimes for profit, too, but it also enabled many to obtain food that was unavailable through legal channels. In whichever case, small-scale black marketeers were more vulnerable to police enforcement; they did not have access to the protection that highly placed officials could guarantee.

Soon, the black market controlled a major part of food distribution on the island, up to 70 percent of the total in some urban centers. The problem was a serious one. Not only were the illegal endeavors raising the prices of food to exorbitant levels but the volume was so great as to severely reduce supplies available at set prices through legal commerce. Allied authorities ordered the Sicilian police to come down hard on the unregulated trade. The police reacted characteristically. Knowing full well that the big traffickers enjoyed protection, they struck most decisively against the small timers. Salvatore Giuliano, then just short of his twenty-first birthday, was one of those who ran afoul of their crackdown.

Giuliano lived in Montelepre, a mountain town of about 5000 inhabitants to the west of Palermo. It later became practically a suburb of the capital. Back in those times it seemed a world apart, located as it is, beyond the high rim of mountains that forms the backdrop for Palermo. Although picturesque to newcomers in the way that hundreds of Sicilian and southern Italian towns are—perched atop of mountains or clinging to their sides, their narrow winding streets slightly widened here and there to accommodate tiny squares and the ever-present figures of black-clad women—Montelepre on close inspection was backward and poor, like many of the world's quaint and picturesque towns. Even the view was largely desolate, revealing little more than barren, almost colorless, sun-drenched mountains, although in the far distance one could sometimes see the sparkling blue of the Tyrrhenian Sea.

Montelepre's inhabitants dedicated themselves to small-time commerce, stock raising (mostly sheep), and agriculture. As was common in the region, the people were congregated in towns, often travelling long distances daily to reach their plantings in the countryside. There was little wealth in Montelepre, and Giuliano's father, also named Salvatore, was poor. He was better off than most, however. Like many Sicilians, he travelled to the United States several times, working in places as far apart as New York, Texas, and California. Giuliano's mother, Maria Lombardo, also lived for a time as a girl in New York, although she and Salvatore met and were married in Montelepre. Salvatore's ventures to America were not spectacularly successful, but he did accumulate enough capital to buy a parcel of farmland outside the town. This set him apart from numerous of his fellow townspeople who, possessing no land of their own, farmed only rented plots or worked as day laborers on the property of others.[4]

Giuliano's childhood and youth scarcely suggested the life that would be his in adulthood. Salvatore and Maria's fourth and last child, he was born on November 16, 1922. At age 10, he began to study in the town school but dropped out after three years in 1935. Although Giuliano later attributed his leaving school to impulsiveness, he added that he also had to help his father on the farm, in the place of his brother who had been drafted for military service. However, young Salvatore (nicknamed Turridu, short for Salvatore, to distinguish him from his father) did not much take to the drudgery of the farm and soon began to look around for some other way to make money. Anyway, the times were sad and the Giulianos badly needed extra income.

Learning that olive oil sold more dearly in Camporeale than in Montelepre, Turridu went into business. He transported oil over the 30 kilometers to the neighboring town on his bicycle, earning in this way 6 to 7 lire a day at a time when farm laborers earned only a little over half that amount. In fact, when his father needed help thereafter, the boy hired a substitute. Clearly, the young teenager was already demonstrating some of the resourcefulness that would later typify his other endeavors.

As war came to Europe in 1939, employment opportunities for Giuliano widened but, even so, he had some difficulty in keeping jobs. Not accepting authority easily, he lost two in disputes with his bosses, the first in telephone line construction, the second in installing guard rails on highways; and when the Allied armies arrived in Sicily in 1943, the soon-to-be bandit was again selling oil.

Turridu's entry into the black market was almost routine. His brother, having returned home from military service on the defeat of Mussolini's regime in Sicily, bought a starving horse from soldiers camped nearby. Giuliano himself purchased a pistol, a 9-mm. Beretta, from a soldier whom he encountered. There was nothing unusual in that, for Sicily at the time was overflowing with arms. Equipped with his brother's horse to transport goods and a pistol to defend himself from the many marauders then loose in the countryside, Giuliano began to deal on the black market.

His life took a sudden turn on the morning of September 2, 1943, as he was transporting two sacks of grain from San Giuseppe Jato to Montelepre. Unbeknownst to him, a temporary check point to intercept black marketeers had been set up on his path at Quattro Molini on the Jato River. When he stumbled upon the four agents of the law guarding it, two of them, *carabinieri* (Italy's elite police), they ordered him to dismount while they checked the contents of the sacks. Certain that the grain had been purchased illegally, they commenced to question him. They wanted to know from whom he had purchased the grain, but Giuliano, unwilling to implicate others, insisted that he had bought it from someone he did not know. The agents then informed him that he would be taken to the American authorities in the town of San Giuseppe Jato for further interrogation and, it seemed likely, formal charging.

Giuliano begged them to reconsider. He protested that he was a poor, simple youth, trying desperately to keep himself and his family alive in those hard times; that the grain was only for their personal use, and that, after all, it was only two small sacks. He was truly sorry, he said. He implored his captors to keep the grain and let him go. They had heard all of those stories many times before, they replied. The reality of the matter was that the police were being pressured by the Allied Military Government to crack down on the black market, and no matter how hard and sadly the youth begged, they refused to let him go.

At that moment, the agents saw another party approaching, which they thought also might be black marketeers. Two of them went to investigate. Giuliano quickly decided to run, but he needed his identification card first, which the *carabiniere* nearest him had confiscated. He suddenly pulled out his concealed pistol, intending to demand the return of the card. When the *carabiniere* reacted by raising his own weapon, Giuliano shot him at close range. He also fired at another agent who stood not far away but missed. Aware now that the other two agents had also been attracted by the firing, Giuliano fled toward a heavy stand of cane some 15 meters away. As he ran, he was hit in the back.

Giuliano escaped, in spite of his wound, but at a heavy cost. He had fatally shot an agent of the law. Circumstances justified his action, he thereafter maintained, the core of his contention being the threat to him of severe punishment for an act that others committed with impunity. That many of the others were large scale traffickers who enjoyed the protection of the political establishment added weight to his view. Admittedly, there was a kind of rustic, if self-serving, logic to what Turridu said; it was a tragedy that he got caught in the police net at Quattro Molini. Even so, his impulsive, foolhardy act of resistance was the opening to a much larger one.[5]

Outside the Law

Although Giuliano was an outlaw when he ran into the canebrake at Quattro Molini, he was not closely pursued during the immediately following weeks. The police had too much else on their hands; moreover, they had his identification card and could look for him in due course. In fact, eluding his pursuers until his death, he never paid specifically for the crime, in spite of the twenty-four-year prison sentence that he was given for it in absentia at Cosenza, on the mainland, in 1947.[6]

The patrol at Quattro Molini did not take chase to Giuliano because their wounded comrade was calling for help. He died the next day. Had they run after Giuliano they might have caught him easily; he was bleeding and in pain and, having thrown away his pistol, without a weapon. Only six or seven hours later, he arrived in Partinico, travelling the entire distance of approximately 25 kilometers on foot. There, a friend gave him first aid and refuge for the night. The next day, Giuliano returned to Montelepre on a borrowed bicycle, going to a relative's house, afraid that his own was under surveillance. His family sent him to Palermo that night, where the bullet was extracted from his side. He remained in the capital city with friends until he was well.

Back in Montelepre after a month, Giuliano lived as a fugitive in the family home at the edge of town. There seemed to be little interest in him—no news of the crime appeared in the press nor was he apparently being sought—but the family was apprehensive. They watched during the day while he slept; at night he kept a vigil of his own. His upper-floor room, which opened onto the terrace, offered a ready route to the adjoining countryside in the event that he had to flee.

Many weeks later, early on Christmas Eve, the authorities came for him. Giuliano's father was on his way to church for the Christmas novena when he was stopped by *carabinieri,* who told him to accompany them to his house. Knowing that his son was in danger, he called loudly to his wife as he approached, informing her that the police were with him and wanted to enter. She quickly sent her daughter, Mariannina, to warn Giuliano to flee. The police searched the premises but found nothing suspicious. When they looked into the room that Giuliano had just vacated, Mariannina was in the bed feigning illness. Before leaving, the police produced a document ordering Giuliano's arrest and demanded to know where he was. Not getting any satisfactory answers, they marched off to the station with the elder Salvatore in tow.

It was soon evident that he was not the only one in trouble; the town was under a state of virtual military occupation. Among dozens of others arrested were more of Giuliano's relatives, including an uncle and a first cousin. The authorities had not forgotten about Giuliano; they had merely waited to try to apprehend him in a general roundup. To carry that out, a contingent of some eighty troops had come to town.

Meanwhile, the morning's events were being noted by an unexpected observer. Far from being in the countryside in flight, Giuliano had skirted the police patrols and was following their movements. Peering from behind a half-closed door well above the main square, he saw the police bringing in their suspects, including, in turn, his own father. Giuliano was quick to anger, especially when he believed that members of his family were being mistreated. Seeing his father in police custody made him furious. Armed with his rifle, he stealthily worked his way down the narrow streets to a point angling onto the square. But he did not foolhardily rush into it with rifle blazing, for the area was filled with *carabinieri.* He waited until a patrol approached his position. Opening fire then, he saw two or three men fall, one of them fatally, before he turned tail and headed for the mountains. The surprised and disoriented troops hardly knew what had happened. The young desperado escaped unscathed.[7]

The Christmas Eve attack brought Giuliano instant renown and served warning that he was no ordinary criminal. He further distanced himself from that class only a few weeks later with his daring participation in a jailbreak in Monreale. Several of those who had been taken on Christmas Eve were incarcerated in nearby Monreale, among them Giuliano's esteemed first cousin, born on the same day as Giuliano and also named Salvatore. He sent word to Giuliano for help. Unable to free his own father, who was under heavy guard in Sicily's capital, Giuliano answered his cousin's call. Inside the jail, using a smuggled-in hack saw, the prisoners had been cutting through the interior bars on an outside window. Giuliano had the job, once they finished, of removing the exterior window guard, a crisscrossed grille that had to be dug out of the surrounding wall. Luckily for the prisoners, the window opened onto a garden that usually was not watched.

Giuliano, having learned from an intermediary that the interior work was completed, arrived outside the jail near noon on January 30, 1944. He whistled to attract the attention of his friends inside, but they told him to return during the night, that the jail was too full of guards at the moment to attempt the escape. Under the cover of darkness, he came back, bringing a ladder and the necessary tools. The work of removing the grille took about three hours, but when it was done the eight prisoners in the cell crawled down the ladder and, scattering to confuse any pursuers, headed out of town for the mountains. A few days later, they came together again with Giuliano to discuss their situation. All expressed gratitude for his assistance, and six of them, his cousin and uncle included, begged to stay with him. Seeing little chance of resuming a normal life soon and hungry for companionship, he consented to their staying. In effect, he had formed his band and passed an important milestone on his road to fame. By himself, he might have earned a place in the history of Sicilian outlawry by his headstrong valiance and youthful appeal, but it is unlikely that, alone, he would have ever become its premier figure.[8]

Giuliano and his men hid out on Sagana Mountain, in actuality a massive mountain chain on a portion of whose lower northern and western slopes sits Montelepre. Long denuded of its forests, like so much of Sicily, its upper reaches stood out bleak and seemingly inhospitable. Giuliano, nonetheless, found Sagana to be a near ideal refuge. He knew its expanses, trails, and caves intimately, having roamed the area as a boy. Few soldiers and police, typically from the mainland or other areas of Sicily, could match him there. From it, he commanded a view of the surrounding countryside, most of it closely grazed or devoted to cultivation and as devoid of tall or thick vegetation as the mountain itself. Little could happen and virtually no one could approach without attracting his attention. Moreover, he soon learned (or already knew) the farmers and shepherds who travelled daily from the villages to their fields and pastures; most of them became his informers. He was likely to recognize intruders almost instantly. Too, he was in Montelepre's backyard, more than close enough to observe the town's comings and goings, and at least in the early part of his career, to go down just about any night to visit his family. Geography was important to Giuliano, as it usually was to rural bandits anywhere; they seldom lasted long unless they had some advantages over those who pursued them. His survival during those crucial early years and Sagana were intertwined. It became his fortress, and it was not long before some were calling him the King of the Mountain.

Banditry in Sicily

On Sicily, in the immediate postwar period, Giuliano was not the only outlaw chieftain. The number of rural bands of brigands then was near three dozen. They were composed of men who became criminals for diverse reasons. Some had run afoul of the authorities over small-scale black-marketeering like Giuliano. A goodly portion came from the 600 or more prisoners who escaped from incarceration during the Allied bombardment that accompanied the invasion, while others were men who in better times would have led normal lives. Some fell outside the law with little foresight; others did so deliberately.

The bands typically had their own exclusive territories and engaged in a variety of criminal activities, among them assaulting cars, trucks, busses, and trains; robbing isolated agricultural warehouses; stealing horses and cattle; abductions for ransom; and extortion. With arms easily available, the bands were fearsomely equipped. One lone outlaw, of which there also were many, was unusually fearsome. In addition to a full complement of weapons, Lautieri carried the well-preserved head of a man. Removing that for display, from the goatskin bag in which he kept it, was enough to bend the will of almost anybody.[9]

The postwar years were not, of course, the first time that Sicily had problems with banditry (the Mafia is treated in the following chapter). The island's bandit traditions, however, were considerably weaker than in some areas of the mainland, where, for example, large-scale brigandage was part of the turmoil of the 1860s that marked the period of Italian unification. Nor did Sicilian banditry ever approach the widespread and sustained level that has existed in Sardinia from ancient times.

Sicily's bandit image was drawn mainly from the lives of a few colorful brigand chieftains. Other bandits, possessing little to set them apart from common criminals, soon faded from memory. Of those who were recalled, a common theme told of a young man who was pushed outside the law by a gross injustice, often at the hands of a soldier or other agent of the law. Whether he thereafter attracted favorable public attention, however, depended upon his qualities as a bandit. Generosity—furnishing a dowry for a poor maiden, for instance—was certain to bring him favor, as would excessive courtesy and boldness. A romantic inclination, especially unusual amatory prowess, also helped. Among memorable Sicilian bandits was Francesco Paolo Varsalona of east central Sicily in the late 1800s who had a "wife" in each of the fourteen communes that he dominated, coming before his death to head a veritable tribe of concubines and offspring. Antonio Cantinella of the early 1700s had foreshadowed him. His preferred activity was robbing convents, and although loot was his main aim, he was widely alleged to have granted favors on request.

Of course, the bandit image had a dark side, marked by overbearing strength and excessive vengeance. This side was cultivated assiduously by the bandits, since, to survive, they had to create the impression that within their area of operation their power was invincible over all opposition and their retaliation for lack of cooperation and disloyalty was massive and certain. Such an impression protected not only their lives and freedom but also guaranteed the efficacy of their extortion activities, the most reliable source of income for successful bands. Yet, many middle- and lower-class Sicilians saw nothing abnormal or particularly reprehensible about them, their parasitic natures and cruel excesses notwithstanding. The bandits did wrong only when provoked, it was often argued, being, for the most part, content to exact their income from those who could afford to part with it.[10]

Astute brigand leaders over the centuries had built this image, because it variously reflected their native instincts, struck their fancies, or helped them survive. Passed from generation to generation, it still had vitality in the mid-twentieth century. What is remarkable is how quickly the public saw the image in Montelepre's young desperado and how well—and often consciously—he conformed to its essential outlines. Scarcely had his career gotten underway when the public began to note that there was something exceptional about him. The circumstances of the killing at Quattro Molini, the daring Christmas Eve attack in the center of his hometown, and the rescue of his cousin in the Monreale jailbreak pointed to the kind of man he was. Other evidence of it was not long in coming.

The Making of a Bandit

Upon becoming a fugitive, Giuliano faced the major problem of how to stay out of the clutches of the law. And the law wanted him. Few crimes disturb police more than the killing of their own; he already had killed two. Knowing that Giuliano was extremely dangerous, and with far more criminals to track down than they had time and man-power for, the police sought to entrap him by the use of informers. Although the monetary rewards that they could offer were modest, even modest sums were sufficient to tempt some of Montelepre's impoverished inhabitants. The tactic placed Giuliano's freedom in jeopardy. It was widely known around town that he was on nearby Sagana. Many knew also that he came down occasionally to see his family and that they frequently took provisions or information to him. Spies were a serious problem and, to survive, he had to demonstrate that collaboration with the police was unwise.

Giuliano early decreed that the penalty for spying or informing on him was death. His first killing for this reason soon occurred. The victim was an 18-year-old boy who allegedly had been promised money to let the police know when the fugitive came down to visit his mother. After seeing the boy frequently lurking around the family home, as Giuliano himself told the story, he warned the boy's father to tell his son to leave him alone; when the suspicious actions per-sisted, Giuliano shot and killed the youth one day as he arrived at a mill to leave grain to be ground.[11]

While Giuliano never killed without a reason, he was capable of the cold-blooded murder of anyone who stood in his way, as the murder of the boy revealed. The total number of spies whom he executed was not known, although the known list was long enough. He frequently wanted knowledge of the killings made public, and it became his practice to attach notes to the bodies attesting to his action. Such notes served as warnings to those who might think of cooperating with the police; they also, Giuliano said, made it less likely that the slayings would be blamed on innocent persons.[12]

Giuliano's introduction to the survival arts of outlaw life included more than learning how to deal with spies. He quickly found his obligations on several fronts multiplying, especially his need for money. The meager support that his family could offer him did not count for much after he acquired a band. For that matter, his family was in worse shape than ever, now that he no longer was a breadwinner. The needs of his band members and their dependents also had to be met. But that was not all. Arms, ammunition, and medicines had to be purchased, as did commonplace necessities—all at outrageous prices. It was risky for the bandits to go into town to purchase food, as it was for their families to buy it and try to get it out to them. The best solution to the problem was to contract with others, preferably ones whose activities would not arouse suspicions. The farmers and shepherds who came daily to the countryside were obvious candidates. Many of them were inclined to cooperate, either because they sympathized with Giuliano or because they feared him; or because the profits were so good. He commonly paid his agents up to ten times the normal retail price for the items that he needed, such as bread, cheese, and wine, the staple foods of the Sicilian peasant.[13] One trip for Giuliano could earn a shepherd the equivalent of a week's normal wages. Giuliano paid well not only out of necessity but also from the recognition that a satisfied collaborator would not be lured easily into the ranks of police informers.

Under these pressures, Giuliano turned into a bandit. As such, he did what most successful Sicilian bandits had always done: He exacted his toll from the wealthy. He did so not only because his moral convictions and nascent feelings of class solidarity dictated leaving the poor with the little that they had but also because only the affluent had the sums of money he required. His crimes against property consisted of robberies, abductions, and extortion; all common enough but, in his case, committed now and then with an uncommon flair. In reality, the number of his crimes was not large and their occurrence sporadic during the first year and a half of his career. His financial needs were not nearly as great as they were to become, and moreover, some of his crimes rendered handsome rewards. The abduction of a prosperous landowner in nearby Giardinello in the summer of 1944, to cite one, was rumored to have produced a ransom of 20 million lire.[14]

Although the total take from another feat a few months later was never publicly revealed, it was believed to have amounted to more than four times the Giardinello ransom. It was the robbery of the Duchess of Pratameno on her rural estate between Partinico and Alcamo. The young chieftain and his band arrived at the family's ancestral castle in the late afternoon of November 5, 1944. Knowing that the duchess was there, Giuliano instructed his men to treat her with dignity. As for the young bandit's own performance, it could only be described as masterful. He walked into her quarters before she even knew there were desperadoes in the vicinity and, in the humble manner of the Sicilian peasant, presented himself and requested her blessing. Less humbly, he kissed her hand and asked for her jewels. When she answered that she had nothing of worth with her, that all of her valuable things were kept in Palermo, he threatened to kidnap her young nephews and nieces who were on the estate with her. That prospect was sufficient to frighten her into opening the safe. Noticing a diamond ring on her finger, he demanded it, too. The noble lady protested that she could not bear to part with the ring, which had been a gift from her husband. Giuliano replied, as he took it from her finger, that knowing how much it meant to her would make him treasure it all the more.

Upon taking leave of the duchess, Giuliano picked up a book from a table and perused it. It was John Steinbeck's *In Dubious Battle,* in Italian translation. Giuliano thought that he would like to try to read it and asked for its loan, assuring her that he would return it. Meanwhile, during the time that the head bandit was dealing with the lady of the house, his men were loading whatever they liked of her possessions into a truck. They departed, considerably richer and well satisfied. As for the book, it was sent back a few days later with a respectful note thanking the duchess for its loan.[15] News of the robbery spread rapidly and struck public fancy. It was a reenactment of the old tale of the meeting of the handsome and courteous young bandit with the noble lady.

Not all of the news that came from Giuliano's camp had the appeal of this story. Much of it, dealing with his day-to-day struggle for survival against the authorities, had its sordid and bloody aspects. His actions worried the police and they badly wanted him, but in the months following his attack on Montelepre's main square he kept them effectively cowed by sporadic action. When a confrontation took place, it oftentimes was by his provocation and more often than not he came out better than they. In early April 1944, he attacked the *carabiniere* station at Piano del Occhio, in retaliation, he said, for the over zealousness with which the detachment sought to arrest small time black marketeers. In them, he saw himself.[16] In June, on Sagana, he ambushed a patrol, killing the captain that led it. He attacked the *carabiniere* station at Borgetto later in the same day.[17]

Two days of violence in mid-September left another officer dead. It started on September 15, when Giuliano set up a highway ambush to kill a young lieutenant who had sworn to get him. It failed, but the next morning, he unwittingly set off a chain of events that gave him another chance. He killed a man early that day who had been extorting bread, pasta, and cigarettes from Montelepre families in his name; the police, learning quickly of the crime, sent three men to bring in the body. They set up a roadblock near the scene, stopping all passersby in an attempt to gain knowledge of Giuliano's whereabouts. One of those they detained was the bandit's aunt, and suspecting that she might not be telling all she knew, they threatened her. Giuliano, unbeknownst to them, was watching from a hidden point nearby. Unable to contain his anger, he shouted to the soldiers that they were to surrender at once or face immediate death. After sizing up their exposed position and his secure one, the three surrendered. They were in danger still, for Giuliano's hatred of police was already well developed, but in this early period his magnanimity sometimes extended to even them, as it did in this case. He heeded their supplications for mercy and, after relieving them of their arms, set them free.

His generosity was not met in kind. No sooner had the soldiers reached town than a force of twenty men was sent out to search for him. Heading the column was the same lieutenant that he had tried to kill the day before. Upon its arrival, Giuliano, already stationed high above the road, opened fire and killed the officer. He also wounded two others in the column.[18]

The operations of Giuliano and his band continued in much the same way through the remainder of 1944 and well into the succeeding year. Acts of extortion, robbery, and abductions were interspersed among occasional conflicts with agents of the law. Actually, the police were not certain Giuliano was responsible for all of the crimes attributed to him; there were, after all, other criminals in the region. But since the rule of *omertà,* the conspiracy of silence, was so strong, finding out exactly who had committed which crime was almost always difficult in Sicily. Frequently, unrelated acts were blamed simply on the area's best known desperado. This may have contributed to Giuliano's growing reputation, especially as other criminals realized that the substitution of his name for theirs was a useful ploy in extortion and kidnapping attempts.

The authorities recognized Giuliano as a skillful, daring, and very dangerous foe. He gave them no reason to doubt, as he told a peasant one day, that he and his men were "hunters of rural guards and police." [19] The police were no match for him, and their record over the first year and a half of his career was poor. Realistically, they faced a multiplicity of problems. Police manpower was grossly inadequate to deal with the high level of crime that then existed in virtually all parts of Sicily. Large numbers of troops could be brought to any one location only under exceptional circumstances, as in the 1943 Christmas Eve roundup in Montelepre. Montelepre's force was permanently increased when Giuliano was recognized as a serious threat, but even then to only about sixteen men. Policing in Montelepre, as in the rest of Italy, was done by the *carabinieri* and the public security police, both answerable ultimately to the Interior Ministry in Rome. The first were military policemen, members of the army, while the second were a civilian force. Regular army troops also could be sent in temporarily when conditions were especially bad.

Montelepre's police were given a new commander in the summer of 1944, 38-year-old Giuseppe Calandra. He found that his men were reluctant to go outside the station, so fearful were they of Giuliano. Much of the problem, he thought, was their lack of equipment.

Not only were there not enough shoes and uniforms to go around, the same was true of weapons. Even the few that they had were old, consisting of outdated revolvers and manually fed rifles. Giuliano's band, in contrast, was armed with clip-fed pistols of German origin and automatic rifles, not to mention a bountiful supply of hand grenades. Indeed, the first automatic rifles that the Montelepre detachment possessed were taken from the bandits. Calandra also thought that part of the bandit's success against the police lay in the knowledge that he had acquired when working as a telephone lineman. Giuliano, he said, regularly intercepted police messages by tapping the wires. The new commander eventually received additional men, hand grenades, and two automatic weapons. When, even with the added strength, his forces were still ineffective, he resorted to mass arrests of the bandits' suspected informers and suppliers. The effects of his efforts on Giuliano were negligible.[20]

"One of Their Own"

Underlying the mass arrests was the assumption that Giuliano got substantial help from his fellow townspeople. The assumption was correct, for other than his determination and cunning, his major asset was the support that Montelepre gave him. The authorities hotly argued that the only ones who assisted him were his family and those whom he either paid well with stolen loot or intimidated through fear. There was some truth to what they said. Giuliano did have the fanatical devotion of his family, he was generous to those who cooperated with him, and his name was sufficient to put fear in the hearts of those who would cross him. But, even so, he also had the sympathy of virtually the entire population of Montelepre and the surrounding area, as many of the authorities themselves admitted—at a later and safer time.

The help he received from his countrymen, both passive and active, was based on some things that were peculiar to Sicily, as well as on others that were related to him and his image. Sicilians had long been distrustful of authorities, a not uncommon trait elsewhere but one that in the Sicilians' case, was accentuated by centuries of domination by foreign conquerors and alien ruling houses. Their history after unification with the rest of Italy, under the mainland House of Savoy, did little, if anything, to reduce the mistrust. Their primary loyalty was to their towns; and, in no way, was this sense of localism violated more than by the almost total monopolization of police power by the central government in Rome. The police who came to pursue Giuliano and his bandits were sent to Montelepre by that distant authority; they often also were not Sicilians but mainland Italians. Thus, Montelepre was protecting one of its own against outsiders. *Omertà*, or the conspiracy of silence before the state, also played its role. The Mafia had done much to establish the practice as an inviolate rule of conduct, but it was also linked to a code of honor in which disputes among individuals were held to be personal matters to be settled privately.

None of these traditional standards of conduct was hard and fast, and alone they did not explain adequately the devotion with which Montelepre protected Giuliano. Maybe, had he been a common bandit, devoid of saving graces, they would have watched passively as the police liquidated him. In his case, the traditional standards came into play because Montelepre believed him to be deserving. At Quattro Molini, they saw a poor, hard working, upright boy, whom the law singled out for prosecution while others who were more guilty than he went free. They understood his killing of the *carabiniere*. His Christmas Eve assault on Montelepre's square was explained by the anger that he felt upon seeing his father mistreated. Even the killing of the spies could be fitted into the same mental framework, as could other crimes. If, indeed, one believed that Giuliano's original crime was committed under circumstances that, because of their inherent injustice, largely exonerated him, then the subsequent crimes he committed to maintain his freedom could be construed to fall under similar terms. At least, that was the way Montelepre saw him.

Yet, to construe Montelepre's predominant attitude toward Giuliano as pity would be to misunderstand the nature of it. He was not so much pitied for having fallen into an unfortunate situation as he was admired for how he dealt with it. He was respected for his strength, his courage, and his use of violence, traits to which Sicilians attached considerable importance. The primary question was not always whether a man's actions were good or bad but rather whether in a duel with others he was able to impose his will. Such was the main ingredient of Sicily's popular cult of manliness, and as Giuliano struggled and survived against high odds, he was seen as an outstanding example of it. He was every man's and every woman's superman.

Still, it should neither be thought that the sole source of his popular favor was brute strength. Not only had he been mistreated; not only was he strong; he was just and generous as well. The conception of Giuliano as a just man came partially from his refusal to submit to the injustice that the state tried to inflict upon him. It was related also to his punishment of imposters who engaged in often petty extortion in his name, acts that angered him greatly. He not only wanted the exclusive use of his name for extortion purposes, but he also disliked any association of it with petty criminality. Giuliano, he wanted the world to know, was a bandit of class. Had he been honest with himself, he might have admitted something else: that petty crimes did not produce the kind of money he needed. He once came close to making such an admission when he explained to a journalist why robbing trains was not sufficiently profitable. If you took the money of every passenger, he said, you got no more than 3 million lire. "Too little money and too much risk," he concluded.[22]

More broadly, the Sicilian conception of Giuliano as a just man came from his role as an enforcer of justice. Well known was his slaying of Montelepre postal official Salvatore Abbate, an event that happened not long after Giuliano first became a fugitive. Abbate, it was believed, was stealing money from letters sent by Italians in America to their kin in Montelepre. One of the alleged victims was Giuliano's sister.[23]

Giuliano's intervention on behalf of a group of Montelepre peasants in the spring of 1944 also helped to form the image. The peasants wanted to lease land on a large estate on Giuliano's mountain range. The problem arose when the estate manager, acting for the absentee corporate owners, refused to accept tenants from Montelepre and favored instead those who came from his native Giardinello. A group of the rejected peasants appealed to Giuliano for help. In answer, he took his band to the property's headquarters on the day when the company director and his lawyer came to make the seasonal contracts with the tenants. A conversation and a show of force were all that was needed to produce the desired change. While he talked, his men drove the rival peasants away by firing just over their heads. By the time the bandits left, the estate director and his lawyer had changed their policy.[24]

Although young Giuliano had rudimentary concepts of justice, he understood, too, that a person who was beholden to him was a valuable asset. When a peasant or shepherd who brought him supplies was generously remunerated, Giuliano received more than just the items. He gained admiration, loyalty, and often, friendship, as well as the promise of someone to serve him in riskier ventures in the future. Similarly, when he gave money to a poor family to buy food, to finance an operation for the grandmother, or send a sick child to the doctor, he did more than dispense charity; he also spread goodwill and extended his network of mutual obligations. Even the authorities, in some of their more candid moments, conceded that Montelepre's people looked upon Giuliano as a benefactor. To many an agriculturist and shepherd, a police officer later admitted, "Giuliano was a god."[25] Sometimes, in keeping with the image, his gifts of money arrived in envelopes immodestly bearing the inscription "Divine Providence."[26]

Giuliano was already becoming a celebrity by the summer of 1945.

A Palermo daily newspaper asked: "Who has not heard of him?" The author of the story went on to write that the young bandit was the most common topic of conversation in Palermo's coffee bars, where men gathered daily to exchange news, opinions, and camaraderie. The public, he said, was attributing to him an "exquisite chivalry worthy of the times of yore." [27] Such descriptions helped to increase Giuliano's fame to the point that it was becoming clear Sicily had a major bandit legend in the making. It was not known publicly, however, that the leaders of the Sicilian independence movement had an even more impressive future in mind for him.

CHAPTER TWO

The Struggle for Power in Giuliano's Sicily

MOST OUTLAWS IN HISTORY HAVE LIVED on the margins of society, and except for family and friends, touching only those unfortunates who became their victims. If the 1940s in Sicily had been ordinary times, Giuliano likely would have done much the same, for little in his early record suggested a future for him other than a short career as an unusually capable bandit. But Sicily in the 1940s was not passing through ordinary times, and Giuliano did not spend his outlaw years in isolation.

Following liberation, Sicily was a boiling cauldron of social conflict and partisan passion, the configurations of its future unclear. For certain, its past would lie heavily upon any subsequent course. But, if fascist rule and World War II had not exactly fractured the past they at least had suspended and weakened some of its aspects. The choices that confronted Sicilians were remarkably open; they were also basic. They would determine both the structure of Sicily's society for decades to come and its immediate ties to the Italian nation. In the latter instance, the separatist movement that blossomed with liberation appeared at first to have broad support, then quickly faded in the face of adversity. The independence question was supplanted by a conflict over land reform, an immediate concern to virtually everyone. This question produced much of the turmoil of the postwar years, as the agrarians and the politicians of the right defended wealth, tradition, and privilege against the aspirations and ambitions of the peasants and their leftist allies. In the midst of Sicily's major controversies, but especially the one over land, reemerged one of the weightier burdens of the island's past, the rural Mafia, which now struggled to regain the power and influence that it had lost during two decades of fascist persecution.

Montelepre's clever young bandit became a participant in all of these conflicts, usually, though not always, in league with the defenders of the old order. To a degree that is remarkable for a bandit, consequently, the larger events of his times form a part of his own story.

The Separatists

The Sicilian separatist movement, which was soon to seek Giuliano's help, had deep roots in the island's history. Sicilians had seen many invaders and conquerors come and go. In modern times alone, they were ruled successively by the Aragonese, the Hapsburgs, and the Bourbons—all foreigners. When, in 1860, they welcomed Giuseppe Garibaldi and his "one thousand" and accepted incorporation into a unified Italian state the next year, they thought they were gaining freedom from tyranny. Instead, many of them later concluded, they had replaced one foreign tyrant with another. They had not joined a federation of autonomous Italian states, as they had been led to believe; rather, they had been annexed by the mainland. The House of Savoy of northern Italian origin looked little less foreign than its predecessors.

The center of interest in the new Italy lay in the productive and prosperous north, and Sicily's welfare was subordinated to northern needs. Tariff policies, which often harmed Sicilian industries, reflected this, as did taxation and government expenditures. Tax revenues grew in Sicily following unification but not much to Sicily's benefit, since a disproportionate share of the money was sent north. Public services in Sicily—roads, railroads, water projects, and irrigation—remained backward. While the north was being integrated into Europe's burgeoning industrial order, Sicily, along with most of the rest of southern Italy, languished in the continent's backwaters, suffering from neglect, economic stagnation, and rapid population growth.

Although Sicily's representatives in parliament often lambasted government policies on their infrequent visits to their districts, in Rome they voted with the government. It seemed to matter little to them that their votes supported northern interpretations of national welfare. Some of them, believing Sicily's problems to be incurable, doubtless thought that they were acting in a statesmanlike manner; others shamelessly sought only to advance their political careers and personal fortunes. But, also underlying the attitudes and actions of Sicilian deputies was another matter of supreme import: They wanted Sicily left alone. They did not want the government to intervene in a way that would upset those who kept them in Rome term after term. One of their main preoccupations was shielding conservative interests in Sicily from reform-minded politicians of the more progressive north. Especially, the dominant groups in rural Sicily, the agrarians and the Mafia, wanted guarantees against rule by law, land reform, and a truly liberated peasantry, all of which would undermine their own power. It was with the connivance of Sicily's dominant classes, therefore, that so little of the promise of the *risorgimento,* the Italian revival that led to unification, was realized in the south.[1]

If anything served to alleviate the poverty of the masses of Sicilians in the late nineteenth and early twentieth centuries, it was the sizeable portion of the island's population that emigrated to other lands, mainly to the United States. Many left Italy permanently; others, like the elder Giuliano, travelled back and forth, as desire and circumstance dictated. It was not long before virtually every Sicilian had a close relative in America. Those Sicilians who did not go to America often received remittances from a family member who had gone there.

With such close links to the United States, the people of Sicily had difficulty making sense of World War II. Benito Mussolini, Italy's wartime dictator and effective ruler since 1922, may have enjoyed considerable popularity there earlier, especially in the 1920s, but other than for his ruthless suppression of the Mafia, he gave little attention to the island and its problems. When, after 1940, his foreign aggressions increased, with the consequent suffering, casualties, and deprivation—and news came of Italian defeats on nearly every front—some Sicilians began to reexamine their loyalty to the nation. By the time the Allies invaded in 1943, plots already were underway to realize an independent Sicily.[2]

Most of Sicily's separatist plotters were rightists. Representative of them was Lucio Tasca Bordanaro, a large landholder and author of a booklet that defended Sicily's landed class. A resident of Palermo, he attracted a following of independence-minded conservatives, among them the island's best known Mafia boss, Calogero Vizzini. Tasca saw as one of the main benefits of independence the protection of Sicily's privileged classes from a postwar Italy that might be ruled by a radicalized north.

But not all of the separatists came from the right. On the far left was the already-seasoned conspirator Antonio Canepa. Born in

Palermo in 1908 and trained in law, Canepa led a checkered life of controversial activities, including a stint in prison for his participation in an unsuccessful antifascist attempt to seize the tiny republic of San Marino in 1933. Released from prison because he was deemed mentally ill, he later publicly embraced Mussolini's cause, apparently in order to conceal his continuing antigovernment activities. World War II's onset found him leading a double life in Catania. He was, to the public, the scholarly professor at the university who wrote treatises on fascist political theory. But under the name of Mario Turri, by 1943, he was circulating underground antifascist writings, including his own proseparatist tract, *La Sicilia ai Siciliani* (Sicily to the Sicilians), and, with a small circle of followers, engaging in acts of sabotage. In ideology, Turri was a communist who envisioned wrenching Sicily out of its past by revolutionary means. He was the main inspiration of the small, often isolated and in the end impotent, left wing of the independence movement.[3]

By the summer of 1943, amid excitement over the impending Allied invasion, enthusiasm for independence seemed high. Separatist slogans appeared in many places around the island. The government's appeals for support went unheeded, and when the British and Americans landed on the coast in the second week of July 1943, they were welcomed as friends. Sicily was free of German and fascist forces by August 16, while mainland Italy was still under their control. All of a sudden, as it were, the island's ties to the mainland were severed.

Public leadership of Sicily's separatists was assumed by Andrea Finocchiaro Aprile when, with liberation, a limited degree of public political expression became possible. On July 28, he announced the formation in Palermo of the Committee for Sicilian Independence. On the same day, he presented the newly formed Allied Military Government with a proclamation requesting the establishment of a provisional government, to be followed by a plebiscite on independence. The committee was formed by about forty of Palermo's citizens, many but not all of the baronial class. Its secretary was Antonino Varvaro, an attorney of decidedly leftist leanings from Partinico, just down the mountain from Giuliano's Montelepre. The inclusion of a few like Varvaro gave the effort a broader base and increased its usefulness as the main organizing vehicle for an independence party when, several months later, full political activity was authorized.

Finocchiaro Aprile was well known in Sicily.[4] Born there in 1878 but educated in Florence, he was the son of a deputy who long represented one of the island's interior districts. He, like his father, also went to the Chamber of Deputies, sent there by the Mafia-dominated district of Corleone, to the south of Palermo. Before his career was halted by the advent of fascist rule, he rose to serve as the assistant secretary of war in one cabinet. His qualifications for leadership of the separatist movement, other than his political experience, included a fairly clear record of opposition to the fascists—he could not be called a collaborator, the kiss of death to a political aspirant in the postwar years. Beyond that, he was a man of distinct bearing who looked a little like America's Woodrow Wilson. Possessing a certain elegance and a reserved, cold personality, albeit a passionate oratorical style, he particularly called Wilson to mind when he wore his pince nez spectacles. Also like him, he was a former university professor, having taught the history of law at both Ferrara and Siena.

Finocchiaro Aprile was ideologically flexible, a useful characteristic for leadership of a movement whose unity was extremely fragile. For, while separatists were united on the desirability of independence, they disagreed on just about every other issue that affected the future direction of the island's society. In his earlier political career, Finocchiaro Aprile, an ardent Freemason, had adhered to the Liberal Party, Italy's anticlerical grouping of classical liberals. Now, in his separatist phase, he was sometimes described as a radical on the right, but in reality, it was seldom clear where he stood. He professed a belief in the ideals of communism but not in the reality of the Italian Communist Party. He spoke of the need for land reform but, in recognition of the productivity of many large properties, warned against their division into small, uneconomic holdings. He talked vaguely of large collective farms. But none of these positions was clearly defined. In general terms, he was a populist who maintained his ties to the dominant class from which he came. His main interest, in the 1940s, was independence. What was needed, he often declared, was a broad-based movement not a political party. After independence was secured, the movement would dissolve, political parties would be formed, and crucially, the issues that divided Sicilians could then be settled by Sicilians alone.

Finocchiaro Aprile, like other separatist leaders, knew that the Allies held the key to independence. They were in actual possession of Sicily, and only with their support and recognition could it win and sustain its freedom. However, the question of Sicilian independence was not paramount to the Allies in 1943. To them, the island was a stepping stone to the continent in a war whose end appeared to lie frighteningly far in the future. Yet, they were not initially antagonistic to the idea. Their relations with the independence forces were good, as was evinced by the nomination of Lucio Tasca as the mayor of Palermo. Indeed, some 90 percent of the Allied-appointed mayors came from separatist ranks. Their popular support and identification as antifascists doubtless carried greater weight than their separatist views in determining their selection, however.

In the end, Allied policy in Sicily was decided by military strategy and geopolitical considerations rather than by perceptions of Sicilian wishes. Separatists had thought that an anti-Mussolini, anti-German, independent Sicily would appeal to the Allies as a base for the continuing European campaign, but unforeseen, fast-breaking political changes on the peninsula undercut their cause and dashed their hopes. On July 24, the fascist Grand Council voted to bring Mussolini's one-man dictatorship to a close, and on the following day, King Victor Emmanuel dismissed him and had him arrested. The king then named Marshal Pietro Badoglio to be the new prime minister. His subsequent defection to the Allied side opened the possibility of a southern Italy under a friendly government, with Sicily as an integral part of it. To the Allies, that was a better option than a divided and mutually antagonistic south, especially since the road north to Naples, Rome, and the nation's industrial heartland was now defended by Germans, who filled the vacuum left by the fascist collapse. The Germans also rescued the imprisoned Mussolini in a daring raid on September 12.[5]

The failure of the Americans and British to support Sicilian independence was probably sufficient to doom it; but, to make things worse, the Soviet Union was also opposed. The Soviet representative to the Advisory Commission for Italy, Andrei Vishinski, came to Palermo in December 1943 to assess the situation. During his short stay, he talked with Allied authorities and secretly saw Giuseppe Montalbano, then Sicily's number one Communist Party leader. The director of the Soviet purges of the 1930s and, more recently, deputy foreign minister met Montalbano at Palermo's Hotel Excelsior, where they conversed alone in French without the aid of interpreters.

Montalbano explained the political situation in Sicily to the Soviet representative, and they talked of the threat of the separatists and of the relative weakness of Sicily's communists. It was certain, they doubtless noted, that a Sicily independent of Italy would be staunchly anticommunist and even possibly, as some separatists were hoping for at the time, annexed to either Britain or the United States. The most realistic hope for the Communist Party was the preservation of a united Italy, to the end that the south could be dominated by the north, where the party's strength lay. Before leaving the capital, Vishinski stated publicly that his government was firmly opposed to Sicilian independence; Montalbano, for his part, passed Moscow's wishes on down to the party's rank and file, some of whom, caught up in mass enthusiasm and lacking authoritative instructions from above, had been flirting with the separatists.[6]

For the moment, British, American, and Soviet interests coincided, and especially following the Allied decision of February 1944 to turn over the administration of Sicily to the mainland Badoglio government, separatist hopes for an easily won independence under Allied auspices faded quickly. Although some British and American officials in Sicily still were sympathetic to the separatists, it was evident that the movement now had to reach its goal on its own and against great odds.

Finocchiaro Aprile, never daunted much by adversity, devoted himself to organizing the effort. He camouflaged the setback by repeated claims that Franklin Roosevelt, Winston Churchill, and virtually every other major figure in the Western world supported independence. In truth, the movement was supported by a sufficiently large number of Sicilians that the separatist leader's fervor was not wholly unjustified. The transformation of the movement into a political party proceeded rapidly, although chaotically, following the authorization of the formation of political parties in early 1944. By the fall of that year, police reports indicated, the new party, the Movement for Sicilian Independence or MIS (*Movimento per l'Independenza Siciliana*), constituted a formidable force, especially in the key provinces of Palermo, Messina, and Catania, where it had its best organizations. Even where the party was poorly organized, authorities believed that its goal of independence enjoyed widespread favor.[7] Indeed, if elections had been held then, the separatists might well have emerged as the strongest single party. As such, they would have been able to press for the fulfillment of their hopes from a position of strength. Elections, however, were far away, even their scheduling awaiting the conclusion of the war on the continent.

Many things prejudicial to the separatists happened in the ensuing two years. The Allied armies made their way slowly up the peninsula, increasingly aided by antifascist partisans until, in the waning days of the European war, the Allies and the partisans dealt the faltering Germans a quick and decisive defeat in the upper part of the nation to the north of Florence. Almost simultaneously, the war was successfully concluded in Germany, Hitler committed suicide in a Berlin bunker, and Mussolini was caught and brutally executed by partisans, his body subsequently displayed hanging by its heels in Milan. By early May 1945, Italy had entered the postwar period, its territorial integrity intact, and due to its early deposition of Mussolini and the actions of its partisans, its honor largely restored. Desirable as these events may have been, they nonetheless increased the obstacles that the separatists had to overcome. Wrenching independence from a restored Italy, looked upon benignly by the world powers, was hardly conceivable.

The effects of the events on the continent could be seen most notably in the growing opposition to the separatists. The traditional Italian parties, all of which opposed Sicilian independence, had appeared to be too weak in 1943 to resist the separatist hurricane; this was no longer true by mid-1945. Not only had they had the ensuing period in which to reorganize and recruit, but as Italy's prestige grew with the successful military effort and final liberation, so did the standing of the parties linked to it. To be sure, some of them never made much of a comeback, for example, the Liberal Party, which was unable to recover most of its former support.

The task of combatting the separatists fell mainly to the Socialist, Communist, and Christian Democratic parties, especially the latter two. Sicily's communists, fairly few and substantially leaderless in 1943, grew rapidly in numbers and effectiveness thereafter. Much of their success was attributable to the direction given them by veteran-communist Girolamo Li Causi, who returned to his native Sicily in August 1944 after an absence of some two decades. He brought with him orders from party chief Palmiro Togliatti, himself recently returned from long exile in the Soviet Union, to take control of the party. Under Li Causi's capable, even charismatic command, Sicily's communists, usually in cooperation with the socialists, built a potent leftist presence on the island that was impressive especially for the support that it attracted from segments of the peasantry. Subject to a program elaborated on the mainland and ultimately answerable to the Soviet Union, the party became fervently antiseparatist.[8]

The Christian democrats, postwar Italy's premier party, originated in a turn-of-the-century Catholic reform movement, which in 1919 became the Popular Party. Led by a Sicilian priest, Luigi Sturzo, this party of "Christian democracy" advocated a broad range of reforms, including the endorsement of peasant aspirations for land and justice. It was of major importance by the time Mussolini suppressed his political rivals in the mid-1920s. But in the immediate postwar period the Sicilian branch of its successor, the newly formed Christian Democratic Party, was weak, its leadership either still in exile or tainted by collaboration with the fascists. Its subsequent rise to influence largely paralleled the growth of the parent organization on the mainland. By 1948, the year of postwar Italy's first parliamentary elections, the Catholic party emerged as the main party of the status quo, although not without considerable internal tension. There were those who wanted to hold it to its original reformist aims. Overall, however, it moved rightward and made the accommodations necessary to electoral success. If unproven allegations may be given credence, one of its more prominent Sicilian leaders, Bernardo Mattarella of Castellammare del Golfo, even enlisted Giuliano the bandit in the crucial 1948 effort.[9]

The combination of the reestablishment of Italian authority in Sicily in early 1944 and the subsequent rejuvenation of the traditional political parties placed the separatists under severe handicaps. They now stood in stark opposition to national policy, and suspected of being potential if not active subversives, their operations were subjected to the disapproving surveillance of nervous officials. Unrest on the island, whether based on political or economic conditions, was blamed on them, and from time to time separatists were arrested on suspicion of having committed acts of violence or engaging in other antigovernment activities. Major episodes of violence occurred in early 1945 in southeastern Sicily, where there were revolts of surprising strength in several towns. While these were kindled more by resistance to the military draft than by separatist sentiment, officials were uncertain of the situation and very worried.[10]

Meanwhile, the traditional parties were eating into separatist strength by their own recruiting, particularly among peasants. The separatists had counted on this group, which traditionally was subservient to the agrarians and the Mafia, to provide the majority of their own votes. But the socialists and communists were making inroads among them in some areas while the Christian democrats, emphasizing the humanitarian aspects of their philosophy and utilizing the authority of the priests, were drawing away many others.

At the same time, the Italian political establishment moved to undercut the separatist cause. There might be a way to grant the Sicilians their essential demands without fracturing the Italian nation, it was suggested. Such a path would entail restructuring the national state so as to provide Sicily with meaningful autonomy. The central government, as the first step to show its self-professed good faith, proclaimed the establishment in February 1945 of a regional consultative body. The body had no real power, but the move, together with similar actions later, convinced significant numbers of separatist sympathizers that the likeliest fulfillment of their aims lay in compromise rather than confrontation.[11]

In the face of these setbacks, separatist leaders appeared to be unable to react decisively and in concert. Finocchiaro Aprile continued to exude confidence. His talk still was of a plebiscite on independence under the benevolent watchfulness of major world figures. Many other separatists recognized the unreality of his rhetoric and looked for alternative ways to reach their goal. In the end, some of them stayed with him, while others sought to salvage what they could through compromise. Still others turned their thoughts toward armed revolt. When, on April 21, 1945, the MIS headquarters in Palermo was destroyed by a progovernment mob and when the government subsequently closed many other party offices, anger fueled the likelihood that the core of the movement would support a resort to arms.

The Mafia

At the same moment, Sicily's mafiosi were also pondering their possibilities, for they too had important stakes in the future of the island. The Mafia of the immediate postliberation period consisted of the remains of the "old mafia," characterized by its location in the rural towns of western Sicily and its ties to the agricultural economy and the traditional class structure. The outlines of the urban-based "new mafia," of often incomparably greater wealth, were barely perceptible as yet. The Mafia of 1943 was poorly organized and weak, but, with the end of fascist rule and the arrival of the Allies, mafiosi found opportunities to regain their power and guarantee their future. Naturally, the question of who would control Sicily was of prime importance to Mafia bosses and their followers.

Studies of the origins and development of the Sicilian Mafia through the nineteenth and early twentieth centuries are many, and their number continues to grow.[12] As it does, brief summaries of its history become more complicated. The Mafia often has been presented as a monolithic, tightly organized criminal conspiracy—references to one dominant Mafia boss have been common. But, in reality, the Mafia was more varied and amorphous than this conception allows. Oftentimes the term *Mafia* more properly denoted types of behavior, both criminal and noncriminal, than organizations. Still, mafiosi and Mafia associations did exist, and it would be hard to argue, as many Sicilians have done, that the Mafia existed only in the imaginations of Sicilian detractors.

Historically, the Mafia might be defined as a complex of individuals and associations, loosely held together by shared attitudes and practices, that became especially recognizable in rural areas of the western Sicilian provinces of Palermo, Trapani, and Agrigento during the mid–nineteenth century. It was so well integrated into society, had such fluid organizational structures, and was rooted so firmly in popular attitudes that it often could not be readily identified. Many Sicilians who recognized its existence defined it in a way that complicated its clear identification and tended to neutralize its more sinister aspects. They saw it only as a set of attitudes common to the mental framework of Sicilians: a distrust of public authority, a preference for finding solutions to problems and resolving disputes privately, and a conception of honor and respect that rested upon the power one exercises over others. Giuliano's nephew, Giuseppe Sciortino, reflected this view when I asked him about the Mafia in present-day Montelepre. He adroitly skirted my query by defining the Mafia in such terms, then diplomatically concluded "We are all mafiosi."

The Sicilian word *Mafia,* which originally was in reference to admirable personal qualities of beauty, individualism, strength, and the like, began to be used in reference to crime or criminal gangs only in the 1860s, following Sicily's adhesion to a unified Italy. It was employed particularly by northern Italian officials to describe the lawlessness that they found there. What they were talking about— vendettas, banditry, cattle rustling and horse thievery, smuggling, deep-seated suspicion and noncooperation before the state by ordinary people, extreme senses of individualism and personal honor, and other examples of general unruliness—were historically common to Sicily. However, perceptions of a critical state of affairs during the last three to four decades of the 1800s were grounded in reality, for Mafia behavior was flourishing as it seldom, if ever, had before.

The origins of the worsening conditions may be traced back at least to 1812, during the Napoleonic wars. In that year, Sicily's parliament, then under strong British influence, adopted a constitution that, among other revolutionary acts, abolished feudalism. The results, however, were not the society of free citizens, private property, and an unfettered labor market that the constitution's liberal architects had envisioned. The attempt to implant liberalism in Sicily ended with the restoration of full Bourbon control in 1816, and Sicily's peasants found themselves in a bad situation. In 1812, they had lost the collective property rights and other privileges and guarantees that the feudal relationship had imposed, and after 1816, they were without the freedom and adequate protection of the law that the constitution had promised. In general lines, they came to be dominated by either the former feudal lords, or they fell under the dominion of a new class of ambitious entrepreneurs and power brokers who arose chiefly from their own ranks. By the end of the century this latter class was being called the *Mafia*.

The Mafia rose to its position of influence during the liberal regime that lay between Italian unification in 1860 and the imposition of the fascist state in the mid-1920s. For, like its predecessor, liberal Italy also failed to establish effective state authority in rural Sicily; this, despite its constitution, which placed virtually all public authority in the central government. Its failure to guarantee peace, security, and law enabled mafiosi and Mafia associations to rise to power.

The precise origins of mafiosi and the nature of their activities varied from time to time and from place to place. It has been argued for long that their origins were related particularly to two occupational groups of growing importance in those times, rural guards and *gabelloti* (singular, *gabelloto*). The guards, frequently former peasants or herdsmen, protected estates from bandits, cattle rustlers, and other outlaws. *Gabelloti* were leaseholders, a class that had developed over the past two or three centuries as rural barons shifted their main residences from their farms to palaces in Palermo, Naples, and even farther afield. When they did so, they left the land in lease to *gabelloti*, who, in turn, sublet it to peasants.

Rural guards and *gabelloti*, wielding armed force in the case of the first and controlling the main resource to livelihood in the case of the second, were natural contenders for power and property in a society where the predatory urge met little resistance from public authority. Yet, mafiosi were not tied exclusively to these occupations; many others became mafiosi also. What characterized their kind were not so much occupations as attitudes and activities. Above all, they could be identified by their demand for "respect," through the exercise of overbearing individual power over others. Although it may not have been true universally that one had to demonstrate the ability to take another human life before achieving "respect" in Mafia circles, this popular belief probably was not far off the mark.

As to Mafia activities, they too were more varied than often has been pictured. Much of the literature on the Mafia points only to the illegal endeavors of mafiosi, when, in fact, their activities ranged widely over legal and extralegal areas. That most, if not all, of them engaged in criminal activities was true, of course. Most also pursued legitimate occupations; full-time, clandestine criminality on the order of the traditional rural brigand was not a Mafia characteristic. Indeed, much of what differentiated mafiosi from ordinary criminals was their integration into lawful society, often on high levels. They may have violated the law on a grand scale, but they were not outlaws in the sense that pertained to traditional brigands. Brigands lived outside the law whereas mafiosi pursued their illicit activities within the confines of legally constituted society.

In the extralegal realm, the influence of mafiosi was pervasive in the communes they controlled. In effect, these aggressive sectors of local society appropriated state power to ensure their own power and autonomy. They were the "law," and the local population saw them in that light. In this regard, their rule had a kind of legitimacy.[13] The citizenry probably saw them in general as more legitimate than the central government. The latter, which normally paid them little mind, was little known, except for its sporadic and sometimes fiercely harsh exercise of police power against virtually the entire community.

The relationship between these de facto local rulers and the central government was generally one of pragmatic accommodation. The Mafia rightly saw in the state at least a potential adversary and recognized the need to neutralize its power; they also wanted access to public monies. In return for local autonomy, the Mafia offered the politicians its power over the electorate, a particularly important consideration after a series of electoral reforms, the first in 1882, expanded the suffrage. The result was a cozy one. The Mafia boss served as the local representative of the district's deputy in Rome. When he came to visit, the boss accompanied him and dictated who had access to him, and the deputy's favors to the area were channelled through him. The access to the central government apparatus that was acquired in this way was invaluable to the Mafia head, particularly with respect to the police. They were centrally controlled, and the right words given to headquarters in Rome by a deputy, or a minister with whom he had influence, could often produce the desired results on the local level. Uncooperative police found promotions slow and transfers imminent. So well known were the links between the Mafia and the deputies from the west of Sicily by the twentieth century that little more than cynical boredom greeted the many assertions with which those same deputies disclaimed not only ties with the Mafia but denied that such a thing existed in their homeland.

The rise of mafiosi to positions of power in Sicily's rural communes was not as orderly as the foregoing survey might suggest. This was attested to by the stories that came out of western Sicily in the late nineteenth century of thievery, beatings, mutilations, and murders, as well as the destruction of citrus and olive groves, vineyards, and other property. Not all of this was Mafia violence, since Sicily suffered from a broad variety of malefactors, but much of it doubtless was the doing of mafiosi. It was directed against competitors and recalcitrant peasants, as well as against absentee landlords who did not submit readily to letting management of their resources fall into Mafia hands. Some of the barons were even afraid to visit their lands, so bad was the situation there, and were forced into selling them, usually to *gabelloti.*

When mafiosi consolidated their power in a commune, violence usually declined through a recognition of a hierarchy of force within their ranks. They divided power, territory, and activities in this largely spontaneous manner. Peace among them was often tenuous, however, and wars between Mafia groups remained a not uncommon occurrence. The ordering produced a local Mafia boss and at least the appearance of an organization. Where Mafia interests collided in a larger area of contiguous communes, a similar ordering might also occur. All together, the various groups made up western Sicily's Mafia. It, too, was sometimes described as having its boss, but in reality, the many parts of the Mafia were much too diverse and locally centered to be ruled by one man.

Central to the success of the Mafia was *omertà,* the code of silence. Crimes went unreported, even by their victims. When public officials attempted to gather evidence or prosecute alleged perpetrators, people usually disclaimed all pertinent knowledge. If they did give evidence to the police, normally only under extreme duress, they repudiated it at the trial. In the end, no one had done anything, no one had seen anything, and no one had heard anything.

From one vantage point, *omertà* appeared to be the moral solidarity of the community against the state, and there was some truth in the appearance. Public power was mistrusted and held to be illegitimate; resort to private power in the settling of disputes, in contrast, was held to be proper. This attitude gave *omertà* a kind of legitimacy in the popular mind, but at the same time, the concept rested heavily upon fear. Death was the standard punishment for revealing knowledge to the police of crimes committed by mafiosi or their friends, and to leave no doubt as to why the execution had taken place, the tongue of the victim was cut out.

By the 1920s, many mafiosi were politically influential, economically affluent, and socially effective. They owned businesses and industries, especially those dealing in the purchase, processing, and distribution of agricultural products. Some of their sons were university graduates, who were knocking on the doors of the island's establishment. But, however far the Mafia had come from its origins, it found itself in deep trouble after 1925, the year in which the fascists consolidated their control. The new regime was openly hostile to the Mafia, and its political usefulness was quickly eroded. By the end of the decade, its role in elections had been undercut by changes that left Mussolini's party the only legally recognized one. Nor did it any longer have influence over the police, who now moved against it with a zeal and vengeance, including the unrestrained use of violence, that rivaled its own record.

The history of the Sicilian Mafia under fascism is unclear in precise terms. Apparently, however, many mafiosi adjusted to the new circumstances, especially those who had legitimate business interests to which they could shift their major efforts. Others with education and professional standing managed to fare quite well, also extricating themselves from clearly illegal activities. Those who probably experienced the most difficulties were the uncultured country mafiosi. They continued to lease and sublease land and deal in farm products, but their lucrative illegal undertakings, like cattle rustling and exaction of the "rake-off" from the unlawful enterprises of others, were very circumscribed. The marked growth of state police power lay at the heart of their difficulties, especially the state's monopolization of violence, and fewer people paid them the respect that they formerly had commanded.[14]

If the beginning of World War II found the Mafia in a much weakened state, the liberation of Sicily in 1943 brought opportunities for a spectacular comeback. The end of the dictatorship enabled old Mafia groups to reorganize and new ones to be formed, little bothered by police surveillance or fear of prosecution. Freedom of action was all that mafiosi needed. The conditions that existed in the interior, especially with respect to the landholding system and the poverty and weakness of the peasantry were at least as favorable as before the fascists came to power. Furthermore, the reestablishment of a democratic system opened the door again to political influence. They easily resumed their electoral functions. The newly formed parties, hastily jockeying for positions, accepted support from almost anybody. Mafiosi found themselves cast in especially favorable light for their opposition to the fascists, a valuable political asset at the time.

Little else, however, did more to breathe new life into the Mafia than the favors bestowed upon it by the British and American armies of liberation. The extent of the participation of the Mafia from both sides of the Atlantic in the Allied invasion and subsequent occupation of Sicily may never be known fully. Suffice it to say here that the United States forces actively recruited men, officers, and special agents from among Americans of Sicilian birth and ancestry for the invasion, at least some of whom were mafiosi.[15] Sicilians found much to comment upon when known mafiosi from both sides of the ocean appeared among the Allied staff, including some in the Palermo area civil affairs office, which was headed by ex-lieutenant governor of New York Charles Poletti. The most impressive gains bestowed on the Mafia by the Allies, however, was on the commune level. With the Allied conquest, the existing fascist town administrators were swept away and new ones named. Large numbers of the new appointments went to mafiosi or their political friends. Charges that this was a plot may be doubted. More likely, the Allied authorities did not much care who the new mayors were, as long as they were not fascists or communists. They wanted men who could wield power effectively in the chaos of those days, and mafiosi were logical choices.[16]

Calogero Vizzini, perhaps the island's most prestigious mafia chief, was named to head Villalba, a commune some 50 kilometers northwest of Caltanissetta. Vizzini had been born some sixty-six years earlier to a Villalba family of modest circumstances. The family's main distinction was the number of priests it produced, a sizeable contingent that included two of Don Calo's brothers. He, in contrast, went the other way. He obstinately refused to attend school and, following the common pattern of mafiosi, got into trouble with the law before many more years had passed. In 1917, the commanding officer of the Caltanissetta division of the *carabinieri* described Vizzini, then about age forty, as "a dangerous repeated offender who is given to the Mafia and capable of anything." Yet he already was rising to a position of power in Villalba, a commune that, lying in a region of landed estates and mafia rule, was often described as one of Sicily's most backward. He particularly profited from the relative prosperity of the first world war by acquiring land and sulphur mines. By the time the fascists began to direct their repression at the Mafia in the mid-1920s, Don Calogero was wealthy, powerful, respected, and widely known. In appearance, and as others usually saw him, he was not out of the ordinary. Known as a good family man, his manner was affable, and in maturity, he had a rotund belly and a not at all unfriendly look.[17] But, then, Mafia bosses were not commonly distinguishable from other eminent personages in appearance and manner. They were politicians and businessmen, they looked respectable, and they could be seen sitting daily in the coffee bars chatting with friends or the police and walking with their wives and children.

At war's end, the separatists and most of the Mafia were political allies. They often, in fact, appeared to be one and the same. Around 90 percent of western Sicily's new town administrators were separatists; about three-quarters of them were also mafiosi.[18] Few separatist leaders saw anything unseemly in working with the Mafia; that had been, after all, the traditional way of doing politics in Sicily. But one of the weakest links in Finocchiaro Aprile's coalition was the Mafia, for its leaders were likely to support the separatist movement only as long as its cause looked promising. When, in 1944 and early 1945, its prospects began to decline, they increasingly looked with greater favor on the traditional parties.[19] Even so, when in the spring of 1945 separatists began to seriously consider armed revolt as the means to their goal, many leading mafiosi still supported them. Calogero Vizzini still did, although some wondered if his commitment was firm. They noted that in his own Villalba the Christian democrats were led by his trusty nephew. They correctly surmised that Don Calo was hedging his bets.

The Struggle over Land

Sicily entered the twentieth century with one of its most pressing problems unresolved, the backwardness and poverty of its rural masses. The roots of the problem were complex and many: the concentration of land ownership in few hands, absentee landownership, the leasing of land to peasants through intermediaries, the extensive and uneconomical use of resources, and the lack of improvements, among others. Moreover, it seemed evident that the problem had worsened during much of the century that had just ended.[20]

The abolition of feudalism in 1812, as noted in the previous section, aimed at a social and economic system based upon private property and free labor. Its aborted effects on Sicily's peasants produced neither. They lost the use of the common lands, which were turned into the private property of the landed barons, who in the main were the former feudal lords. Without any real rights of their own, or other recourse, the peasants became simple tenants or day laborers. It was not always the landed barons for whom they worked, however. Increasingly through the century, as earlier, the barons absented themselves from their lands and leased them to *gabelloti,* who then also lived from the peasants' labor, sometimes even more parasitically.

Through the years, the Bourbon kings and various of their officials were concerned about the conditions in rural Sicily, and from time to time they made attempts at reform, but their actions were either ill-conceived or too feeble to produce beneficial results. Meanwhile, the aggrievement of peasants grew. They harbored memories of a time when life had been easier, and in any village, it was said, they could identify the lands that had once been theirs to use. In revolutionary years such as 1848, these lands were likely to be targets of peasant agitation.[21]

The coming of Garibaldi and the end of Bourbon rule in 1860, followed by the union with Italy, brought hopes for quick reform. In contrast, little resulted. Garibaldi's hastily given promise of land to peasants was not heeded by the new rulers. Later in the decade, a possible first step in that direction, a radical proposal to confiscate the Church lands and distribute them to peasants, was thwarted. The anticlerical government confiscated the lands, to be sure, but then sold them at public auction, a policy that predictably benefitted few penniless peasants.

The plight of the majority who lived in Sicily's rural zones was exceedingly grim through the remainder of the century. Exploited by both landowners and *gabelloti,* they were hurt also by population growth, which devalued their labor and placed severe strains on limited resources. The tenancy contracts in some regions were grossly unjust; the wages of day laborers were equally unrewarding. Severe deprivation, on a scale Sicilians had not known in normal times, was a constant reality in the lives of many.[22]

During the nineteenth century, Sicily's peasantry occasionally demonstrated a propensity for violence in their futile attempts to reclaim their rights; perhaps, it was their only recourse. By the end of the century, however, there were reasons for hope that their discontent might be channeled toward more constructive solutions. The *Fasci Siciliani* (Sicilian Leagues) of socialist inspiration were the first significant manifestation of this hope. They reached the peak of their influence in 1893. In that year, deep in the interior at Corleone, they held the first peasant congress in Sicily's history. At it, they set forth improved terms for the renewal of tenancy contracts, and subsequently those who adhered to the movement refused to work unless their demands were met. The strike sufficiently alarmed landowners that they succeeded in bringing harsh government action against it. The *Fasci* were crushed, but the seeds of a better organized and more focused peasant agitation had been planted; socialist attempts to organize the peasants continued.[23]

In addition to socialism, Christian Democracy also appeared, one of the results of Pope Leo XIII's *Renum Novarum* of 1891. This movement, which began soon after the *Fasci,* worked to establish community-based institutions for the benefit of smallholders and tenants. In Sicily, rural credit banks, peasant leagues, and cooperatives were formed. The principal aim of the cooperatives was the leasing of land directly from the owners, a strategy which eliminated the *gabelloti.* Though the reform movement was soon stunted by conservative opposition, including action by Pope Pius X in 1904, it nonetheless helped to raise the social consciousness of segments of the peasantry. Through his work in it, the young Sicilian priest Luigi Sturzo concluded that political action was also necessary. He later would be the main figure in the formation of the Popular Party in 1919, the forerunner of the post World War II Christian Democrats.[24]

By the early years of the twentieth century, the social, economic, and political context of Sicily was undergoing significant change. Doubtless, the new liberalism of Giovanni Giolitti, who frequently was prime minister after 1900, had some effects there. A prime minister who believed that agricultural workers had the right to strike, and who refused to order state action against them, was an innovation, in any event.

Of greater consequence was the large-scale emigration from the island. To French Tunisia, the United States, Argentina, Brazil, and other destinations, some 1.5 million people left before the outbreak of the first world war.[25] This exodus of people valorized labor as never before. Contracts began to be offered tenants that afforded greater security of tenure and encouraged improvements and better use of the land. More landowners also began to live on their properties, or at least, to attend to them with greater interest. Of major effect, too, was the money sent home by family members who emigrated or brought home by those who returned. For the first time, significant numbers of peasants could purchase land. The plots that most could afford were small, like the one that Giuliano's father bought. In some areas, the fractionalization of properties into hardly viable economic units began to appear.

Social tensions fell among those who acquired land but rose among those who could not, and agitation over the land question continued. A major episode in its history followed World War I. During the war, well over one-half of Sicily's adult male peasants became soldiers. To try to maintain the loyalty of its peasant conscripts from Sicily and elsewhere, in the face of economic difficulties at home and losses on the military front, in 1917, the government promised them compensation in land at war's end. After November 1918, these men came home in full expectation of collecting their pay.

The results generally were disappointing. The government did not move quickly to effect the thorough agrarian reform that would have fulfilled its promise. When it did not, angry veterans responded with widespread land occupations between 1919 and 1921. To these disorders, the government took a generally ambiguous but perhaps politically realistic course. It did not attempt to crush the peasant movement—confronting hundreds of thousands of angry veterans over Italy was hardly an inviting prospect; nor did it seek vigorously to meet its demands. Rather, it maneuvered to control developments, mediate among opposing parties, and legalize a restricted number of land seizures. Its tactics, it appears, included both delay and partial satisfaction, in anticipation that the need for more decisive action would be forestalled.

Meanwhile, more ex-soldiers and other peasants took advantage of the relative lack of restraints to seize land. At the same time, many landowners sold their properties, cognizant that the state of affairs guaranteed them little security. Since the prosperity of the war period and the continuing flow of checks from America produced an unusually large amount of ready cash among Sicilians, including peasants, potential buyers for land were numerous.

A deeper reform might have been carried through if the peasants and those who tried to lead them had been better organized and more united. But suspicion, antagonism, and conflicting interests made it difficult for veterans, nonveterans, tenants, day workers, and smallholders to act together. The divisiveness was worsened by the professional activists who sought to define and lead the movement. Most prominently, these were socialists and, under the banner of the Popular Party, Catholic reformers. Although both professed deep interest in the plight of peasants, both also had distinct political aims. The radical majority in the Socialist Party hoped to instill class consciousness in the peasants and harness them for the revolution, while the Catholic activists aimed to halt the spread of such secular radicalism by milder reform. In the end, many peasants worked through their own organizations. They were suspicious of both political factions, but especially of the socialists, among whom sympathy was minimal for those whose highest aspirations reached only to private ownership of their own small farm.[26]

By 1922, rural Sicily was settling down. Its land tenure situation, which remained quite stable during the years of fascism, was a mixed one. Anything over 200 hectares was considered to be a very large property; in 1946, only approximately 28 percent of the land fell into that category. On the other hand, very small properties of 5 hectares or fewer accounted for about 35 percent of the land.[27] Figures such as these, however, did not adequately describe reality. Extremely large estates, true latifundia reminiscent of the past, still were predominant in parts of the interior; very small properties, in contrast, were numerous near the coast and around the large cities. The Montelepre area was typical of the latter. Although large properties, like the Lo Zucco Estate, existed there, small holdings were the rule, many no larger than 1 or 2 hectares.

It was the remaining landed estates that drew the attention of peasants and leftists when, with the end of the dictatorship in 1943, social passions were again unleashed. Scarcely had the Allied armies arrived, when Sicily's already active Communist Party called for the overthrow of the privileged class and the creation of a socialist state. The pronouncements of the majority of socialists were equally strident. Soon, under the auspices of both parties, peasant leagues and labor unions were formed. The confiscation of large estates without compensation to their owners formed the basis of a program that the left hoped would draw the landless to its ranks.

Sicily's barons were alarmed. They saw little chance of help from Rome, since the Minister of Agriculture in the coalition Badoglio government, Fausto Gullo, was himself a communist. The revolution seemed very near when, in April 1944, Comrade Gullo came to Messina to attend a regional meeting of communists as the official representative of the party's central committee.[28]

Whether the left could actually mount an effective campaign for social change appeared doubtful. Confusion reigned within both socialist and communist ranks. Neither had strong leadership. At the Communist Party's Messina conference, the factions that had long divided the left emerged again. One argued in favor of piecemeal reforms as a temporary tactic, whereas the other would settle for no less than the immediate and total nationalization of all property.[29] The latter position hardly appealed to the island's normally conservative peasants, who only wanted their own plot of land. Lack of understanding and conflicting interests between the left and segments of the peasantry still made a close union of their forces difficult.[30] Many peasants looked instead for help from the Christian Democratic Party, whose commitment to both agrarian reform and private property seemed firm.

Only in midsummer 1944, with the arrival of Girolamo Li Causi, did the uncertainty on the left begin to turn into firm resolve. Li Causi had been away from his native land for more than twenty years.[31] Born in Termini Imerese on the northern coast of Palermo province, he had become a socialist at the age of 17 in Venice where he was a student; in 1923, he defected to the communists, who themselves had split from the socialists two years earlier. Li Causi rose quickly in Communist Party ranks and, following the consolidation of fascist control in 1925, was a member of the inner circle that ran the party in the underground. Arrested in 1928, he spent the next decade and a half in prison. He regained his freedom in 1943 and in the next year was sent to Sicily by Togliatti. A good indication of the importance that Togliatti attached to the island was demonstrated by his choice of the tough, proven Li Causi to direct party affairs there. Once in Sicily, Li Causi went to work immediately, imposing discipline on the party's disorderly factions and squashing any of its lingering sentiment for separatism.

His speeches set the tone for the party's public program. At Termini Imerese, he stated that, in the "historic phase" in which the nation then found itself, the communists would seek neither the violent conquest of power nor the imposition of the doctrinaire proletarian state. Rather, he assured his listeners, the party's aim was "progressive democracy," in close cooperation with intellectuals, workers, and peasants. The central problem to be confronted, he declared, was the continuing existence of the large landed estates. Togliatti himself seconded Li Causi's emphasis on the land question a few days later in Palermo's *La Voce Comunista* (The Communist Voice). For reasons of strategy, and maybe conviction as well, Li Causi was trying to move beyond communist sectarianism to a broader-based party that, at least in this phase, would present a more moderate image. He hoped to attract all segments of the peasantry to it, including smallholders and those who aspired to such status, by avoiding rhetoric about the socialization of rural properties. Li Causi, not long thereafter, would announce his support of a united front with the Socialist Party, the majority of whose members, unlike virtually all other European parties of that persuasion, were almost indistinguishable from the communists.[32]

Few who knew Li Causi doubted his courage, but perhaps even a close associate or two were surprised when he scheduled a public appearance in the central square of Villalba, Don Calogero Vizzini's own lair. Li Causi had few natural enemies as dangerous as he. Vizzini's concern for land reform was firsthand. Like many Mafia bosses, he was a *gabelloto,* a major one, in his case. He knew that the kind of land division proposed by the communists and socialists would alter radically, if not totally undermine, the structure of absentee ownership, leases, and powerless peasants that undergirded the rural Mafia's power.

The wonder of Li Causi's trip to Villalba, a small town well inside the rugged interior region southeast of Palermo, arose from the knowledge that while there he would be on his own. Don Calogero's near-absolute control of his hometown was undoubted. Li Causi's principal contact there was young Michele Pantaleone, later to become one of the most powerful anti-Mafia voices among Sicily's writers. A land surveyor from a locally prominent family, in 1944 he was the secretary of the town's Socialist Party.

Li Causi appeared in Villalba on September 16. By the time the meeting started in late afternoon, Li Causi thought he had assurances from Vizzini that he would be permitted to speak, but he had been warned not to mention the land question or the Mafia. The leftists took their position in one corner of the square, opposite the Christian Democratic Party headquarters. There were only two other groups there, both of them small. One, near the Christian Democratic Party office, was with Mayor Beniamino Farina, Don Calo's nephew; amid the other, in the middle of the square, was Vizzini himself. Groups of peasants, who had been told to stay away, could be seen just beyond the square.

Disregarding Vizzini's prohibitions, Li Causi launched into a fiery attack on what he labelled the two "parasitic" classes of agrarians and *gabelloti,* then denounced the situation at one nearby estate, on which, in fact, Vizzini was the *gabelloto.* Vizzini loudly and angrily retorted: "It isn't true, it's a lie." A Li Causi partisan shouted to him to shut up, whereupon altercations started. According to the leftists, the first aggressive moves were made by the other side, but before the affair ended, both sides had resorted to gunfire. Remarkably, no one died in the fray, although fourteen persons received wounds, including Li Causi in the knee.

The affair at Villalba was one of the most talked about events in Sicily in the immediate postwar period. The Italian left made it a cause celebre, hoping to put Calogero Vizzini behind bars. An investigation was conducted and judicial proceedings initiated, but long-drawn-out maneuverings that included appeals, lost records, amnesties, and presidential pardons kept Vizzini and his henchmen out of prison. When he died in 1954, at age 77, he died a free man. He had too many ties to high public offices not to be dealt with gently.[33]

However lightly Vizzini was treated, Li Causi's side in the struggle was not without strengths of its own, for the communists were an influential part of the provisional government. At about the time that Li Causi recovered from his wound, his fellow communist at the Ministry of Agriculture initiated a series of postwar measures that eventually would radically alter the land tenure system in Sicily. The first of the two main Gullo decrees (October 1944) regulated the division of production in owner–tenant contracts in a scaled manner that was tied to the type of land in question. For example, the most favorable contracts for tenants were for undeveloped land, from which they would keep 80 percent of the yield. Such liberal provisions brought the owners so close to rebellion that the High Commissioner for Sicily interpreted the decree to make it less onerous to them. This move angered the tenants. Eventually, a 1946 revision stipulated that for most productive land the division of yield would be 55 percent to the tenant, 45 percent to the owner.

Such liberalizing regulations helped to reduce peasant discontent; in those areas, that is, where they were effected. For, in other places, where the peasant leagues were weaker and traditions different, little changed. In whichever case, they did not satisfy peasant aspirations for land ownership. The second Gullo decree (December 1944) had aimed in that direction by providing for the concession of unused land to peasants. But little land changed hands, since responsibility for implementing the law fell to prefects, who generally had close links to the landowners.[34] Peasant and leftist frustration thereafter grew from the government's failure to do more—and greater violence was yet to come.

CHAPTER THREE

Colonel Giuliano

IN THE SPRING OF 1945, GIULIANO TOOK his first step toward greater fame. In a typewritten manifesto that appeared in San Giuseppe Jato on April 26, he proclaimed his support of an independent Sicily.

> Sicilians! The solemn hour of the Sicilian revolution is ready to strike. Imitating the heroic moves of our forefathers . . . who liberated us from the French yoke, we will sever this Italian chain which under the guise of protecting us oppresses and suffocates us. . . . We will fight and inevitably win that independence for which we have yearned so long . . . at the shout of liberty take up arms and gather in the town squares where you will find men to lead you in the realization of the highest aims of the Sicilian nation.
>
> Giuliano[1]

Many in the separatist high command also believed, by this time, that independence could be achieved only by armed revolt; otherwise, their movement would be strangled by repression from the mainland. Sorely short of competent military leadership—and with inadequate troops besides—some of them saw hope in seeking the help of the more capable chieftains of the island's criminal bands. Giuliano quickly came to mind. Not only was he known to favor their cause, but in any event, they needed his cooperation. Younger separatists were trying to persuade the movement's senior leaders to permit them to recruit and train troops in the mountains back of Palermo. That area, however, was Giuliano's. If they were to work there, they had to come to an understanding with him.

The leaders of the Separatist Youth League asked Lucio Tasca to set up a meeting for them with the brigand chief. Palermo's former mayor easily arranged it through his vast network of contacts. On the appointed day in mid-May, Attilio Castrogiovanni of the youth group talked with Giuliano for about an hour near Montelepre's cemetery. The bandit assured him that he was a separatist "by instinct" and readily offered to support the insurrection. More than pleased, Castrogiovanni explained that Giuliano soon would have the chance to meet the top commander of the revolutionary army.[2]

The Death of Antonio Canepa

Before another encounter was arranged, the movement's major military figure and de facto commander of its only army fell as a martyr. Antonio Canepa, the Catania radical, had left Sicily after the arrival of the Allies to fight with the Italian partisans against the fascists and the Germans in the north. He returned to Catania in the fall of 1944.

By the beginning of 1945, he was recruiting and training troops in preparation for going into action, at a time when others in the movement were also concluding the struggle could be won only by armed insurrection. Antonino Varvaro, the leftward-leaning Partinico lawyer who served the MIS as its secretary, proposed that Canepa be brought in as the commanding officer of its military arm, the Voluntary Army for Sicilian Independence, or EVIS (Esercito Volontario per l'Indipendenza Siciliana), existing as yet mostly on paper. The conservative MIS executive committee, suspicious of Canepa's leftist ideology but desperate for experienced fighters, agreed to a compromise. Nominal command of EVIS would go to a middle-aged nobleman of the Carcaci family of Catania but Canepa would be offered a brigade within it, to be trained in the mountains of northeastern Sicily after the manner of the renowned Yugoslav partisans. Canepa accepted the assignment, aware, no doubt, of the ineptitude of the separatist leadership and convinced that he could act independently.

The recruiting and training of his army proceeded. In one minor action, they seized and briefly held an isolated forest guard post but, in anticipation of the arrival of a force sent to retake it, Canepa concluded that the effort was premature and ordered retreat. Military action, he told his men, would be resumed in the fall.[3]

It is to be doubted that Canepa's planned return to action would ultimately have made much difference in deciding the destiny of a movement that had so much going against it. In any event, he was not to get his chance. Early in the morning of Sunday June 17, 1945, according to the police report, Antonio Canepa (alias Mario Turri) was fatally shot at a roadblock on the Randazzo–Cesarò highway, not far from his clandestine camp.

As befitted Canepa's mysterious past, the police statement was doubted; and, in fact, some portions of it had been falsified. The official version related that the roadblock had been set up in response to reports of the presence of bandits in the area. When the troops saw a truck approaching with ten or more young men aboard, they were suspicious and ordered it to halt. Instead, the vehicle speeded up. The shots that the soldiers fired into the air to scare the occupants into stopping resulted in a full scale conflict. In the course of it, a man riding in the cab tried to hurl a hand grenade at the soldiers, which, however, exploded prematurely and killed him. By the time the battle ended, three of the truck's riders were dead and two others were wounded and in custody. The remainder escaped.

The police further stated that the truck was transporting an EVIS force from a secret military camp somewhere in the Catania or Messina area and that they found arms and ammunition on board. The mature man killed, they said, was EVIS commander Antonio Canepa, who, they added, was carrying large amounts of money.

While portions of the police report were true, other parts of it were not; much was left unsaid, in any case. Canepa was dead, to be sure, but he had not died instantly as the police claimed. He and his men had been subjected to an attack without warning as they travelled down the highway. They then succeeded in reaching Randazzo, where the truck's driver left the dead and wounded before making his own getaway. Canepa was already dead by then or died soon thereafter.

The police wanted the public to believe that they had killed the separatist leader in a casual encounter, unaware of who he was, whereas they had been told of his expected route and had the ambush in place when he arrived. The story was designed to protect their informers. As to who these were, suspicions fell heavily on Catania's rightwing separatists. Mistrustful of the radical professor, it is held, they were anxious to terminate his services to their cause out of fear that, if his efforts succeeded, he would become the leader of a mass-based separatist movement of the left. Yet, such allegations have never been publicly confirmed. If they are true, neither the police nor Canepa's betrayers understandably have been willing to confirm them. Antonino Varvaro, with his good connections to both right and left separatists, promised to reveal the real story someday, but he still had not done so when death overtook him in 1972.[4]

A Pact with Giuliano

After Canepa's death, military command of the EVIS brigade was passed to Concetto Gallo. The son of a former mayor of Catania, Gallo, then 32, was in business with his father. Although a one-time fascist, he had been with the separatist movement from its beginnings. His exuberance, energy, and courage seemed best to fit him for leadership of the armed struggle. He also looked the part. A tall, athletic man with a family, he stood in sharp contrast to the small, reserved, studious bachelor whom he succeeded.[5]

The uprising was set for the fall of 1945 and, early in September, the MIS executive committee gathered at Lucio Tasca's villa in Mondello, the fashionable beach town near Palermo, to give its final approval. Virtually all the prominent movement leaders were there, eleven in all, among them Tasca, two dukes from Catania, a baron or two, Varvaro, Gallo, and Finocchiaro Aprile, who presided. Mafia boss Calogero Vizzini was also present. While from Villalba, he often was in Palermo, where he maintained a second residence in a suite in one of the city's hotels.

Major discussion at the meeting centered around the idea, strongly pushed now by Gallo, of incorporating bandits into the separatist forces. Not only should Giuliano be invited to join but so should the formidable Niscemi area bandits of the southeast, Gallo urged. Enthusiasm for the proposal was generally high. Tasca had already approved it. The only dissent of much significance came from Varvaro, who opposed the use of irregular forces; but he had little influence over the conservatives who dominated the committee.

Calogero Vizzini liked the idea. He stated that he could guarantee the bandits' cooperation with the separatist forces, in answer to some apprehension about enrolling criminals in the movement. He gave assurances, furthermore, that he could "completely paralyze" police resistance to the insurrection.[6] The Mafia boss's confidence about his influence was debatable. At the moment, in a portion of the rural zone adjacent to Palermo, it was not the Mafia, certainly not Don Calo's group, but Giuliano who ruled. Actually, Vizzini's assurances with respect to the police also were exaggerated. He and his fellow Mafia bosses often could influence the state's use of force, but they could not guarantee control of it, especially when the army became involved.

The decision to enroll bandits having been made, it was necessary to arrange another meeting with Giuliano. The separatists wanted him to meet them near Catania on a property of the Duke of Carcaci, but Giuliano, with his customary caution, declined to travel so far from his refuge. So, they went to him. The conference was held in the middle of September near Sagana Bridge, on the other side of the mountain from Montelepre. Representing the separatists were Gallo and two prominent leaders of the movement's youth section, Duke Guglielmo di Carcaci, who was actually forty-four, and Baron Stefano La Motta, in addition to one or two others. As Giuliano invariably dictated when he met outsiders, they did not know the location of the meeting place in advance. As instructed, they drove along a designated highway until they were hailed by an agent of his who took them to the well-guarded site.

The negotiations between the separatists and Giuliano were both wide ranging and to the point. They made it clear that they needed him and assured him that, with the victory they hoped for, he would achieve legitimacy and fame for himself and his men. For his part, he convinced them of the depth of his separatist convictions. On one major point, their wish to set up their military headquarters in his zone, he balked. He found the idea untenable for the reason, he told them, that provisions for a large number of men could not be readily obtained there. Perhaps, there was some truth to his contention, but his principal fear went unstated. Although inexperienced in the ways of politics, he had the mind of a shrewd peasant. He knew to keep his distance from those whose trustworthiness had not yet been proved. He was willing to work with the separatists but unwilling to entwine his destiny too closely with theirs, and letting them set up their headquarters on his mountain was much too close.

They also discussed money, a subject brought up by Giuliano. He told the separatist leaders that he wanted an initial sum of 10 million lire to support his proposed activities in the uprising. In answer, one of them reminded him that he had his own ways of raising money and another, with an insider's knowledge of Sicily's upper class, said that he could suggest targets for Giuliano's actions. Giuliano bristled at the implication that he was a common bandit. He insisted on financial support from them. In the end, they promised it, one of them pledging a million lire of his own.

The separatists had not gotten everything they wanted, for Giuliano had been a hard bargainer, but they were satisfied. They offered him the rank of colonel in the independence army and bestowed upon him the movement's red and yellow flag. They also suggested that he might become the chief of police in the new government. Still, he wanted time to think over the matter. They departed, except for Gallo, who remained behind in hopes of convincing the young brigand to accept the proposal. For two days they stayed together, talking much, moving frequently, and sleeping in caves at night, taking turns at standing guard. Not long after Gallo left, Giuliano sent word that he had decided to accept their offer.[7]

Giuliano's commitment to the separatist cause was genuine. He fought for it harder and longer, and with considerably more skill and success, than did anyone else. Long after he was dead, a journalist asked the others to recall their memories of the legendary bandit with whom they had once dealt so intimately. While they hedged on some details and denied others—they had made their peace with the Italian establishment years earlier—they conceded that Giuliano was sincere and well meaning. Pressed further, they revealed more of their feelings. Of the bandits of the postwar years, Castrogiovanni asserted, "he was the only one capable of having ideas and lofty sentiments." Giuliano, he said, kept his promises to the movement in full. Gallo remembered him "as a good boy, with a profound sense of justice and a profound resentment for the way he had been treated by the authorities." One who had been a young volunteer in EVIS said it more effusively: "Giuliano was for us not only a legend but also a heartening reality. We did not consider him a bandit, but the most courageous fighter in our army. We admired the audaciousness, the effrontery, of his actions against the state forces and we were proud that he did them beneath the colors of the red and yellow."[8]

Preparations for Revolt

Before the separatists and their bandit allies could organize their forces for action, the authorities took counter measures of their own. They formed a new command, the General Inspectorate of Public Security in Sicily, to assume overall direction of the antibandit efforts. Although under the command of a public security police official and answerable to the Interior Ministry, the subordinate officers and men were drawn from both the public security police and the *carabinieri*. Ettore Messana, a veteran police official and native of Sicily's Agrigento Province, was named to head it.

Alarmed by incendiary independence oratory, seditious broadcasts from a clandestine radio station in eastern Sicily, and the certainty that the separatists had formed a military arm, the authorities struck directly at the MIS leadership. On the evening of October 1, they arrested Finocchiaro Aprile and Varvaro in a Palermo coffee bar and, within hardly more than an hour, had them aboard a boat headed for the Mediterranean island of Ponza. The two separatists had fallen victims to Italy's infamous confinement policy. Such a measure required a minimum of judicial proceedings.[9] The detainees were not incarcerated, but they had to remain within the limits of the town to which they were sent, they had to sign up daily with the local police, and they had to be inside their living quarters during the hours of darkness. The sentence of confinement was useful to the Italian state as an easy means of removing troublesome political figures and criminals from their locales. Ponza in 1945 was almost a world away. The Carcacis of Catania and Lucio Tasca took over the leadership of the movement.

Only days later, Giuliano added his own propaganda to that emanating from the broadcasts on the other side of the island. His was a proclamation posted in Palermo and area towns. In it, he offered the grand sum of 100,000 lire per month to those who would join him "for the sole purpose of fighting against the enemies of liberty." He warned against spies and counselled potential recruits to seek specific instructions as to how to enlist in his army from those who were known to be his friends. Giuliano also invited women to participate in the campaign. Whether he actually intended them to become soldiers in battle was not clear, but, if that was his aim, there was precedent for it in the history of Italian banditry. Peasant women had joined bands of brigands in impressive numbers during the social convulsions in the south of the 1860s. A general of that era particularly remembered one female brigand who, with a pistol in each hand, had intrepidly confronted his cavalry.[10]

In and around Montelepre, where Giuliano's call met intense interest, getting in contact with him entailed no more than a few discrete inquiries. Word soon got around that the man to see was one of the town's barbers. Potential recruits could express their interest to him without arousing suspicion, since barber shops are common men's gathering places; and, if Giuliano wanted them, they would be contacted later. That was what happened to Frank Mannino, who with other recruits was taken that night by the barber to meet Colonel Giuliano.[11]

Some men tried contacting Giuliano directly. One who succeeded in doing so was 17-year-old Francesco Barone. He was in Peppino's barber shop, awaiting his turn for a haircut, when two well dressed and obviously important men came in to confer with the barber in his living quarters back of the shop. The boy, curious as to the goings on, asked a fellow customer who the men were. He was told that they were separatist leaders and that one of the biggest figures in the entire movement was none other than Giuliano. Francesco, the poorly educated son of a Montelepre peasant, had never heard of separatism, though he knew much of the famous brigand and on occasion had seen him. When the separatist aim of securing independence for Sicily was explained to him, it struck him as a worthy idea.

When Francesco's turn with the barber came, he was too timid, too much aware of his youthfulness, to pursue the matter with Peppino in the presence of all the others. Knowing that Giuliano frequently came to town by night to see his mother, he resolved to try to contact him in person. His subsequent vigil finally paid off when one night he saw Giuliano emerge from the house just before dawn and head for the mountain. The ever-alert bandit, seeing that he was being followed by a lone individual, waited with revolver drawn. When Francesco told him that he wanted to enlist in his army, he was informed that he was too young and asked if perhaps he had not run away from home to escape a whipping. Convinced by the boy's sincere pleading, Giuliano accepted him. For young Barone, it was the beginning of a long adventure.[12]

By December, Giuliano had set up camp on Sagana and was actively enlisting men. The number was never large, no more than 40 to 60, for he was thinking only of a small guerrilla force. Each man received a rank and was issued a uniform consisting of a jacket, pants, and a beret, all made of American-type military khaki. Each also wore proudly the symbol of the separatist movement. Cast in metal and known as the Trinacria, the ancient name of Sicily, it was a striking insignia of three bent legs projecting at balanced intervals from a winged human head.[13]

Realistically, Giuliano's handful of separatist warriors had little chance of success. Yet, those men and boys who joined were impressed by what they saw. The Sagana camp had all the appearances of a military base. The uniformed men, the stocks of arms and ammunition, the motorized vehicles, and the intense activity engendered enthusiasm and confidence. In those hungry times, when sufficient food at affordable prices was in painfully short supply, the chance to consume cheese, olives, bread, and wine in unlimited quantities was also no small matter. Colonel Giuliano's western army was ready for action.[14]

All of this activity cost money, a lot of money, far more than the band had ever had to spend before. Nothing came cheap, for Giuliano was still paying premium prices for his supplies. His payroll also increased with the growth in the band's size. Contrary to the attractive proposition that he had made in his proclamation, offering 100,000 lire per month to recruits, he actually paid a more realistic 400 lire per day to ordinary recruits—still good wages at a time when agricultural laborers earned no more than half that figure. Real labor costs, nonetheless, were much higher, since Giuliano saw to the needs of his men's families also. In addition, he remitted funds to the separatist high command.[15]

Giuliano had known that the uprising would require extensive financial support. That was why at the Sagana meeting he had asked for commitments from the movement's leaders. If they gave him any, it was very little; as they had suggested to him when the matter first came up, he had ways of raising money on his own. The abduction of well-off persons for ransom, or the threat of such, was one of his most lucrative activities, as it had been traditionally for Italian bandits. Often, he did not have to actually execute the abduction, nor, for that matter, even mention the word. A request for money from him carried an implied threat of reprisal in case of refusal to pay. As to candidates, he already knew the area well and knew which of its inhabitants were wealthy; Lucio Tasca reputedly suggested additional names. Giuliano then wrote them letters requesting large sums. Some paid on the request, either willingly because they favored the separatists or unwillingly because they feared reprisals. Others negotiated for lesser amounts, while a few refused to make any contributions at all. These were threatened with abduction. They then usually paid off.[16]

No longer a bandit but a rebel leader, Giuliano tried to make his demands for money appear to be legitimate. He often paid for his supplies, but when he did not he issued revolutionary script in the form of an IOU bearing the movement's name and signed by himself. He also sometimes told those whom he abducted that the ransom money would be returned after Sicily won its independence.[17]

By December, separatist mobilization was proceeding in preparation for the commencement of action before the end of the month. Earlier plans for attacks on several fronts had been scaled down by then, since the large armies that the separatist leaders once visualized were not in evidence. There had been much talk and little effective organizing. Final plans, though still vague, called for two initial actions. Gallo and his allegedly numerous forces, operating from their base at San Mauro, near Caltagirone, were to go on the attack in the east, in concert with the Niscemi bandits. The ultimate aim there was the capture of Catania. Simultaneously, Giuliano would assault police outposts in his area to draw troops out of the capital. A large separatist army would come from Enna to occupy it. Other actions would follow, some separatists even still anticipating intervention on their behalf by the United States, once the revolt started.

Such, at least, was the plan. Little that subsequently happened, except for Giuliano's actions, made it appear to be other than a half-baked plot resting on fatally flawed assumptions. A high level military report, prepared just before the revolt came off, was close to the truth. Brunetto Brunelli, the general commander of the *carabiniere* corps, told the government in mid-December that the separatist army was made up of a few romantics, most of them students, and not much else. The state should be vigilant, he warned, but probably there was not much to worry about.[18]

Giuliano and his men, on Sagana, did not know of the weaknesses of their fellow conspirators. Young, naive, and isolated, they were taken in by the titles, smooth talk, and promises of the EVIS command. A hopeful and confident Giuliano called his men together in late December for the beginning of the campaign. He told his approximately four to five dozen men, some of them no more than 17 years old, that uprisings would occur at the same time all over the island. Some would die, he cautioned, but, to counter that sobering thought, he read aloud an encouraging letter from one of the separatist leaders. He then raised the red and yellow flag and, with his men, swore loyalty to it. A toast, "vivas" to an independent Sicily, and a feast ended the convocation.[19]

The Revolt

Giuliano's first attack under separatist colors occurred very early in the morning of December 27, 1945. The timing was dictated by the

EVIS command, which was trying to divert attention from Gallo's San Mauro camp. The existence of that post, separatist leaders had learned, was known to the authorities, and it was hoped that vigorous action by Giuliano in the west would buy Gallo time in the east.[20]

The post at Bellolampo was Giuliano's first target. Miles from any town, lying on the main Palermo–Montelepre road, its isolation made it an easy target. A two-story building of heavy masonry construction, it, like other rural police stations, housed both the offices and living quarters of the military assigned to it. The station had had an uneventful history, so on December 27 the three men stationed there retired early, as they normally did, in expectation of a quiet night. Their peace ended just after midnight, when they were awakened abruptly by the sounds of automatic weapon fire. Jumping from bed and grabbing their own rifles, they concluded that they were being assaulted by a group of about fifty well-armed men—Giuliano said he had ten men with him. The attackers called on them to surrender, but the three fought back as best they could. Only after about an hour, and with one of their number wounded, they capitulated. The bandits entered the station and started to tie up the soldiers. Giuliano saw the wounded man and, after briefly ministering to him, ordered one of the other soldiers left free to help him. The bandits then set to work, burning the station's records and loading arms, hand grenades, and ammunition into their truck. In reaction to the raid, 100 troops were sent to search for Giuliano.[21]

Two days later, shortly before midnight, Giuliano's separatist band struck again in a near reenactment of the Bellolampo raid. They attacked the isolated *carabiniere* station at Grisi, near Partinico, blowing up one of its wings and forcing its defenders to yield after an hour's battle. They tied up the soldiers without harming them and burned the station archives. The amount of arms and ammunition that they carted off was said to be abundant. The station was left burning and in ruin by what the press called the gang's "vandal-like fury."[22]

Over in the east, Gallo at near the same time fought his only engagement in behalf of the separatist cause. Giuliano's moves, contrary to hopes, had not saved San Mauro from attack. Once the authorities learned of its exact whereabouts—the camp was located on a property of the commander' wife—they reacted swiftly. A force that was variously said to range from 600 to 2000 men was sent to attack the encampment. They had little reason to believe that it amounted to much but were cautious nonetheless. After all, separatist leaders had talked of large armies. The defenders of San Mauro actually totalled some 200 at most.

Firing began near dawn on December 29. Most of the rebels, after assessing their chances for victory, or out of simple fear, began to sneak away with Gallo's consent. He and five men courageously, if foolheartedly, fought from behind the wall of a ruined building until they were overwhelmed. Just at the end, Gallo killed a soldier at point blank range. The state later formally arraigned him for the slaying. Fatalities in the battle included only one or two on each side; fewer than a dozen were wounded.[23]

With the news of the San Mauro disaster, the other separatist armies, including the allegedly large one from Enna that was supposed to proceed to Palermo, quickly disintegrated. Only Giuliano's army of the west was left to hold the red and yellow aloft, except for some of Gallo's eastern bandit allies who for a while yet were capable of committing acts of terrorism. In the worst of these latter actions, Rosario Avila's Niscemi bandits abducted eight military police at an isolated station near Caltagirone and offered the lives of the captives in exchange for Gallo's release. When, after eighteen days, the demands were not met, the brigands killed the soldiers. Following this bloody reprisal, the Avila band itself was soon eliminated.[24]

The fiasco at San Mauro ended the "regular" separatist military effort but not that of Giuliano's. He stepped up his action. He lacked the experience, sophistication, and temperament to realize the futility of the struggle. Moreover, there was much of the showman in him, and realistically he did not have much to lose. He already was an outlaw. Besides, his desire to justify himself, together with his marked romantic nature, dictated that fighting in the name of a just cause, even a lost one, was preferable to being a common criminal.

In early January 1946, Giuliano attacked the police posts at Pioppo and Borgetto, without notable success in either case. The authorities, reacting to his earlier attacks, were strengthening their defenses.[25] This frustrated Giuliano, but he was also angry. The state and the censored press were refusing to recognize him as an authentic rebel, calling his actions mere violence and vandalism.[26] They were not linking him publicly with the separatist movement; yet, ever since Bellolampo he had left his own personal brand of separatist propaganda on the walls of the police stations he attacked. Giuliano had prepared for this campaign several months before. In the previous summer, he commissioned Frank Mannino to make a large ink stamp to imprint a picture on walls. Portrayed in the design were Giuliano's hope for the annexation of Sicily to the United States. The proposal was not original with him. Talk of a union with America, or possibly England, had been heard since liberation. But Giuliano's design was striking, nonetheless. One man stood atop the United States pulling on a chain that was attached to Sicily on the other end, while a second, armed with giant scissors, cut the chain that tied the island to Italy.[27]

To demonstrate his continued dedication to the cause, Giuliano initiated the most spectacular campaign of his career. If it did nothing else, it forced the authorities to take due note of him. Action began around 9:30 P.M. January 7, 1946, with an attack on the Montelepre police station, located at the edge of town. The size of the force that attacked the station has been a matter of dispute. Giuliano said that it was composed of himself and two others but, as was characteristically the case when Giuliano was involved, the police thought it a more numerous one. The exchange of fire lasted for near an hour and could be heard in Partinico, several kilometers away. Giuseppe Calandra, the commander of the Montelepre detachment, telephoned for reinforcements. Calandra's move was exactly what Giuliano had anticipated; he now hurried back to Belvedere Curve, about 300 meters from Montelepre on the Partinico road, to join his other men and await the arrival of the additional troops.

At about 11:00 P.M., the reinforcements approached Montelepre. Comprised of a company of *carabinieri* and a detachment of regular army troops, they travelled in a truck, which was also carrying ammunition. In addition, there were several motorcycles and an armored car. When they rounded Belvedere Curve, Giuliano and his men, positioned advantageously above the sight, subjected them to automatic rifle fire and lobbed hand grenades and fire bombs at them. A series of explosions rocked the truck as the ammunition went off, and the vehicle itself caught on fire. In the midst of this, the able-bodied troops were trying to rescue their wounded comrades from the flames while the rebels mercilessly continued the attack. Some thirty government troops were wounded. Finally, the armored car, damaged but still mobile, retreated to Partinico to send a message for further reinforcements. The call for help was urgent; the number of rebels involved in the night's two assaults, it appeared, was surprisingly large. A Catania newspaper, basing its story on reports from Montelepre, estimated the attacking force at 1000 men.[28]

The morning after the Belvedere attack, Montelepre's residents awoke to a surprising sight. On top Monte d'Oro (Gold Mountain), the steep, cone-shaped formation that arises from the town's side, proudly and defiantly flew the separatist flag. Giuliano's challenge was, to Commander Calandra, "intolerable." He called to Palermo for more help. Before midmorning, Giuliano and his small band of insurgents opened fire from atop the mountain. With the arrival of reinforcements from Palermo, the government troops mounted their own attack. They blasted him with everything they had, including mortars. Additional troops continued to arrive throughout the day, until the number that had come from Palermo alone exceeded 550—all, however, to little avail. When, toward evening, the rebels vacated the mountain, stealthily and in small groups, they were still unharmed. Government casualties amounted to fourteen.[29]

The officials understandably were reluctant to admit the size of the force they threw against Giuliano, afraid the that the public would know the truth about the military's ineffectiveness. But, in Montelepre, the people had seen it all. Their native son was clearly the hero of the day. Giuliano, for his part, did not want it known how few men he had. That same evening, with a bare half dozen, he attacked Partinico in an attempt to create the impression that he commanded large numbers of men, divided into groups and engaged in action in several areas.[30]

Alarmed by the apparent strength of the rebels, the government placed Montelepre and surrounding towns under martial law on January 13 and maintained it for the succeeding 126 days; mass interrogations and arrests took place. Older boys and young men, known separatist advocates, and Giuliano's relatives and friends were special targets. But anyone who was believed to be sympathetic to the rebels, a category that included most citizens of Montelepre and immediately adjacent towns, was likely to be arrested upon the slightest suspicion. Many were sent to jail in Palermo, even though there was no substantial evidence against them. They were held merely on hopes that someone might later implicate them. Nor were prominent citizens excluded. The town lawyer found himself among those arrested, and so did the doctor.

As the headquarters of the military command, Montelepre appeared to be the center of a war zone. Portions of four army divisions, not to mention police and *carabinieri*, were there at times; artillery and armored cars moved continuously through the central square; the Giuliano family home was itself sequestered by the authorities for the use of the Garibaldi division's commander. From 5:00 P.M. until 7:00 A.M., citizens were forbidden to leave their homes. Ordinary activities almost came to a standstill. Transportation was critically disrupted. Many staple foodstuffs were unavailable for days at a time. Water was carefully rationed, not because of a shortage, but in an attempt to ensure that little if any was available to sneak out to bandit rebels in their barren mountain hideouts not far from town.[31]

The townspeople were being terrorized, but for the most part Giuliano was left alone. Fearful of being attacked, the troops stayed in town and left the countryside to him. At night, they holed up in their barracks and gave him the town, too. Such a state of affairs much impressed one Palermo reporter who went to Montelepre in late January.[32] He first journeyed to Partinico on the train, in expectation of hitching a ride on to his destination. Drivers, however, told him that they were avoiding Montelepre. So he doggedly set out to cover the 9 kilometers on his own power. Along the way, he saw neither policeman nor bandit; for that matter, not a single soul. The few houses that he passed were deserted. He noted that the terrain provided ideal settings for guerrillas. Troops who fell under attack on that road would have little chance of organizing effective defenses. Only when he reached the town did he encounter anyone. There, civilians were grumbling and soldiers were jittery. Escorted to the military command post, he asked for news from the battle lines. News, he found, was scarce. What one learned from the military in Montelepre, he discovered, was much like the government releases that had come from the disastrous Italian campaign in North Africa during the late war. They were brief and revealed nothing.[33]

In the following weeks, Giuliano's actions declined in frequency but were still often enough and with sufficient ferocity to keep the government's concern at a high level. In the most disastrous of these, he and his men ambushed a truck convoy of soldiers between Montelepre and Partinico on the morning of January 18, killing three soldiers and wounding others. An afternoon attack on a military jeep resulted in another fatality.[34] Riskier and much less successful were his repeated efforts to capture a radio station near Palermo. The risks were worth taking, for he wanted to knock out telegraph facilities housed there, as well as broadcast a separatist proclamation. Nonetheless, the station's defenses held, the attacks doing little more than momentarily interrupting a program or two. A predawn raid on the Monreale jail was equally unsuccessful.[35]

Prudently, however, fears of what Giuliano and his band might still do could not be taken lightly. In view of this, Minister of Interior Giuseppe Romita offered a reward of 800,000 lire for Giuliano's capture. Maybe Giuliano was offended by the paltry sum the state was willing to pay for him—he made many times that amount in one kidnapping. His answer was an insolent flyer that promised 2 million lire to anyone who would deliver the interior minister to him, dead or alive.[36]

CHAPTER FOUR

Political Boss and
Enterprising Kidnapper

THE DEFEAT AT SAN MAURO, TOGETHER with the failure of the regular separatists to attempt any other actions, left Giuliano's dramatic but isolated revolt sputtering and, in the end, with nowhere to go. As disillusionment set in, the band began to disintegrate. Giuliano took the desertions hard, for he had no intention of laying down his arms. He believed in Sicilian independence and would continue to espouse it but, more to the point, his freedom was at stake. Unlike many of his men, there was no chance that he could sink back into the anonymity of the peasantry.

Yet, faced with complaining band members and recognizing in them the same bitterness he felt, he did not try to keep them by force or fear. He had the right to shoot deserters, he told them one day, but, if they wished, they could go home. He asked only that they think about it overnight. The next day, almost all of his men informed him that they wished to leave. He told them as they departed that they were still his friends and could always depend upon him. Remaining with Giuliano were only a lifelong friend and 17-year-old Francesco Barone.[1]

The bandit chief knew that turning loose men who knew his habits was risky. The large reward on his head could tempt even good men. He thus made the effort to keep track of his ex-followers, sometimes gathering information on them through the boy Francesco, who could wander around town without attracting much attention.[2]

Giuliano's caution was well taken. He learned shortly that four of his former followers in San Cipirello were guiding the police on night patrols over his old trails. He moved quickly. Just minutes past midnight on April 25, now with a reinforced band, he arrived outside the house in San Cipirello where the culprits, the three Misuraca brothers and their brother-in-law, were asleep. Knocking on the door and calling out in the name of the police, the bandits told the young men that they were wanted at the station to accompany a patrol in search of Giuliano. They fell for the ruse and soon found themselves backed up against a wall on the main square threatened with immediate death. They ran at that point, not having much to lose, but Giuliano's gunmen killed two of them anyway. They explained their failure to kill all four by the night's darkness. On the dead bodies, the bandits left notes claiming credit for the executions.[3]

The June Elections

Following the failure of their pathetic revolt, the separatist leaders sought to revive their movement through participation in the June 1946 elections. To do so, they needed the release of their two top leaders from confinement, the legalization of the separatist movement as a political party, and amnesty for those who had taken part in the recent revolt.

Negotiations on these matters were pursued by the MIS with the government, mainly through the good offices of the commander of the army in Sicily, General Paolo Bernardi, who was sympathetic to them.[4] The government set two conditions for the success of the efforts: the renunciation of violence by the separatists and the surrender of arms still in their possession. On the first, Lucio Tasca spoke for his party in a letter to the authorities in which he denied any links between the MIS and EVIS, asserting rather that the armed group had had an entirely independent existence.[5] Tasca's denial was patently untrue, but it allowed the party to disassociate itself from its violent past without, at the same time, admitting guilt. To meet the second condition, the separatist leaders had to have Giuliano's cooperation.

Giuliano was suspicious. Although he longed for the peace and respectability that politicians could grant him through amnesty, he was afraid to give up his arms, to place his fate in the hands of the state. He held long, often heated, and not very fruitful discussions with Tasca, Carcaci, and others on the matter. The sticking point was his demand for a guarantee of amnesty for himself and his men, something that the separatists could not get the government to concede. All that the separatist leaders could offer him ultimately was a promise that when they came to power they would grant amnesty. That was not enough.[6] He would not lay down his arms. In the end, the government overlooked the failure of separatist leaders to obtain Giuliano's cooperation. In view of the weakness of his band at the moment, he was not regarded as very important.

The elections scheduled for June 2, 1946 were crucial for Italians. They would decide whether the nation would remain a monarchy or be transformed into a republic. They also would elect an assembly to write a new constitution for the nation. The association of the throne with Mussolini and the wartime German alliance augured ill for the monarchy in the referendum, and to bolster its fortunes, King Victor Emmanuel abdicated in favor of his son, Umberto, on May 10. Even so, prospects for preserving the monarchy were not good.

Prospects for the separatists in the elections were also unpromising, although some things went well for them. Negotiations for the release of Finocchiaro Aprile and Varvaro bore fruit with the return of the two in March. An amnesty was announced in the same month for participants in the separatist uprising. Excluded from its provisions, however, were common crimes, as well as other illegal acts committed either before or after the revolt. Giuliano and many of his men stood to gain nothing from it.[7]

One of the main problems for the MIS was its lack of clarity on major issues, particularly on the question of whether it would remain committed to total independence or accept some kind of autonomy within the Italian state. But, added to the confusion was the additional question of whether it was monarchist or republican. In actuality, it embraced all of these views, and the actions and statements of the party leaders in the weeks before the election did little to cover the contradictions. It was known that both Finocchiaro Aprile and Varvaro had renounced total independence in favor of autonomy as a condition of their release. Few could fault them on this, since hopes for independence had faded rapidly, but another apparent concession by them threatened to split the movement apart. Again to obtain their release, both of them gave at least nominal assurances that their party would uphold the monarchist position in the referendum. Once out, however, Varvaro advocated the republican view. The party chief, on the other hand, supported the king. So did Tasca. Others in the party also did as they pleased.[8]

Some party members saw in the monarchists the chance to achieve outright independence. Tasca, Carcaci, and others plotted to move the House of Savoy to Sicily in the event of a republican victory in the referendum. Allegedly, their plans met with some favor in Umberto's court, but the effort predictably came to nothing.[9]

Separatist lists for the constituent congress were entered in only two provinces, Catania in the east and Palermo in the west. The absence of candidates elsewhere reflected the party's organizational shortcomings. In those two districts, vigorous MIS campaigning attracted much attention. Finocchiaro Aprile and Varvaro were the leading candidates in the west, whereas, in the east, the one who drew the most interest was Gallo, in jail and charged with the murder of the soldier at San Mauro. His election, under law, would guarantee both his release and immunity from prosecution during his term in office.

Meanwhile, Giuliano geared up his electoral machine in the separatists' behalf. His endorsement of the MIS virtually ensured its victory in Montelepre and some surrounding towns. His support of the party was whole hearted, in spite of the mistrust that he felt for its leaders. Like others in the movement, however, he had his own views. He was a republican of liberal leanings, something after the pattern of Varvaro, but, on the question of the movement's ultimate goal, he still favored annexation to the United States as its forty-ninth state. Now, he announced the formation of the Movement for the Annexation of Sicily to the American Confederation (Movimento per l'annessione della Sicilia alla Confederazione Americana). In reality, MASCA was never much more than Giuliano. Still and all, it was an imaginative act that, among much else, set the King of Montelepre apart from run-of-the-mill bandits.[10]

Giuliano's role in the 1946 campaign was impressive. As a fugitive, he could not appear publicly in behalf of the party, but he made his views known anyway. He opened a party office in his home town and invited the citizenry to enroll. As the mayor at the time remembered it, among the many who accepted the invitation were the town's most prominent people, some of them, the mayor thought, more from fear of Giuliano than sympathy for his party.[11] Giuliano placed cars and trucks at the party's disposal and convinced others to do likewise. His financial contributions accounted for a substantial portion of the funds expended by the party in the campaign.[12] It seemed not to trouble the separatists that the money came from the bandits' continuing extortions and abductions.

Most of all, Giuliano's support of the MIS effort could be seen through the participation in it of his sister. Then in her midtwenties, two years older than he, Mariannina entered the campaign on the urging of party leaders, who recognized her potential. Taken under the wing of Varvaro's wife, Jolanda, herself a prominent MIS campaigner, she toured with the separatists for some two months. She carried the party flag at rallies and sang the party hymn, dressed in a red and yellow blouse of her own making that bore the party symbol. Pretty and high spirited, she helped to attract crowds and work up enthusiasm.[13]

Inspired by the fervor of the crowds, the separatists were enthusiastic about their prospects as election day drew near. Finally, after three years of waiting, their aspirations would be vindicated by a vote of the Sicilian people. They seemed unaware of the ill effects that their record of overblown expectations and attendant disappointments, including the failed revolt, had had on the public. In many ways, they gave the appearance of still living in the heady days of postliberation 1943, when independence had seemed to be within their grasp.

In fact, much had changed since then, including the aims of the movement, as party spokesmen had backed away from the advocacy of outright independence and endorsed autonomy. Then, in a propitiously timed move, the government undercut the party on that issue, too, in the month before the election. The provisional government decreed on May 15, 1946, the Statute of Sicilian Autonomy that had been in preparation for several months. No matter that its major promises would go unfulfilled and its principal feature—a Sicilian high court with inviolable powers—would be nullified by a controversial ruling of Italy's supreme court, the blow had been administered. Disillusionment for Sicily lay in the future; for now, the parties that composed the provisional government had neutralized autonomy as a political issue.[14]

In the end, the separatists were unable to hold the majority of their potential voters. Some likely support, especially among the peasants, was won over by the Socialist and Communist parties on the social question. This complex issue, the core of which was land reform, was generally avoided by MIS campaigners. Most of them adamantly opposed any such reform; those who looked upon it favorably were too afraid of antagonizing the party's agrarian and Mafia support to talk much about it. Many others, peasants, agrarians, and Mafia included, moved over to the Christian Democratic Party. After all, there was not much reason to stay with the separatists once the likelihood of independence disappeared; and, as for autonomy, the Christian democrats claimed to be among its true architects.[15]

The results of the June vote were predictably disappointing to the Movement for Sicilian Independence. Its votes came to 166,609, a small 8.71 percent of the total. Only four MIS candidates won: Finocchiaro Aprile, Varvaro, Castrogiovanni, and Gallo. The election's clear winners were the Christian democrats, who emerged first with 33.63 percent of the Sicilian vote. The combined island totals for the socialists and the communists came to just over 20 percent.

It was not Giuliano's fault that the separatists had done poorly. In Montelepre, the party amassed 1694 votes, compared to 588 for the second running Christian democrats. Equally impressive, separatist victories were garnered in Giardinello and Monreale.

As to the Mafia, it was evident that its support of the separatists had greatly weakened. Mafia-dominated towns generally voted for the Christian Democratic Party or the Democratic National Union, a rightist coalition in which the Liberal Party played a major role. Yet, the Mafia's desertion of the MIS had not been complete. Many Mafia towns gave it disproportionately large numbers of votes. Even in Villalba, where the Christian Democrats won over their major local rivals, the communist-socialist group, the separatists took over 20 percent of the vote.[16]

It also was evident that the Mafia had not spoken with one voice. Instead, the many parts of it had allied themselves with whichever conservative party suited local inclinations. The Mafia's failure to give solid support to the MIS was not surprising. Vizzini's drift away had been clear by the April preceding the elections, when he had refused to attend a party meeting in Palermo.[17] Anybody who knew Don Calo would scarcely have expected anything else. His kind were not known for chasing after lost causes. If Sicily was to remain a part of Italy, mafiosi recognized the wisdom of finding a political home in one or another of the parties linked to Rome.

In the referendum on the monarchy, the nation voted for a republic, but Sicily, like the rest of the south, voted heavily for the king. On the island, the monarchists accounted for 65 percent of the vote.[18] King Umberto II went into exile upon learning the results. But at its Enna congress following the elections, the MIS declared itself to be monarchist, and in so doing underscored its lack of political realism. The action profoundly antagonized the party's republican wing.[19]

Still a Bandit

Although Giuliano was an active participant in the electoral campaign, he did not limit his activities during those times to politics alone. He still attacked the police when a low-risk opportunity presented itself or when he was moved to anger by their actions. He found an easy mark in late March, when he cold-bloodedly murdered a soldier in Pioppo, a village on the Monreale–Partinico highway. The act was in retaliation for a challenge that Francesco Sassano had posed to him. The young *carabiniere* was a part of the Pioppo detachment when it was assaulted by Giuliano's band earlier in that same month, and after the attack, he said publicly that he would like to be transferred to Montelepre to confront the brigands face to face. Giuliano, who liked the police scared and humble, arrived outside Sassano's home on March 25. He and two of his band barged into the house—three more stayed outside to guard—just as the surprised soldier and his two sisters sat down to their evening meal. The desperadoes took Francesco to the edge of the village and murdered him, then left a note on his body claiming credit for the act.[20]

Angered by police harassment of members of his family, his mother and sisters included, Giuliano tried to kill the commander of the Montelepre *carabinieri* on Monday, April 1, 1946. Giuseppe Calandra, he had learned, would be aboard the bus that ran the Palermo–Montelepre route. The bandit prepared his ambush. He chose as the site one of the many steep, hairpin curves not far from the Bellolampo station, where his men could operate from their superior positions with little fear of effective retaliation.

Minutes before 4 o'clock Monday afternoon, by which time the bandits were in place, the lookouts let Giuliano know that the bus was coming. He placed on the road a grass-stuffed, life-sized dummy, which when drenched with red liquid appeared to be the body of a badly shot-up man. Armed to the teeth, the outlaws waited. When the bus halted as its occupants spied the form, two soldiers descended to investigate the apparent homicide. The outlaws commenced their fire just as the soldiers saw that they had been tricked. The surprised troops offered as much resistance as was advisable under the circumstances but, in the main, tried to save their lives by fleeing. Three of them were hit, one of whom soon died. Calandra escaped unharmed. Giuliano was angered by the failure of his macabre April Fool's Day scheme, and this would not be the last time that he would lie in wait for his pursuers on the treacherous Bellolampo curves.[21]

The bandits' violence against the police led Commander Calandra, in early summer, to attempt to reduce the conflict with a personal call on the man who had plotted to murder him just weeks before. He wanted to try something new, he wrote later, since the methods then being used to eliminate Giuliano were not working. He spoke of his desire to Antonio Lombardo, Giuliano's uncle, who told him that he would speak about the matter to the bandit's mother. Some days later, Maria Lombardo told the commander that a meeting with her son was possible, but only if he went unarmed and alone. Calandra accepted the conditions. About two weeks later, a boy handed him a message saying that he should go immediately to Antonio Lombardo's butcher shop. The butcher informed him that the moment had arrived, that if he would stroll along the town's main street he would be picked up by an automobile.

Calandra, as nervous as he was excited, rushed back to the station, where he quickly penned a letter to his family, telling them that if he did not return they should make inquiries to Giuliano's mother. Leaving behind the letter, his ring, and his watch, he began to walk slowly along Castrense di Bello Street, armed with his pistol. He strolled for nearly a half hour before a car stopped and its driver invited him to get in. They next picked up Antonio Lombardo, who relieved Calandra of his weapon, and then drove to the foot of Saraceno Mountain. There, as they approached an uninhabited house, they were met by two heavily armed youths. One of them, Calandra saw, was Gaspare Pisciotta, already known as Giuliano's best friend.

The bandit himself stepped from behind the house, and although he cordially offered his hand and invited the commander in, the meeting did not get off to a good start. Giuliano first asked Calandra what he wanted, but then interrupted his reply with a torrent of complaints about the arrests of innocent people and the terrible difficulties that his town was undergoing. Losing his temper, Calandra retorted that the people did not consider him a hero, they did not appreciate him, and they said that he was "yellow"; or at least that is what the commander said he told the famous desperado. Immediately on his feet, an even angrier Giuliano informed his adversary: "Here, we are not in your office where you shout at poor people. Here, we are in the mountains, and he who commands is I." With that, the commander mellowed his attitude. The rest of the conference proceeded without additional outbursts and concluded amicably with an agreement that neither side would aggressively pursue the other.

The two met on Saturday. On Monday, Calandra hurried to Palermo to tell his superiors of the meeting. A reduction in the violence, he told them, would save lives and, by making Giuliano less fearful, foster an atmosphere in which he might be more easily captured. Their reaction was not favorable. The role of the police was to fight bandits, not arrange truces with them, they told him, and within fifteen days he was transferred.[22]

A Way Out

Following the collapse of the separatist revolt and the disappointing June elections, Giuliano and his followers seemed not to have much of a future. It would have been a good time to quit. Giuliano might have gone abroad, as Giuseppe Calandra had suggested to him when they met.[23] But the bandit chief was willing to consider seriously giving up his outlaw life only in the unlikely event that the state should grant a comprehensive amnesty to him and his men.

Many of the men, in contrast, were very disillusioned and desirous of finding an immediate way out.[24] By the summer of 1946, Giuliano had rebuilt his band to include some twenty regular members. As always, he could hire additional help when he needed it. Although a few of those now in the band were new recruits, most were not. These latter had dropped out following the failure of the separatist revolt; they came back from disappointment over the turn of events, especially the failure of the amnesty to include Giuliano's regular bandits. After then, their hopes rested on a MIS victory in the June elections, only to run out afterward. Too few MIS candidates were elected to have any real influence on the government, and in any case, the party had never shown much concern for the troubles of those who had been its most successful soldiers. Giuliano's conclusion that the party had abandoned him and his men was correct.[25]

A prominent churchman's efforts to persuade the outlaws to surrender in the summer of 1946 met some favor among the men, though not much in Giuliano. Cardinal Ruffini of Palermo made his plea on a pastoral visit to Montelepre. In return for the bandits' surrender, the cardinal promised to intercede with the government on their behalf. The offer, made privately through town mayor Steffano Mannino, was accompanied by a public call from the pulpit to Giuliano to repent of his sins. While the head bandit had some interest in the prelate's efforts, he also had serious doubts. How much influence Ruffini had with the authorities, how he and his men might fare in the hands of the police, and how the system of justice would eventually dispose of their cases were questions that profoundly troubled him. As to repentance, he never much saw himself as a grave sinner. In essence, that is what he told the churchman when he rejected his intercession.[26]

Some of Giuliano's men, less cautious than he, were inclined to accept the offer. Antonio Terranova, famed and feared for his kidnapping skills, was one of them. He sent his wife to the cardinal to secure guarantees that if he turned himself in he would not be jailed. Satisfied with the reply, he was on the verge of surrendering when he received a call from Giuliano. Giuliano warned Terranova against accepting the offer and advised him not to betray him.[27] He said the same thing to others who were considering Ruffini's offer. He did not want his closest companions to fall into the hands of the police, for they knew far too much about him and his habits. Still, he may have convinced his men not to desert mainly because he did not want to end up alone. Most of those closest to him agreed to remain.

Giuliano never insisted that all of those who had accompanied him in the separatist campaign stay with him; he was concerned chiefly about the core of his followers. For the remainder of his career, he preferred his band lean and efficient. He also knew better than to keep men against their will. To those who genuinely wanted to leave, he gave his blessing and made the arrangements for their departure abroad, where, hopefully, they would be safe and not endanger him by falling into the hands of the Italian police.

One of those whom Giuliano assisted was young Francesco Barone, who, after the collapse of the separatist revolt, had remained with his chief almost longer than anybody else. But eventually he, too, drifted back to town. When Giuliano asked him to return, he replied that he did not want to come back but to work and get married. Giuliano warned him that things were not as they appeared to be; that he soon would be arrested if he stayed in Sicily. He had two choices. He could return to the band or go abroad, either to Tunisia or the United States. Barone chose America.

His departure was soon arranged. Two men contacted him, saying that they had been placed in charge of his clandestine journey. He travelled to Naples, accompanied by "Vincenzo," who, on their arrival, placed him in the care of "Mr. Milone." After being concealed in a room for some days, Francesco's father and brother unexpectedly arrived to bid him farewell. The next day, he boarded the ship like any ordinary passenger—his Naples contact had provided him with an exit permit. When he went to his cabin, he was greeted by another man, who, with the aid of others on board, kept him hidden for the rest of the voyage.

The day of his arrival in New York was cold and snowy. There, he was turned over to "Sammy," who, bestowing upon him the new name of "Pino Abate," told him that he was to obey him absolutely. The youthful fugitive had thought that he would probably settle down in the big city, but, instead, he soon found himself in the hands of "Carmelo" in a small Wisconsin village. The arrangement, he was told, had been decided by none other than "Frank," the big boss himself. Francesco was dazzled. While he had known mafiosi in Sicily, they shared the modesty and rusticity of the towns, like Montelepre and Borgetto of their birth. Not so the American Mafia, which was, as Sammy described it, "colossal." Clearly, the network of Giuliano's contacts was extensive in area and impressive in power. Francesco never learned how much his flight had cost his former chief, but it must have added up to a sizeable ransom or two.

Over the next few years, the Sicilian fugitive grew to manhood, still frequently on the run and never in charge of his own life. Back to New York, residing with a family that taught him English; then to Chicago; followed by Detroit, where he was told that an emissary had been sent to Sicily to bring Giuliano himself to America; next to San Francisco, there hearing on the radio of the great bandit's death—Barone's itinerary in America reads almost like that of an affluent European tourist of a later time. Even the city of his last residence in America was appropriate. He was finally arrested, at a time when the Italian government was making an intense effort to bring Giuliano's former henchmen to trial, as he gazed out on the Atlantic Ocean from the sands of Miami Beach. The rest of his story breaks the parallel. Sent first to Florida's then notorious Raiford Penitentiary to await the disposition of his case, and later to Camp 35 of a prison road gang, he was appalled by the fierceness of his fellow inmates, not to mention the harsh discipline and hard labor. Finally flown to Italy, after extradition proceedings were completed, he was tried, found guilty, and sentenced to a long prison term.[28]

Back in Italy during the summer of 1946, the authorities stepped up their campaign against Giuliano, much of the action directed at his alleged supporters. A major roundup on a Sunday night in early July resulted in the arrests of over 100 people, including the mayor of Torretta. In retaliation, Giuliano ambushed three *carabinieri* as they rode in a truck with civilians on the Monreale–Pioppo highway; one soldier and two civilians perished in the incident.[29] For Giuliano, the most troubling event of the times was the arrest of his mother and Mariannina near the end of August. They were taken on the highway between Montelepre and Trapani as they travelled home in an automobile. Among other suspicions, the police thought that they had been to see Giuliano. Although the authorities believed that the two were vital links in Giuliano's organization, they released them after a period of incarceration in Palermo.[30]

A Lucrative Enterprise

The police efforts against Giuliano during the summer of 1946 were closely related to his continuing abductions. If he did not attack the police or stir up such public attention that he could not be ignored, he was not usually bothered by the authorities. The intensive manhunt and mass roundup in early July were largely an attempt to discover where he had hidden a prominent Palermo merchant.

The abduction of Gino Agnello, a dry goods wholesaler, took place within Palermo just after noon on June 7. The multimillionaire had stepped out of the house of a friend—he was there on a tryst, said one of the bandits who had done the groundwork for the event—and headed for his parked car nearby when he was accosted by four armed men who instructed him to get into their own elegant automobile. Blindfolded, he was raced out of town. Only later did he learn that he was in the hands of Antonio Terranova, Giuliano's most skillful kidnapper.

Agnello surmised that the first stop was near Bellolampo, where he was locked in a small room for a few minutes, before being whisked away in another vehicle toward Montelepre. After travelling for some two hours, the car came to a halt in the open country. From there, he was taken on a mule to a dilapidated rural cottage and locked up again. After removing his blindfold, his masked caretakers forced him to eat under the point of a gun. The terrified Agnello had begun a captivity that was to last for forty-three days.

Confined to a small room, the days passed slowly, each one like a century, he said. Soon, the bandits forced him to write a letter to his wife requesting a large ransom. He did not know whether it reached her, for no one told him anything. Nearly three weeks passed, and, thinking that his end was near, he went on a hunger strike. Jarred out of it a few days later by a move to a new location, then to still another at which a battle took place, he realized that the frequent moves and the battle must mean the police were on his trail. His hopes began to rise. At the last location, he was lodged in a cave, where he learned that there were two other captives, at least for a time. Although he had no direct contact with them, he found out later that they were Antonio Vanella, a well-to-do landowner of the Corleone area, and Antonio Ugdulena, a young engineer of Torretta.

While Agnello pondered his fate and worried about his wife and two children, Giuliano directed his attentions to the business end of his kidnapping enterprises. He took time, nonetheless, to visit Agnello and apologize for the poor quality of the lodgings and the other discomforts. Maybe Giuliano was sincere, for he did possess some of the qualities of a gentleman, but more than that, it was a role that he loved to play. What interested him most, however, was ransom money. He wanted 100 million for Agnello, 15 million for Ugdulena, and 10 million for Vanella. But Giuliano in such dealings was reasonable, and the exact amount was usually open to negotiation.

Vanella was released first, reputedly for 3.5 million lire. The small amount, the bandits said, was out of gratitude for his support of the separatist movement. When he left, he carried notes for the Agnello and Ugdulena families. In their cases, negotiations dragged on for weeks because of various difficulties. One agreed upon meeting between the outlaws and the Agnello family fell apart when Gino's brother informed the police of it. Giuliano, not easily fooled, kept his men away from the proposed meeting place.

Eventually, a mutually satisfactory ransom of 50 million was decided, and Agnello's brother was told how to deliver the money. He was to drive back and forth along a designated stretch of deserted highway in a tiny Fiat that the Italians called the *topolino* (little mouse) until he was flagged down. Predictably, the highway was one with a long stretch that could be seen easily from nearby vantage points. The site offered no opportunities for the police to be present without being seen—the car was much too small to conceal anyone— and the transaction was completed uneventfully on the morning of July 30. As for Ugdulena, his family pleaded poverty. If they paid Giuliano anything, it was a modest ransom.

The release of the two captives came on the afternoon of July 30. They were left blindfolded not far from Alcamo and told not to move for half an hour under the threat of being shot. Before leaving, their escort gave both of them cigarettes and Ugdulena a small sum for a bus ticket home. They waited, as instructed, then, bearded and dirty, walked into town. Ugdulena wondered thereafter what had happened to his Alfa Romeo, which the bandits had taken when he was captured. He never recovered it, although he learned months later that parts of it had been seen at the home of a Montelepre peasant.[31]

The abduction of persons for ransom was a favored means of raising money for Mediterranean area bandits. Corsica, Sardinia, the lower part of the Italian peninsula, and Sicily were all known for it. Certainly, it was one of Giuliano's most lucrative enterprises. Unlike many others, however, he did not abduct children and, very rarely, women. Almost without exception, his victims were men. Also, as elsewhere, extortion or the protection racket was profitable for Giuliano, but, since these acts attracted less attention than kidnapping, not a lot is known of them. Single acts of extortion did not yield the immediate sums that a lone kidnapping could produce, but the advantage lay in the ability to collect payments over a sustained period of time. The wish to avoid the large damage and dreadful experience of an abduction led wealthy persons to regularly meet Giuliano's demands. Yet, to a wealthy family, an abduction, however costly, had one advantage over an extortion. Under Giuliano's rules, if they paid the ransom, they were immune from any further molestation by his men.[32]

Giuliano did not engage in petty robbery nor was he much of a highwayman, but he was not likely to pass by the opportunity for grand larceny. The most financially rewarding act of his career reputedly was the 1944 robbery of the Duchess of Pratameno, in which the "take" in jewels alone was said to have exceeded 60 million lire.[33] His band infrequently engaged in horse theft or cattle rustling, two of rural Sicily's most common crimes. Perhaps, it was because, as Frank Mannino said, such could never compare in yield to a well-chosen, well-executed abduction.[34]

Giuliano needed money and a lot of it. His expenses, always large, grew rapidly with his entry into politics. The frequency of his abductions increased markedly in the fall of 1945 and continued at a high level throughout most of the rest of his career. Only during the final period of his life, when his activities were intensely restricted by police pressure, did his abductions fall off and practically come to a halt.

How many abductions Giuliano executed in the course of his seven-year outlaw career was difficult to establish. The known cases came to around forty, but a complete list would have been substantially longer. Many abductions were never reported to the authorities, and in reality, there was little reason to inform them. They generally were ineffective against Giuliano's careful schemes; moreover, their interference might jeopardize the captive's safety. It was more prudent to work out the details of the transaction personally or turn the job over to a knowledgeable third party, usually a mafioso. For both sides, his involvement provided an efficient and risk free means of closing the deal. Fees for his help ranged between 5 and 15 percent of the total ransom.[35]

If one did not choose to use the Mafia, discrete inquiries might reveal other intermediaries, such as, for instance, Montelepre's physician, Dr. Francesco Lupo. The doctor for long was free to come and go at will without arousing suspicion, even when curfews, roadblocks, and other restrictions prevented ordinary citizens from moving about. Now and then, as a cover, the doctor gave the police bits of information about the bandits, maybe an indication of where some of them were supposed to be at the time. The bandits must have been privy to his revelations, since by the time the police arrived they were always gone. But Lupo's collaboration with Giuliano eventually became known, and he was sent to confinement on Ustica Island, off Sicily's northern coast. Later released, he was rearrested, charged this time with helping to negotiate a 30 million lire ransom.[36]

The initial amounts of the ransom requests normally fell between 10 and 100 million lire. As a rule, the bandits levied a sum calculated to approximate one-half of the family fortune. But the amount was flexible, and substantial downward adjustments could usually be negotiated. The bandits often settled for half of their first demand, sometimes for much less. For Alfonso Anzalone of San Giuseppe Jato, Giuliano reduced the ransom from several millions to 1 million lire when the captive told him of the troubles that he had supporting his wife and their eight children in addition to his mother. A Carini lawyer talked his way to freedom by convincing Giuliano that his assets were exceeded by his many debts.[37]

Giuliano's leniency notwithstanding, he collected on ransom demands over the course of his career what must have amounted to a fabulous sum. His success was attributable in no small way to his patience. He would hold a captive for whatever time it took to either exact a ransom or determine that the family was incapable of paying. Agnello was held for 43 days; Giuliano's record was 108 days.[38]

In any case, the bandits seldom settled for less than their expenses. Once, they abducted the grandson of a prominent mafioso of San Giuseppe Jato. The mafioso was humiliated, to say the least; such an act negated all he stood for. Sure that Giuliano would understand, he sought him out. The outlaw chieftain was duly sympathetic and agreed to release the captive. All he wanted was 1 million lire to meet the expenses that his men had incurred in kidnapping him.[39]

The initiative for abductions normally came from within the individual squads, but almost always, Giuliano was told of them in advance and always participated in the division of the ransom. His best known kidnapping squad was the one headed by Antonio Terranova, a Montelepre native who turned 21 years of age only late in 1946; the four others in it were about the same age. Terranova oftentimes dressed as a *carabiniere* when he was executing a risky abduction.[40]

The bandits preferred safe abductions in the countryside, but if the need was great or the rewards promising, they sometimes acted more boldly. Giuliano told the story of one such effort. Pushed hard by the police in the Montelepre area following the collapse of the separatist revolt, the bandits retreated to Trapani province in mid-February 1946. They found themselves well to the west of Montelepre, out of their home territory and short of money. Casting around for a victim, they learned of Giuseppe Cardella, a rich dry goods dealer and landowner in Custonaci, still farther west, near the coast. They came down out of their mountain refuge and, posting themselves by the highway, hailed and took possession of a truck transporting barrels of wine from Alcamo to Marsala. Stopping near the Greek ruins at Segesta, they unloaded the wine and dismissed the driver, telling him that if he did not go to the police the truck would be returned to him the next day. He agreed and, as usual, Giuliano kept his word.

Once in Custonaci, the outlaws scouted the small town. It presented some difficulties, because Cardella's home was between the *carabiniere* station and the fiscal police post, and very near both of them. Giuliano put one of his men to guard the first, two to watch the second, and took the remaining five to help him get Cardella. The merchant, having seen the strangers arrive, was already suspicious, and when they knocked on his door, he began to shout for help. With that, the police opened fire. The bandits returned it and in the melee kicked down the door and dragged Cardella out. Making their getaway in the truck, they returned to the mountains to demand their ransom and await its delivery. When it came after a few days, Giuliano assured Cardella that the full sum would be returned to him in the future by an independent Sicilian government.[41]

The outlaws usually planned their abductions well. However, if something went wrong and the intended victim was not present, they might substitute any available man or older boy in the family for him. They also might exchange one member of the family for another following the initial kidnapping. This happened, for instance, in the case of Nicolo Colicchia, who, in 1945, took the place of his nephew when he went to Giuliano to negotiate the young man's release. The nephew then went to raise the money to ransom his uncle.[42] Colicchia, a man with an abundant midsection and a twinkle in his eye, savored the story of his misfortune when he told it to a court that tried some of his abductors. Others, too, who had been kidnapped by Giuliano seemed to value their memories of him, despite the hardships that he caused them. Having encountered the famous—or infamous—figure added a feature to one's life that not all could claim.

Giuliano lent himself to storytelling. Often generous and gentlemanly, he exhibited traits that were uncommon to his trade. Insulin was regularly brought to an abductee who suffered from diabetes; clean stockings were purchased for another whose fastidiousness was doubtless greater than that of most of his captors; two captives were asked every morning what they would like to eat that day, and they conceded that their requests were met as far as was reasonable. One kidnapping attempt, against the tax collector of Borgetto, was aborted, when the bandits found him in the company of his 10-year-old son, who broke into tears and howled loudly when they tried to take his father away. Taking pity on the boy, they settled for the 104,000 lire that the collector had on him, but, finding him without his son a few days later, they abducted him, held him for fifteen days, and charged over 4 million lire for his release.[43]

Few of Giuliano's kidnapping victims complained much about the comportment of the bandits. True, they did not like the confinement, the often rustic quarters, and the worry and boredom of it all, but their captors, they said, treated them humanely. The bandits frequently conversed or played cards with them and, on occasion, expended considerable effort to try to make their ordeal bearable. Giuseppe Geraci, held in a room for three weeks, never saw his guard, for the tiny window through which they talked did not permit an unobstructed view of the outside. But the man read to him every afternoon. The story was terribly dull, Geraci said, and full of antique words, but he had not wanted to complain, even though the reader often paused to inquire if he was enjoying it. As he got to know his guard better, he finally confessed to him that he found little enjoyment in such a melancholy story. They discussed what would be a good book to read, the captive arguing in favor of a swashbuckling novel. The guard arrived earlier than usual the next afternoon and commenced a medieval tale full of battles and duels. He read with great emotion, doing his best to entertain his prisoner and probably himself, too. When Geraci was released, they had not yet reached the end of the tale, so he promptly went to town and purchased a copy of the book for himself.[44]

CHAPTER FIVE

Portella della Ginestra

IN ITS AUGUST 11, 1946, EDITION, ONE OF Palermo's leading newspapers published a lengthy letter from Giuliano. It was not his first statement to the press, but it was the most complete public explanation of his social views that he had given. Against the backdrop of the June elections, Giuliano reminded the politicians that they had promised reforms. He wrote: "June 2 has passed, the Republic has been proclaimed, but the conditions of the people have still not been improved. The situation is always the same ... hunger, unemployment, and misery." Although accusing politicians of hypocrisy, for denouncing delinquency when they were engaging in robbery themselves, he conceded that

> It is just to denounce delinquency. But the common and brutal delinquents must not be confused with those who take a bit of money from the rich to give to the poor. ... Because if it is true that from those who have much you need not take everything, it is also true that to those who have nothing you need to give something. In the name therefore of a great social revolution ... knowing full well that the reforms talked about in the Council of Ministers are never seen in reality, I claim for myself the right to take from the rich, from those who have too much, to give to those who have nothing. ... It is for this that they have wanted to brand ... those who are still dedicated to fighting for the independence of Sicily, as common delinquents. ... It is well that the people know that the men of the Giuliano band are not criminals but soldiers for independence who fight for the people and their land. For those who have been fooled first, then betrayed, forgotten, and cheated.
>
> *Carabinieri,* you also are of us, you also live in misery and want. And do you know why you are sent to fight against your brothers? To defend the rich, who reduce you to starvation. ... To protect those who, while you and we shed our blood on the fields of battle, starve our families and show no pity for our mothers who cry and pray still.

He ended with a warning that the people were waiting for the politicians to act, but "If the wait is useless and in vain . . . and Sicily must remain the last of the Italian colonies, we will again take up arms and return to fight and die, convinced that from our shed blood new martyrs and new heroes will spring." [1]

Although the letter reflected the ideas that appealed to Giuliano then—social justice and independence—the composition of it was not wholly his. He did not write that well. For him, a passable degree of literacy was recent. The tongue he commonly used was the local version of the Sicilian dialect, almost exclusively a spoken language. He had only a meager formal education and little experience in the written language, which was standard Italian. Apparently, only after he made contact with the separatists did he become interested in educating himself. Once recognizing his backwardness, he sought help from anyone who could read and write. One of his teachers was Pasquale Sciortino, who joined his separatist uprising and later became a member of his family for a brief time. In fact, the ideas in the letter also looked much like Sciortino's, who probably helped him write it. It was, in any event, a strange letter to appear over the name of the man who some months thereafter would launch a major terrorist attack on a holiday gathering of peasants and their leftist allies.

The April Elections

During most of late 1946 and early 1947, Giuliano was not very active. He did not much bother the police nor did they pursue him with any zeal. When he resumed vigorous activity, it was to garner votes for his candidate in the April 20, 1947, elections. The April vote was to choose the members of the first Sicilian Regional Assembly, a major step in the implementation of the autonomy statute. The separatists again entered candidates, this time, however, in two opposing lists. A split in the MIS had opened just after the June 1946 elections, when at the Enna party congress Finocchiaro Aprile had proclaimed support of the House of Savoy and criticized his republican compatriots. By the time the party held its next congress, in the resort town of Taormina in late January 1947, Varvaro, as the movement's leading republican, had taken preliminary steps already toward the formation of a new party. When at the Taormina meeting his request to speak was turned down because he refused to sign a pledge recognizing the legitimacy of the gathering, he was expelled. He then turned his handful of followers into the Movement for Sicilian Independence–Democratic Republican (MIS–DR).

Freed of the regular party's conservative majority, Varvaro's dissidents unfurled their true colors. They not only denounced the bloated capitalists of the north for their suffocation of Sicilian industry, a common enough separatist theme, but, also turning their attack on the landed capitalists of Sicily, they endorsed radical agrarian reform. Although the campaign of the dissident separatists foundered badly—most left-wingers in the movement had long since deserted it for the unequivocally radical parties—it found a receptive ear in Montelepre.[2]

Varvaro's strident plea for social justice coincided easily with Giuliano's own views, as set forth in his letter to the press in August of the previous year. Moreover, Varvaro was from nearby Partinico. Maybe, though, the main link between the two was Jolanda Varvaro. Her husband and the bandit had never been close, but she had good relations with the Giuliano family, especially with Mariannina.[3]

As usual, Giuliano's support was worth having. Mariannina again campaigned, and in Montelepre and surrounding towns signs appeared over her brother's name inviting people to vote for List Number 8, the MIS–DR. Varvaro later said that he disapproved of the signs, not wishing to be so blatantly identified with the bandit. Visiting Giardinello, he asked the police there to remove them, whereupon the officer in charge asked him if he looked like he was crazy. He was not going to risk his skin tearing down signs that Giuliano had posted![4]

On April 20, Montelepre's citizens heeded the call from the mountain and voted for the MIS–DR over the next strongest party, the Christian Democratic Party, by a more than two to one margin. Nearby Giardinello did even better. Partinico also went for Varvaro, though narrowly, but the victory there for its native son could not be attributed much to Giuliano. Elsewhere, the party, which contested races only in Palermo and Catania provinces, did poorly. It received 19,542 votes or approximately 1 percent of the total cast, which earned it no seats in the assembly. The regular MIS, which was very nearly blanked in Montelepre, elected eight assemblymen. It received almost 9 percent of the vote and might have done better had not many of its potential supporters opted for the newly formed monarchist party.[5]

After 1947, the separatist political movement went into a sharp decline, all but disappearing by the end of the next decade.[6] To the end, the separatists contended that only they genuinely believed in autonomy, that the others were just posturing for political profit. Justifiable as their view was, it did them no good. For better or worse, Sicily appeared to be irrevocably bound to the mainland.

After 1947, Varvaro saw no future for himself within an ever more isolated and dwindling movement, and he soon cast his fortunes with the Communist Party, which warmly rewarded him with quite lengthy tenure in a seat in the regional assembly. That the former advocate of independence would join so centralist a party did not greatly surprise those who knew already of his equal commitment to leftist radicalism. One, however, who was much disappointed by his move was Giuliano. Ardently pro-American and anticommunist, he considered Varvaro a turncoat and dared him to campaign ever again in Montelepre. When in a subsequent election, Varvaro scheduled a rally there, Giuliano had a party of lemon-throwing hoodlums lying in wait for him. The candidate failed to appear.[7]

The clear winners of the 1947 elections were the communists and the socialists, who, together with two smaller parties and some independent politicians, formed the Popular Bloc. This potent coalition emerged with nearly 30 percent of the vote, compared to approximately 20 percent for the second finishing Christian Democratic Party. The victory of the left posed an ominous challenge to Sicily's rightists—indeed, one that they were inclined not to let pass.

The Rightist Reaction

Sicily's rightists were greatly alarmed by the surprising strength of the leftist vote in the elections and angered by evidence that many peasants had defiantly contributed to it. What they feared most of all, however, was the continuing peasant and leftist call for radical land reform, which had become even louder in 1946 and 1947 than it had been in the 1943–1945 period. In a major manifestation of their demands, 3000 peasants from Piana degli Albanesi had come to Palermo on horse and on foot on June 1, 1946, to demonstrate for land. The Segni decree, with liberal provisions ceding uncultivated land to peasants, was already under discussion and became effective on September 6. However, many peasants, unwilling to wait for the slow-moving government and, spurred on by radical leaders, commenced the unauthorized occupation of estates. Many of these occupations were symbolic and temporary, while others were actual seizures. Over some of them, flew the black figure of the hammer and sickle against a red background.[8]

Agitation for land reform and more illegal occupations of estates continued in 1947 and became major issues in the campaign that led to the April vote. In it, the left's rhetoric was shrill and aimed mainly at the landless, as, for instance, in an election eve rally at San Giuseppe Jato. There, a Popular Bloc orator had exploited class antagonism to the fullest when he spoke of the "furs and jewels" that adorned the ladies of the upper class—luxuries, he asserted, that were exacted from the sweat and misery of his audience. He assured his listeners that a leftist triumph would mean no more tenancy, that the land thenceforth would belong to those who toiled it. A new regime would dawn—"your regime, the regime of the peasants," he shouted.[9]

To rightists, the next day's socialist-communist victory in Sicily presaged nothing less than the imminence of Stalin and Togliatti's red revolution. Some of them sought desperately to hold it back. The upcoming May Day celebration in Portella della Ginestra would be an appropriate occasion to frighten the left and intimidate its peasant supporters, they decided. They had violence in mind, and to execute it, they needed men who were handy with weapons. Giuliano, it occurred to them, was a likely prospect to head the action.

Giuliano and Michael Stern

It may seem incongruous, indeed, that the conservative conspirators turned to Giuliano to head their terrorist action at Portella della Ginestra. After all, just months before, he had spoken in the name of a "great social revolution" and proclaimed his right to take from the rich to give to the poor. Yet, a closer look at him suggests that his acceptance of their offer was not out of character.

At bottom, Giuliano's instincts were with the peasants, his own class. Even the occasional description of him as vaguely socialist in sentiment was not really farfetched.[10] In at least an equal measure, however, he was also anticommunist. He held this view consistently throughout his short adult life. It was shaped by his and his family's identification with the United States, as well as by the conservative politicians—the leftist Varvaro aside—with whom he associated. Beyond these considerations, it would be a mistake to attach much significance to Giuliano's opinions on public affairs. He was young, ignorant, inexperienced in politics, and easily and vainly swayed by others; he switched party preferences four times in fewer than that many years. His record suggests not so much the lack of a consistent ideology, which he knew little about, as a search for pardon or amnesty. To secure it, he was willing to make political camp with almost anybody or any party and do whatever was asked of him. In this practical sense, his terrorist action at Portella della Ginestra fit well enough into the pattern of his life.

A stranger who visited Giuliano early in 1947 may also have unwittingly helped prepare him for the proposal that would be tendered not long thereafter. Michael Stern, an American journalist, was stationed in Rome. Stern, whose journalism was of the sensationalistic variety, was assigned to seek an interview with Giuliano by *True,* an American magazine with a strong appeal to teenage boys and young men—exactly the readership that would be attracted by a young, handsome, dashing, pro-American bandit of Robin Hood inclinations in the mountains of a Mediterranean isle. Stern, as he told it, was not particularly interested in making the considerable effort of looking up Giuliano. But, since he already wanted to go to Sicily to write a story on the eruption of Mount Etna, he thought that a side trip to the other end of the island might be worth his while.

The trip by jeep from Rome to Sicily consumed a whole week. Since the journalist knew little of how to find Giuliano, he stopped in Palermo to see what he might learn. At police headquarters, he met Chief Inspector Ettore Messana. The inspector, "short, stout, and bald as an egg," in Stern's vivid language, was not much interested in his quest but showed him a list of the bandit's crimes and told him that Giuliano could be found somewhere around Montelepre. The next day, he made the two-hour drive to the town, over a rough road with tortuous, hairpin curves. Montelepre was poor and unimpressive, inhabited by suspicious, scared people who would tell him nothing. Some of them ran when he asked about Giuliano. Finally, an old man offered to take him to see the bandit's family. Only later did he learn that he was in the tow of the bandit's father. In the family home on Via di Bello, he met "Mamma" Giuliano, a "short, squat, gray, toil-worn, shrewd" woman who told him that the three outstanding personages in history were Roosevelt, Churchill, and her son.

Stern won the family's confidence, as he was soon to win Giuliano's.

Being an American helped, but that was not all, for he wore the uniform of a U.S. Army captain, which his hosts believed him to be. In fact, he was not in the army then; the uniform was probably leftover from his service as a war correspondent during the late war. Adding to the appearance of an official visit was his "aide," Wilson Morris, who was introduced as a sargeant. Stern knew of Giuliano's pro-American stance and long-standing hope for help from the United States. If he concluded that an American military uniform would gain him the easiest entry into Giuliano's camp, as he appears to have done, he was absolutely correct.

After a few days of waiting, Stern was told that he would be picked up on a certain street corner in Palermo. When the jeep arrived, the bandit's father was among its occupants. They headed west toward the mountains in the direction of Montelepre, coming to a halt at the first severe U-turn where the road begins its steep ascent. There, they were met by Gaspare Pisciotta, Giuliano's lieutenant, who took them on a route through country lanes and fields to an abandoned, war-damaged house. They walked to a small grove of olive trees where three men waited. Two of them had machine guns cradled in their arms. The third, wearing a tan shirt, green corduroy hunting coat, and work pants, was a barrel-chested man who stood with head high, his thumbs in his belt loops. His bearing unmistakably marked him as the chief. To Stern, he looked like Errol Flynn portraying Pancho Villa.

The two men sat under an olive tree for their talk. Giuliano readily warmed up to his guest and enthusiastically discussed with him his pro-American views. He wanted it known that he was a natural ally of the United States and a deserving candidate for its aid. He badly needed arms, he emphasized, if he was to hold up his end of the war against communism. Stern concluded that the bandit was sincere and personable but dangerous.

In the course of their conversation, Giuliano handed Stern a letter he had written in anticipation of the meeting. He wanted the American to read it, check its appropriateness, and deliver it to the addressee. The missive began "Dear President Truman." The bandit first asked the president's pardon for disturbing him, then introduced himself. The press had made much of his life, he wrote, portraying him either as a legendary hero or a common criminal. He supposed, he continued, that the president knew quite a lot about him already. The main body of the letter summarized Giuliano's career, emphasizing his desire to see Sicily annexed to America. He affirmed his hatred of communism and his resolve to combat it. After noting that his home-land was an Italian colony, he begged the president not to forget the hundreds of thousands of people who still awaited the day of libera-tion. In the letter, he included a copy of his placard showing Sicily being detached from Italy to join America.[11]

Giuliano's letter to President Truman was introductory and con-tained no specific requests for immediate aid; instead, he expected Stern to secure aid for him. When none came during the following weeks, he sent a letter to Stern for delivery to the American military headquarters in Rome. In it, he referred to his previous request for aid, a reference to Stern, that had gone unanswered. The Italian po-lice, he continued, were becoming better equipped, with armored cars and other heavy weaponry, and to combat them he needed small cali-ber antitank guns, mortars, and bazookas. He begged for clarification of American aims—whether he was really going to get help. Giu-liano's request never reached Rome. It, along with an accompanying letter to Stern, was found badly damaged by the bullets that killed the bandit who was to drop it off at the post office.[12]

In Rome, meanwhile, Stern was rushing to get his story into print. When he learned that reporters from the *Chicago Tribune* and *The New York Times* had just flown out of Rome on their way also to seek out the bandit, he fired off a telegram to the Giuliano family warning them that two agents of the Italian secret police, posing as American journalists, were headed in their direction. After this, Giuliano became extremely wary of reporters. It was more than a year before he would grant another interview.

Stern's effort proved to be quite a success on his end. He sold stories based on it to *True* and *Life* and several other publications, too, both in the United States and abroad. His account of Giuliano was shallow, no more than an unblushing appeal to popular fantasies. In spite of this quality—or perhaps because of it—the interview marked the be-ginning of foreign interest in Giuliano, at the same time that it in-creased his fame at home. The Italian police were upset over the story. They not only resented their adversary's growing popularity but were also stung by pointed criticism that they were unable to find a criminal so readily located by a foreigner who knew little of Sicily.[13]

Giuliano was flattered by Stern's visit and took it as evidence that the United States was interested in his cause. He had shared the view of the immediate postliberation separatists that America wanted an independent Sicily as a bulwark against Soviet penetration of the

Mediterranean. He now interpreted what he believed to be a visit by an official representative of the U. S. government as a renewed interest in that matter. Likely, the visit made him considerably more receptive to an offer to attack the leftist gathering at Portella della Ginestra as a dramatic demonstration of his anticommunist fervor. If, in fact, Stern did influence Giuliano in that direction, the recklessness of the free-wheeling American journalist was underscored.

A Traditional Gathering

The annual gathering at Portella della Ginestra was well embedded in tradition. It was begun by Nicola Barbato, a physician and socialist of Corleone, who was a leader in the *Fasci Siciliani,* the peasant movement for land reform of the early 1890s. Barbato thereafter was an idol of many peasants, and it became customary for him to speak on May Day at Portella della Ginestra. The speaker's platform, a large, white, flat-topped boulder, was known as Barbato's podium.[14] The meeting place was an open depression between two mountains, Pizzuta to the north and Kumeta to the south. It was easily accessible to Piana degli Albanesi, San Giuseppe Jato, and San Cipirello, the three towns that furnished large crowds for the celebration.

Portella della Ginestra was only 4 kilometers from the town of Piana degli Albanesi, earlier named Piana dei Greci. Unique, even in a unique land, it had been founded over four centuries earlier by Greek and Albanian refugees who fled to Sicily to escape Muslim conquerors. Their adopted homeland was in the mountainous interior of the western part of the island, where, in their cohesiveness and isolation, they preserved their dress, customs, language, and the Greek Orthodox religion. Farmers and artisans for the most part, they had long been known for their radical politics and antimonarchical views.[15] After World War II, the socialists and communists commanded their loyalties so well that in the April 20, 1947, elections the town voted for the Popular Bloc over the next most successful party, the Christian Democratic Party, by a ratio that exceeded five to one. The leftist parties also commanded the largest blocks of voters in San Cipirello and San Giuseppe Jato, though less impressively.[16]

The May Day gatherings had been suspended during Mussolini's rule but were resumed in 1944 with as much interest as ever. Since leftist enthusiasm was at a high point following the Popular Bloc victory in the April elections, the 1947 event was expected to be one of the most memorable ever. Little was it known that the memories of it would be so bitter.

The Mysterious Letter

Giuliano received final authorization to proceed with the May Day attack only in very late April. At the time, he was with four of his men just outside Montelepre when Pasquale Sciortino, who had recently married Mariannina, arrived with a letter for him. The bandit chief read it, then conferred briefly with its bearer. Next, Giuliano burned the letter, after which Sciortino left. Giuliano then startled his companions with his announcements: "The hour of our liberation has come. We are going to attack the Communists, to go to fire on them on May 1 at Portella della Ginestra." One of the men protested, reminding Giuliano that large numbers of women and children would be there. In answer, Giuliano assured the men that no harm would come to women and children. The action, he said, would be against radical leaders.[17]

The question of the contents of the letter that went up in flames that afternoon was of great consequence. It not only gave Giuliano the final word to proceed with the attack and verified an offer of "liberation"—amnesty—for himself and his men in payment for it, but it also probably carried the signature of the chief of the conspirators, or at the least, of someone who represented them. If so, the inevitable query demanded an answer that time would yield only reluctantly and never with complete clarity.

Following receipt of the letter, Giuliano instructed Antonio Terranova to bring his kidnapping squad for the attack.[18] He also recruited temporary help for the action, offering as much as 5000 lire for the few hours' work; the arms would be furnished. Almost all of the recruits were young, some no older than 17. They were told that they should not worry about the apparent illegality of their service, that important government figures stood behind them.[19]

Rumors of Impending Violence

In the towns around Portella della Ginestra, there had been talk of possible violence since before the elections. Some of it was motivated by hopes of intimidating potential Popular Bloc supporters, as in San

Cipirello, where a Mafia boss had warned in a rally that physical harm would befall the families of those who voted for the leftists. With the coalition's victory, fears were raised on both sides. Conservatives expected widespread peasant invasions of estates, probably on May Day, according to rumors, while leftists were afraid that conservatives would actually resort to violence to avenge the Popular Bloc victory. Ominously, a Piana degli Albanesi mafioso told a communist partisan just before the May Day gathering: "Go ahead and celebrate your victory, but, mark my words, wait to see how it ends."[20]

The authorities themselves were aware of the spate of rumors and, surprisingly, had been told that Giuliano was planning an action against the communists. That information had come from Salvatore Ferreri, one of the band's squad commanders, who was giving information to Chief Inspector Messana. Messana insisted, however, that Ferreri told him nothing of the intended time or place.[21] When all of this was revealed later, the leftists were certain that Messana, a conservative of monarchist persuasion, was lying. They suspected that he was pleased with Giuliano's attack on them and had taken no steps to prevent it; or even that he was one of the conspirators. None of the charges, however, was ever proved. In any event, no unusual security arrangements were made for the May Day meeting. There were a few *carabinieri* in attendance, as was common at public gatherings, but not enough to deal with the scale of attack that Giuliano had planned.

The May Day Tragedy

The mood was happy when the crowd began to gather at Portella della Ginestra around 9:00 A.M., arriving by truck, automobile, carts, horses, bicycles, and on foot. The times were highly charged, but rumor on top of rumor had produced skepticism or resignation, and under these conditions, people tended to go about their lives in normal ways. Sicilians, anyway, had long lived with violence. Whole families came, the very young and old, bringing baskets of food, for the celebration was more than a political event; above all, it was a popular festival.

The only disappointment by the time the organized part of the day got underway was occasioned by the absence of any prominent figure to address the crowd. It had been widely expected that Girolamo Li

Causi himself would be the main guest. But Li Causi was at home in Termini Imerese, and many later wondered why he had not come. How better could the island's most noted communist, they asked, have celebrated the recent Popular Bloc victory than at a historic, predominantly peasant May Day rally in the Sicilian town that surpassed all others in its loyalty to leftist causes? His absence led thereafter to speculation that he might have gotten word of the impending tragedy or suspected that violence might occur. He stoutly denied any such allegations, but did not give a satisfactory excuse for his absence. Maybe, he had become more cautious following the incident at Villalba. The finally announced speaker, a young labor leader from Palermo, would have been a disappointing but acceptable second choice, but his vehicle broke down en route and he never got there.[22]

By 10:30, the red flags were flying over an estimated 3000 to 5000 men, women, and children who had gathered in the area between Mount Pizzuta and Mount Kumeta to celebrate the international working class holiday. Unbeknownst to the festive crowd, Giuliano was observing them from his hiding place fewer than 300 meters away on the side of Pizzuta Mountain, where he and his men had arrived around dawn. They had encountered a problem right away. The main force, led by Giuliano, had come upon four early morning hunters at the base of Pizzuta. They were questioned as to who they were, and in particular, Giuliano wanted to know if they were communists. Not knowing their questioner and fearing that the impressively armed young strangers were mafiosi, they answered they most assuredly were not. The strangers told them that their answers were good, that if they had been communists they would have been shot; in fact, two of the men were party members. The bandits obviously could not let the men go, so they placed them under guard in a cave where they would be unable to see what was going on. Giuliano and his squads then took positions to await the arrival of the crowd.[23]

The bands had played, the air rang with the sounds of happy people, and although no noted figure had arrived to speak, the time had come to formally inaugurate the occasion. A substitute orator was recruited from among the lesser celebrities in attendance, and cobbler Giacomo Schirò, secretary of the Socialist Party local at Piana degli Albanesi, began to introduce him. He had scarcely said "Comrades" when a burst of explosions shook the air. Two more bursts followed. They were taken to be fireworks until some of the people, to their horror, heard others cry out and saw them fall to the ground, blood running from their wounds. Most of the people ran in panic. Others tried to help the wounded and dying.

The attack was over almost as soon as it began. Some in the crowd, among them war veterans who had been under fire before, were sure that the shots came from Mount Pizzuta. They also believed that the first two bursts had been fired in the direction of the podium but aimed well above it. The third had hit the crowd. Some of the victims died instantly, whereas others lingered for a while longer. The final count was eleven persons killed, between two and three dozen wounded. Among the dead were a woman and three children: Sera-fino, age fifteen; Vincenza, age eight; Giuseppe, age seven. The toll could have been much heavier. Many wondered why the attackers had killed so few when they easily could have slain so many.[24]

The firing was heard in the town, and within minutes the first of the panic stricken people arrived and related what had happened. The police also had heard the noise but did not rush out to investigate. Instead, they called Palermo for help. Only in the afternoon, after the first of the reinforcements had come—the total number of troops soon reached close to 400—did they go out to the site.[25] By then, Giuliano was far away. He had retired calmly, knowing that as yet he was in no real danger, to regroup his men at a previously designated place a few kilometers distant. There, the men turned in their arms and were paid off. Giuliano told them to return to their homes one by one or in twos and threes so as not to arouse suspicion. The four hunters had been released earlier under warning of death if they told anyone of anything they had seen or heard. Giuliano and his own squad, on their way back, ran into a rural guard whom they believed to be a police informer. They killed him, then dropped his body into a well.[26]

When the bandit left the mountain, he apparently did not know of the tragedy that had occurred. When he learned of it, he was angry that things had not gone as planned. He had intended no harm to innocent people. In his preparatory instructions, he had told his men to aim over the heads of the crowd to create fear and confusion. That was what he himself had done. Apparently, only one man had erred. In confusion or for an unknown reason, he fired his automatic weapon indiscriminately into the crowd. It was later said around Montelepre that the culprit was a 19-year-old boy from Giardinello. Although some denied this, it was a convenient answer to the questions, since, by the time the trial for the slayings commenced in 1950, the boy was dead, the victim of a battle with the police in June 1947.

Letting it be believed that he was the guilty party kept suspicion away from those who were still alive.[27]

Giuliano was remorseful over the deaths, but he also was angry over his failure. He had intended more than scaring the crowd. His plan had envisioned no less than the capture, and probably the execution, of Girolamo Li Causi. Terranova and his men were to descend the opposite mountain to grab the communist leader in the midst of the panic and confusion that the simulated general attack would create. This latter action, first intended solely as a diversionary move, became the main one when Li Causi's absence foiled the original plan.[28] People in the crowd, in fact, reported seeing men on the other mountain, but when the police searched the location for spent cartridges they found none.[29] In truth, none were there, since Terranova's squad, having nothing to do when Li Causi failed to appear, retired when the firing commenced.

Giuliano, and naturally Terranova, too, stoutly maintained thereafter that the kidnapping squad was not at Portella della Ginestra, that Terranova, in spite of his orders, had taken his men elsewhere. The argument was designed to limit the fallout from the slayings by providing Terranova's squad with alibis. Giuliano also pursued this tactic with respect to the temporary help that he had recruited for the action. He simply declared that they had not been there. The only ones who could be justly implicated, he maintained, were a dozen of his own "regulars" whom he had personally led in the attack.[30]

Giuliano never tried to conceal his antagonism for Li Causi. He later admitted that he attempted to abduct him on at least one other occasion. That plan, which was to seize Li Causi at his residence in Palermo, went awry when the leftist leader failed to appear at the expected time.[31]

Who Had Done It?

The Portella della Ginestra incident provoked a reaction throughout Italy on an almost unprecedented scale. There was much genuine shock. Almost everybody, of whatever political persuasion, lamented the shedding of innocent blood, especially that of children. The socialists and communists had reason to be sadder than most, for their comrades had been the victims, and naturally they wanted to see their murderers behind bars. But, they also quickly perceived an opportunity to embarrass the Christian democrats and their conservative allies. That the socialists and communists were then members of the ruling coalition under Christian democrat De Gasperi did not much restrain them; they were on the verge of being ousted from the government and indeed would be out of it before the month ended.

The ability of the left to influence public opinion was impressive. Socialist and communist members of the government were able to draw widespread attention to the issue. The leftist press was widely read, especially *L'Unità,* one of Italy's influential dailies. Even more effective were the leftist-dominated labor unions, which immediately called a nationwide general strike for May 3; their locals also bombarded the Ministry of the Interior with telegrams that indignantly demanded action against those responsible for the incident.

The leftists had no difficulty in deciding the identity of the culprits. The attack, they were certain, was the work of the reactionary right.[32] In it, they included not only the Mafia and Sicily's landed elite but the political parties of the center and right as well. Of course, they did not know yet that it was Giuliano who had actually executed the attack.

Standing against the leftist view was Minister of Interior Mario Scelba, who argued from the beginning that the event was devoid of political significance. It was, he affirmed in Rome, just one more act of "feudal banditry" in a land where such acts were endemic. Whatever he may have known, Scelba, a native Sicilian, was trying to deflect the barrage of accusations that was raining down on the government and specifically on conservative sectors of Sicilian politics, with which he was intimately associated. In the main, the minister stood alone. Even the government's High Commissioner for Sicily believed that the origins of the incident were political.[33]

The police, like most others, concluded that the action had surely been the work of the Mafia. If anyone else was involved, they agreed, common sense suggested that it was the landed elite. Police investigation at the site on the day following the event indicated that the attackers had possessed impressive fire power, whoever they were. They found evidence that nine machine guns had been positioned on the mountain and approximately 800 rounds of ammunition fired. They did testing with their own firearms and wondered why, with the quantity of ammunition that the attackers had expended, so few people had been hit. It would have been easy, they said, to kill just about anybody down below, especially those on Barbato's podium.[34]

Locally, accusing fingers were pointed at various mafiosi. Landowners and *gabelloti* themselves, they were allied politically with other landed interests in the Monarchist, Liberal, and Any Man (*Uomo Qualunque*) parties. Residents recalled what had appeared to be an urgent meeting of area mafiosi on a rural estate two days before the attack. They also thought it strange that the young sons of mafiosi had stayed away from the May Day celebration. Usually they had attended, even if their fathers did not, since the event was a social occasion for almost everybody.

The person first suspected of having organized the attack was 55-year-old Giuseppe Troia, a liberal, a mafioso, and the first Allied-named mayor of his native San Giuseppe Jato. Area residents said that in the evening and night before the Portella incident he was seen in conference with other mafiosi in both San Giuseppe Jato and Piana degli Albanesi, as well as in Monreale, a center of Mafia and reactionary political influence.[35]

The communist press found significance also in the arrival of Calogero Vizzini in Palermo on the same evening, especially when they learned of allegations that he had brought with him a bag of money. That allegation might logically be linked to a later one, which reported that funds had been raised by subscription among area landlords to finance the attack—Giuliano's services always came high. Anyway, Don Calo spent the night in his suite in the Hotel Sole, remained through the morning, and departed for Villalba after news of the attack reached Palermo.[36]

The police moved quickly to arrest and question scores of mafiosi. A good many, learning of the mass arrests, fled the area. Even so, well over a hundred men identified with the Mafia were interrogated. Quite a large number of them were held, Troia and his associates included. They professed their innocence with the convincing alibis for which the Mafia is justly renowned. Most of their claims, moreover, stood up under investigation. The stories of several suspects were uncommonly persuasive. They were, at the time of the attack, with the police chief of Piana degli Albanesi; they had invited him to the estate of one of them for lunch.[37] That alibi calls to mind one of the more memorable professions of innocence in Sicilian history, that of Mafia boss Vito Cascio Ferro in 1909. Under virtually ironclad charges of having personally slain Joe Petrosino, the Italian-American policeman who had come to Palermo to investigate transoceanic criminal links, Cascio Ferro produced a member of the Chamber of Deputies who swore that he was having lunch with the accused when the killing occurred.[38]

Evidence against Troia and his closest associates seemed to be especially strong—eyewitnesses declared they saw four of Troia's men leaving the scene of the crime.[39] Yet, these four, like the others, were released. Although the role of local mafiosi in the incident remained a mystery, nothing substantial proved their innocence, and circumstantial evidence suggested complicity. Locally, their alibis were taken as proof of guilt more than innocence. They were so good that they must have been arranged with knowledge that the May Day event was to end in disaster. The view, widely held in the area, that mafiosi were in on the planning of the crime and in addition may have fired some of the shots, was probably correct.

The reasons why the state dropped the charges against the mafiosi included more than the strong alibis. More central to the decision were the indications that Giuliano and his gang had been involved in the crime. Mafiosi were difficult to deal with, if for no other reason than their political connections, and pursuing them would be a long and fruitless exercise. The bandits, in contrast, were a clear mark, a way to solve the case in an expeditious, unambiguous, and politically acceptable manner.

Inspector Messana suspected Giuliano from the moment he first heard of the attack. Ferreri, of course, had told him that action against the communists was being planned. Two of Giuliano's henchmen who were arrested following the attack revealed something about the matter. Much more was learned when the four hunters who had been detained by the bandits decided to talk. They had not known that their strange encounter was with the famous bandit until they were shown a photograph of him. The photo was furnished by Messana, who got it from Ferreri. On the back of the handsome picture, showing a regal Giuliano mounted on a horse, the bandit had written "Robin Hood." There were also four older boys who had observed Giuliano's retreat from the site, unbeknownst to him. They had been out for a holiday dalliance in the woods with a prostitute.[40] The police connected Giuliano with the massacre within three weeks of its occurrence. In their public announcement, they placed responsibility for it fully on him and made no mention of the Mafia.[41]

The Continuation of the Terrorist Campaign Against the Left

The public announcement of the culpability of the bandits coincided with their next major burst of activity. Travelling by automobile, firing with automatic weapons, and lobbing hand grenades and fire bombs, the brigand chief and his men struck against an assortment of labor union, communist, and socialist offices in Carini, Borgetto, San Giuseppe Jato, Partinico, Monreale, and Cinisi on Sunday night, June 22.

In Partinico, they arrived at the Communist Party headquarters about 10:30, when a good many members were inside passing the time. One man was killed and three wounded in the attack. The noise of the shots and explosions quickly dispersed the crowd that had gathered nearby in Garibaldi Square for the evening's band concert. In Carini, where the Communist Party office was hit in the early morning hours, the raiders were more considerate. They told the several persons inside the building to get out before they threw in two bottles of an inflammatory liquid and ignited it with a grenade. Overall, casualties were light for the number of attacks, but even so, two persons were killed and several wounded. Since the actions came in several locations in short order, the police believed that Giuliano had his band of some twenty men divided into two squadrons. The attacks had been planned, they thought, at a Montelepre meeting presided over by Pasquale Sciortino.[42]

Likely, Sciortino also helped his brother-in-law compose the manifesto that appeared with the raids on the leftist offices. In the crudely typeset statement, Giuliano sought to enlist men in his anticommunist crusade.

> The decisive hour has already struck! He who does not want to be easy prey to that baying pack of reds . . . must today decide. Those people who want at every cost to throw us into the lap of that terrible Russia, where liberty is an impossible fancy and democracy a legend . . . must be fought without ceasing. And I have assumed this responsibility. . . . To the superficial chronicler of events it may seem strange that it would be I who gives life to this Crusade. . . . Resolutely many have wanted to falsify my positions. . . . For nearly four years I have fought unceasingly . . . for a rich, flowering, and prosperous Sicily, and to make it become, as before, the garden spot of Europe. For this I have fought and will continue to fight. . . . He who feels truly Sicilian . . . and wants to cooperate in this great anti-Bolshevik battle knows that there is an estate called SAGANA where I have established my general headquarters. . . . I am certain that many will join me there.[43]

Giuliano's renewed attacks on communists—and the probability that more actions would follow, as his manifesto threatened—again raised leftist anger to fever pitch. In reaction, Prime Minister De Gasperi met in emergency session with the interior minister, the national chief of police, and the head of the *carabinieri*. He then announced that Messana would be replaced as the director of the campaign against banditry in Sicily; he also raised the reward on Giuliano's head to 3 million lire.[44] In fact, the violent phase of Giuliano's anticommunist crusade was over, in spite of the threats in his manifesto. He thereafter remained fervent in his professions of animosity for the left but he did not take up arms against it again.

The Postscript to Portella della Ginestra: Had Giuliano Acted Alone?

The inscription on the marble monument erected in 1949 in memory of those who died at Portella della Ginestra reads:

> On May 1, 1947, here, on the rock of Barbato, celebrating the working class festival and the victory of April 20, the people of Piana degli Albanesi, San Giuseppe Jato, and San Cipirello, men, women, and children, fell under the ferocious barbarity of the bullets of the Mafia and the landed barons, who mowed down innocent victims in order to put an end to the struggle of the peasants for liberation from the servitude of feudalism. The slaughter horrified the world. The blood of new martyrs consecrated in the conscience of the people the resolve to continue the struggle for the redemption of the land in a world of liberty and peace.[45]

It is noteworthy that the blame was laid on the Mafia and the agrarians, not on Salvatore Giuliano. The glaring omission of his name is suggestive of the national controversy that swirled around the event for the quarter of a century following it. A trial at Viterbo in the early 1950s judicially proved the guilt of Giuliano's band but hardly settled the matter. The bandits were guilty, everyone conceded; the dismay came from the state's failure to establish the identity of those who stood behind them. The Italian public was convinced overwhelmingly that Giuliano had not acted on his own.

As to who had contracted with Giuliano to execute the attack, suspicions and allegations varied widely. Some leftists blamed American imperialism. To them, the sinister figure just back of Giuliano was "Captain" Michael Stern, who, they charged, was an American secret agent. Stern initiated a libel suit against *L'Unità,* the Communist Party daily that had printed the charges, and won his case in 1952.[46]

Many others, finding the claims of American involvement shrill and unfounded, believed that a more logical candidate for guilt was the Mafia. But they doubted that the trail of guilt ended there. In the end, it was hard to dispel the notion that ultimate responsibility for Portella della Ginestra rested heavily on those who had the largest stake in the Sicilian latifundia, the landed barons.

The police were discrete in making any such allegations; the leftists were not. Heading their efforts were Li Causi and Giuseppe Montalbano of Palermo. The latter was the most persistent of the "detectives" who tried to solve the case of Portella della Ginestra. Many others may have been content to exploit the issue politically and let it hang in the wind as long as possible, but he genuinely wanted to identify the guilty and bring them to the bar of justice. Born in 1895, his political odyssey paralleled that of many other Italian leftists of his time. He was a socialist at 18 and a communist a few years later. Twice, he was jailed for antifascist activities. At war's end, he became a professor of law in Palermo. He was also, until Li Causi's arrival, Sicily's leading communist. Thereafter, he continued to be important in the party, serving first in the constituent assembly, then in the Regional Assembly, and for over a decade on the Communist Party central committee. In 1957, he deserted the communists to return to his original socialist affiliation. A prolific writer on legal and other socially significant topics, he was also a fearless crusader against the Mafia. That crusade took on an intensely personal character with the disappearance of his stepson in 1949. Montalbano loved the young man as if he were his own and believed that he must have been killed by the Mafia.[47]

Merely charging that the landed barons were responsible for Portella della Ginestra was easy; proving it and naming names were not. The communists tried to blame Sicily's leading conservative parties: the Christian Democratic, Liberal, Qualunque, and Monarchist. It was a logical association to attempt to establish, since all of these parties drew significant support from the agrarian class and the Mafia. If Giuliano was not alone responsible for the terrorist action, then his accomplices almost certainly came from one or more of them.

What appeared to be the first major break in the case came in April 1951 from a person who had been very close to the now-deceased Giuliano. He was Giuliano's most constant companion, Gaspare

Pisciotta, on trial in Viterbo, along with others, for the Ginestra attack. Pisciotta's sensational revelations pointed to the monarchists. The accusation made sense, for not only were they unequivocal champions of the landed barons, but Giuliano's association with individual monarchists was long standing. Most of that persuasion initially were separatists—there were no monarchist parties of note until after the royalist defeat in the 1946 referendum—and Giuliano had gotten to know several of them during his own participation in the separatist movement. Maybe, he had known some of them even longer. Allegations had linked him especially with an influential young monarchist from Monreale, Prince Giovanni Francesco Alliata.

Pisciotta named Alliata and two other monarchists as the ones who contracted with Giuliano to carry out the terrorist action. The other two were Tommaso Leone Marchesano and Giacomo Cusumano Geloso, both of Palermo. Pisciotta admitted that he had seen neither Alliata nor Leone Marchesano with Giuliano. Cusumano served as their representative to him, he said.[48] The most prestigious of the three was the Brazilian-born Alliata, a member of the Sicilian nobility and one of many heirs to the long defunct throne of Sicily. His father was Italy's commercial attache in Rio de Janeiro, his mother a Brazilian heiress. Through her, a landed inheritance in Brazil of considerable magnitude fell to him. He acquired a university education and served in the Italian army until 1943, when he was taken prisoner by the Allies and held for the next three years. Upon his release, he immediately began to play an active role in politics as a rightist.

Leone Marchesano, a lawyer and property administrator for Alliata, was himself a prominent monarchist, counted among the leading founders of the party. He was elected to the Chamber of Deputies in 1948 in the first election for that body of the postwar years. Cusumano Geloso, also a lawyer, did not have the prestige of the other two. A member of the Regional Assembly, he spent most of his time in Palermo—unlike Alliata and Leone Marchesano, whose political careers took them to Rome—and was the one who most frequently dealt directly with Giuliano.

According to Pisciotta, Giuliano made an agreement with the monarchists to perform the service at Portella della Ginestra and subsequently support their party, in exchange for a promise of amnesty for himself and his men. In the event that amnesty should prove to be impossible to obtain, Alliata would see to the bandits' expatriation to Brazil and settlement on his land there. Alliata and his fellow monarchists predictably denied the accusations. For its part, the government showed no inclination to investigate them.

In popular opinion, the accusations were taken seriously, not only because they appeared to substantiate what had been believed in general terms ever since the event but also because the accuser's intimacy with Giuliano strongly suggested that he might know what he was talking about. A nagging doubt was bound to persist, however, as long as the charges stood only on the words of Pisciotta. Nevertheless, Pisciotta's accusations seemed to possess more reliability than any that had yet been made. At his trial, Pisciotta added that Alliata had repeatedly offered him as much as 50 million lire for his silence.[49]

Montalbano, on the basis of Pisciotta's statements, formally entered charges against the three monarchists. They, in turn, sued him for false accusation. Nothing ever came of any of the suits; all were dismissed without fanfare in 1953.[50] So far as the government was concerned, the case of Portella della Ginestra came to a satisfactory conclusion in 1951 with the conviction of Pisciotta and eleven other bandits for participating in it. Many others disagreed, and the controversy continued to be much discussed and written about, although without great effect. Then, over twenty-two years after the massacre, another strange and disturbing revelation was made. Appropriately, it came from the indefatigable Montalbano, who told his story early in 1970 to a parliamentary anti-Mafia commission. Li Causi also sat on it, but, since Montalbano had rejoined the Socialist Party well before then, they were no longer political allies.

On a mid-November evening in 1969, the law professor related, a man came to his home to give him a sealed envelope on which was written: "For Giuseppe Montalbano. To be given to him in the event of my death. December 9, 1951. Antonio Ramirez." The caller who had brought the letter was Giuseppe Ramirez, the son of Antonio, who had died a few days earlier. The letter tended to confirm what Montalbano had long held to be true.

Many years earlier, on December 7, 1951, the elder Ramirez had written, he was visited by a Gioacchino Barbera who revealed to him several matters of grave import: (1) Tommaso Leone Marchesano confessed that he had given Giuliano the orders to launch the Portella della Ginestra attack, although, as Giuliano had always maintained, there had been no intention to kill innocent people. (2) Prince Alliata and Cusumano Geloso, in addition to Leone Marchesano, were always in close contact with Giuliano; indeed, almost all of the bandit's extortion letters were written with Leone Marchesano's consent. (3) Pisciotta's accusations against Alliata and other prominent politicians were true. (4) Giuliano, as Pisciotta had said, was promised amnesty in return for his antileftist actions. (5) Montalbano's stepson had been slain by one of Leone Marchesano's mafiosi. (6) He (Barbera) had decided to tell Ramirez these things, even at the risk of his life, because, while he was a member of the high Mafia, he did not approve of brutal killings. By 1969, Barbera was dead, as were also Leone Marchesano and Cusumano Geloso. Montalbano was then in his mid-seventies.[51]

The Ramirez letter had the ring of truth about it. Any suspicion that Montalbano might have fabricated the story seemed unworthy of serious consideration. Besides, there was a witness in Antonio Ramirez's son Giuseppe. Antonio Ramirez was a respected old gentleman who had played a fairly prominent role in Sicilian politics after the war as a republican. As for Barbera, an unobtrusive lawyer and monarchist politician, his life and professional career were carried on within circles that made it easy to believe he knew whereof he spoke.

Alliata, the only principal in the letter who was still alive when Montalbano revealed its contents, appeared in April 1970 on his request before the same anti-Mafia commission to address the accusations. The 48-year-old prince, who was born one year before Giuliano, categorically repudiated the charges, denying also that he had ever had contact with any bandits. The only thing that the commission learned from him was his resolve to reveal nothing of any consequence about anything. Their extended questioning of him was entirely in vain.[52]

Alliata's continued wall of denial surprised no one, since it was hardly expected that the architects of Portella della Ginestra would ever confess to their own guilt. For this reason, early hopes had been pinned to the possibility that revelations, in one form or another, might come from Giuliano, who at least admitted his participation.

Giuliano had contradictory things to say about the origins of Portella della Ginestra. At times, he claimed that only he was responsible for it. He was angered, he said, by the strength of the communists around Piana degli Albanesi in the April 20 vote and the failure of those towns to support Varvaro. In reality, the three towns that he was talking about were perennial centers of socialist and communist strength and could scarcely have been expected to give many votes to the dissident separatists; Giuliano had little electoral influence in them, anyway. His claim must have arisen from a promise to protect others.

On other occasions he was more candid, as when he talked with the Italian journalist Jacopo Rizza in 1949. Giuliano told him that he had been deceived at Portella. A promise of liberty was given him that was never kept, and other than for that promise, he never would have made the attack. He would not tell Rizza from whom the promise came, although he talked in general terms of his association with the monarchists, especially with an unnamed one at the heart of the movement. As he did at other times, he affirmed that at the proper moment he would reveal the full story.[53]

Giuliano never made his promised revelations, at least in so far as is publicly known. One might still hope for the discovery of memoirs in his handwriting that tell all. Short of that unlikely event, the best answer to the central question of Portella della Ginestra rests on the statements of the police and residents of the area, Pisciotta's accusations, the Ramirez letter, and Giuliano's own limited admissions.

A summary reconstruction of the event on the basis of this evidence indicates that some of Sicily's leading monarchists contracted with Giuliano for the attack, in exchange for their influence in an effort for amnesty and, quite likely, a substantial sum of money, too. The cooperation of the Mafia was easily obtained. Lower-level mafiosi may have participated in the attack; Mafia bosses arranged their solid alibis ahead of it.

Few of those bosses, to be sure, were affiliated with the Monarchist Party, which was weak in their towns. More often they adhered to another conservative party, like the Liberal, Qualunque, or Christian Democratic; yet, they shared a commonality of interests. The monarchists may have stood out in the affair only because they negotiated with Giuliano, while the others remained hidden. How far the trail of guilt led up into the ruling Christian Democratic Party is very difficult to say. Pisciotta made that accusation, too, levelling it at both Bernardo Mattarella, a party leader in Sicily, and Minister of Interior Scelba in Rome, but, as with so many of his charges, he offered no details to substantiate them.[54] Nonetheless, the conclusion that a converging of reactionary interests produced the May Day tragedy was unavoidable, whether or not the prestigious Christian democrats were involved.

Giuliano. (*Scafidi Foto, Palermo.*)

Monte d'Oro. In the foreground, a portion of present-day Montelepre. (*Photograph by the author, 1984.*)

In the foreground, the Giuliano family home. (*Scafidi.*)

Giuliano's mother, Maria Lombardo. (*Scafidi.*)

A Montelepre street scene during the war against Giuliano. (*Scafidi.*)

The police post at Bellolampo, the site, in 1949, of one of Giuliano's most destructive attacks on the state's forces. (*Photograph by the author, 1984.*)

Peasant invasion of a landed estate, c. 1947. (*Scafidi.*)

Don Calogero Vizzini, Sicily's best-known mafia boss in Giuliano's time. (*Scafidi.*)

The fiery Girolamo Li Causi, Sicily's top Communist, whom Giuliano tried to abduct (and perhaps execute) on more than one occasion. (*Scafidi.*)

R. PREFETTURA DI _____

AVVISO IMPORTANTE

Si rende noto che il Ministero dell'Interno
ha stabilito di corrispondere un premio:

1° - Di lire 800.000 (ottocentomila) a chiunque fornisca
esatte notizie che portino alla cattura del bandito
Giuliano Salvatore di Salvatore e di Lombardo Maria, nato a Montelepre il 22 Nov. 1922;

2° - Di lire 500.000 (cinquecentomila) per la cattura
del bandito **Avila** Rosario di Rosario e di Amato
Salvatrice, nato a Niscemi il 12 Febbraio 1899,
capo della banda armata dei Niscemesi; somme
proporzionalmente minori saranno corrisposte per
la cattura degli altri componenti di questa ultima
banda.

I nomi degli informatori saranno mantenuti nel più
assoluto segreto.

LI 18 FEBBRAIO 1946   IL PREFETTO

Fotografia del bandito GIULIANO

Fotografia del bandito AVILA

The offer of a reward for the capture of Giuliano and one of the Niscemi
bandits following the separatist revolt. (*Courtesy of the Archivio Centrale
dello Stato, Rome.*)

The body of Rosario Candela, killed outside of Montelepre in early 1950. (*Scafidi.*)

The home (second from the left) of Gregorio de Maria in Castelvetrano, in which Giuliano was killed in 1950. The opening to the right (totally enclosed by a gate in those days) leads to the courtyard where his body lay. (*Photograph by the author, 1984.*)

Giuliano's body in de Maria's courtyard. To the right, Colonel Ugo Luca; to the left (in dark glasses), Captain Antonio Perenze. (*Scafidi.*)

The handsome Gaspare Pisciotta in chains. (*Scafidi.*)

A partial view of Palermo's infamous Ucciardone Prison, in which, in 1954, Pisciotta died. (*Photograph by the author, 1984.*)

Antonio Terranova and Frank Mannino, both in chains. (*Scafidi.*)

Inside the Giuliano family chapel, Montelepre. (*Photograph by the author, 1984.*)

The privately-erected monument in Montelepre in memory of those who fought and died for the separatist cause. (*Photograph by the author, 1984.*)

PER LA SICILIA !..

SICILIA INDIPENDENTE

SICILIA INDIPENDENTE
FRONTE NAZIONALE SICILIANO

F. N. S.

The Trinacria, the symbol used by the separatist forces, on a 1984 campaign poster of the National Sicilian Front, a small group that still espouses independence. (*Photograph by the author, 1984.*)

A
MORTE I SBIRRI
SUCCHIATORI DEL
POPOLO SICILIANO
E PERCHE SONO I
PRINCIPALI RADICI
FASCISTI, VIVA IL
SEPARATISMO DELLA
LIBERTA   GIULIANO

Giuliano's depiction of his plan for Sicily to become America's 49th state. (*Scafidi.*)

The arrival of Giuliano's remains at the Montelepre cemetery. (*Scafidi.*)

CHAPTER SIX

The Slaying of a Mafia Boss

GIULIANO'S ALLIANCE WITH THE RIGHT and his terrorist campaign of May and June 1947 marked a significant turning point in his career. They tarnished his reputation and led him into ever greater difficulties. Still, for quite a time yet, his reverses were minor and his strength impressive. In any event, much remained to happen in the three years that were left to him. Down his path lay many hazardous turns. He reached one of them in the summer of 1948 when he slew a prestigious Mafia boss, an act that made his ultimate fate more easily foretold. However, much of the year that preceded that event was not especially out of the ordinary for him.

The Death of Salvatore Ferreri

A few days following the bandits' attacks on leftist offices in June 1947, Salvatore Ferreri, Chief Inspector Messana's informant among Giuliano's men, was killed. Better known as Fra Diavolo (Brother Devil), he was already a bandit when he teamed up with Giuliano. Handsome, elegant, experienced, and capable, he soon was entrusted with his own squad. His betrayal of Giuliano was aided by his father, who made the initial contacts with authorities. Following these, the son agreed to furnish Messana with information in return for a promise of clemency. Thereafter, the police were told to leave the inspector's man alone.[1]

Strangely, Giuliano knew of his lieutenant's contact with Messana. Ferreri himself told him, probably from fear that Giuliano would find out on his own and kill him. But Brother Devil did not tell the true story of how it had been arranged. Instead, he fabricated an account of being captured by the police and given a choice of prosecution or turning informant. He accepted the latter, he assured Giuliano, only from desire to escape the clutches of the law and rejoin his chief.[2] Since Giuliano did nothing about the matter, he must have both believed him and not known of his continuing relations with Messana. If so, it was not the last time that the normally astute Giuliano would be fooled in such a way. Ferreri furnished the inspector with several valuable leads. He warned him that Giuliano was planning a major action against the communists and, following it, pointed him toward a pair of brothers who told of Giuliano's involvement.[3]

The squad leader was killed on June 27 following an ambush in Alcamo in which he had been wounded. Taken to the station, he told of his contacts with Messana and produced a safe conduct pass signed by him. There are two versions of what then ensued. The *carabinieri* reported that the bandit was shot and killed when he grabbed for a weapon, but locally it was held that he was killed without provocation. The act was attributed to jealousy that existed between Messana's public security police and the rival *carabinieri;* Ferreri was killed because he was Messana's informant, it was said. This might appear to be another example of Sicilian fondness for conspiratorial explanations, but in fact rivalry between the two police organizations was sufficiently intense at times to override their common aim. There was not much doubt but what such a circumstance produced Ferreri's death.[4]

The dismay created by the action reached all the way up to Minister of Interior Scelba in Rome. In a confidential request for an investigation, he asked why Captain Giallombardo, the commanding officer of the detachment, had deviated from orders without permission from Messana. The captain's action, Scelba wrote, had ruined a sound plan for Giuliano's capture.[5] Giallombardo was transferred to a remote post in Calabria.

Another Big Search

After the mid-June announcement of Giuliano's culpability in the Portella della Ginestra attack, the authorities had to do something to show that they did not condone terrorist attacks on leftists. On Monday night, June 20, just before the bandits raided the leftist headquarters, they sent over 200 men to encircle a mountain near Montelepre on which, they had been told, Giuliano was hiding. As so often had happened, they sadly reported in the end that their prey was not there. Their informants had been mistaken or else he had outwitted them again.[6]

Their next move, in early July, followed the strikes against the leftist posts. It was far more ambitious and, as the press described it, done in "grand style." If people still doubted the government's resolve to bring Giuliano's anticommunist violence to a halt, this was designed to convince them otherwise. The effort was reminiscent of World War II. The campaign included 2000 men, 4 armored cars, and 149 trucks and jeeps. Divided into squads of 60 men each, the troops were to surround Montelepre and vicinity and search every square meter of soil, every cave, and every structure in its confines.

The operation lasted for twenty-six hours. The number of arrests came to only about twenty, among them six "affiliates" of the band and three of its suppliers. Giuliano had not been seen, nor was any of the six an active member of his main cadre. The police, as usual, had exaggerated the significance of their arrests. They often described anyone who was arrested as a key part of the band, even though the person was not closer to it than a friend or relative of one of the bandits or someone who had been active in it in the past.

Arms, ammunition, hand grenades, binoculars, and a military telephone were also uncovered in the sweep. The telephone was found in Giuliano's home in a concealed cubicle that had also sheltered Giuliano on many an occasion. Excavated out of the soil and capable of comfortably holding four men, it could be entered only by removing nine large stones from the ground floor pavement. Mariannina, who was at home when the police came, took the search calmly—the family had grown used to such intrusions—and freely admitted that her brother sometimes came to see the family. But he came rarely, she said, and then only for short visits, preferring to pass his nights in the country. He did not trust anybody, not even his friends, she added. A similar concealed compartment was discovered also in the home of another active member of the band.[7]

The big sweep of early July 1947 was Inspector Messana's last major action. His pending removal as head of the campaign had already been announced, but, because of difficulties in finding a replacement, he had continued in the post. His lack of success in the July action forced his exit. The government needed quick results, so notorious were Giuliano's most recent actions, and little in Messana's past performance showed much promise of his ability to deliver them.

The Departure of Pasquale Sciortino for America

Around the time of the Portella della Ginestra attack, Giuliano had received a letter from a friend in America urging him to leave his outlaw career in Sicily and join him there. Giuliano did not want to go then; instead, he sent Pasquale Sciortino, his brother-in-law, one-time teacher, and fellow rebel. Sciortino, a year younger than the bandit chieftain, came from nearby San Cipirello, where his grandfather was a prosperous businessman; his father was dead. Educated through secondary school in Palermo, he saw military service during the war, lastly as a partisan against the Germans in the north. He was drawn into the separatist movement mostly through his grandfather's acquaintances who were active in its leadership.

Sciortino was arrested in early February 1946, after the EVIS revolt had run its course. Incarcerated in Palermo, he shared a cell with Giuliano's brother, Giuseppe, where he met Mariannina when she came on a visit. Giuliano's sister, then already past 25 years old, was taken with Pasquale—blond, distinguished looking, and self-confident. Thereafter, they corresponded with each other and, following his release from jail, became sweethearts, she said.

Sciortino was freed in early June as a result of the amnesty. Unlike Giuliano's regular bandits, he was accused of no crimes of a nonpolitical nature; his connections to prominent MIS figures also put him in good stead. With his intelligence, charm, education, solid family base, and personal ties to wealthy persons, young Sciortino might have had a promising future—if he had broken his links to Giuliano.

Pasquale and the bandit's sister were married secretly by Montelepre's Padre Di Bella on April 24, 1947; the civil service had been performed already by town mayor Stefano Mannino. Mariannina loved her husband dearly but his affection for her was less than binding. He later maintained that the marriage was forced upon him by Giuliano, who falsely accused him of intimacies with his sister.

Following the marriage, Sciortino found his situation both uncomfortable and threatening. He was living with the Giulianos, and the authorities suspected that he was still a part of Giuliano's band and had participated in both the Portella massacre and the June raids. When Giuliano first proposed Pasquale's expatriation to America, it was understood that Mariannina would accompany him. But, she was pregnant, and in the absence of any strong insistence by her husband that she go with him, it was decided that she would join him later.

The network that Giuliano's money then set in motion carried out its task with efficiency, and Pasquale soon found himself in New York. The next five years were adventuresome ones for the young emigre. Knowing a bit of English already and possessing a level of education that set him above the ordinary Sicilian emigrant, he readily adapted to his new country. Almost anywhere he went—New York, St. Louis, Los Angeles, Detroit, and South Bend, among other cities—contacts already had been established for him by his relatives and friends.

In Los Angeles, he worked for a Sicilian-American owned radio station as a disk jockey, spinning recordings of Mexican and Italian music. There, he called himself Antonio Venza, the first of several aliases that he used in America. After the Korean War began, he enlisted in the American Air Force under still another assumed name. By then, he was charged in Italy with grave crimes, but the matter did not deeply trouble him; for he thought that the door was closed to the period in which his life was enmeshed with that of the Giuliano family. He had written little to his wife and by now had ceased to do so altogether. The birth of his son Giuseppe in 1948 and the death of Giuliano two years later were events that, to him, were linked more to his past than his future. It must have seemed to him that he had escaped his past.[8]

Return to Normalcy

During the last months of 1947 and the early part of 1948, Giuliano's activities took a more normal turn. There was an occasional abduction, continued extortion, and now and then a run-in with the police that was usually provoked by Giuliano rather than by them.

In mid-October, the bandits killed a *carabiniere* and gravely wounded another in an attack on the station in San Giuseppe Jato, and late in November, Giuliano committed one of his more audacious acts of the period. He learned that Lieutenant Colonel Luigi Geronazzo of the detachment of *carabinieri* at Partinico had publicly stated his resolve to put an end to Giuliano's career. Statements of this type usually brought on a quick reaction, for Giuliano regarded them as throwing down the gauntlet.

Close to midnight on October 21, he divided his band in two squads and led them into the town. One of them attacked the officers' barracks; the other went in search of the colonel, who was out for a late stroll with a civilian friend, a pharmacist. The squad fired on the pair at close range, wounding both of them, the colonel so severely that he died three days later. In answer to this brazen assassination, the authorities occupied the area with nearly 1000 troops. Pointing to the many arrests they made, and alleging that Giuliano's force was faltering, they asserted that an ever more constricting circle of "iron" had been erected around the bandits, cutting off "every avenue of escape." With that extravagant claim, news of the big hunt ended.[9]

After that, things were fairly quiet for a while, emboldening Giuliano to make one of his rare public appearances on an evening early in the next year. Another *carabiniere* was assassinated in Partinico on the morning of the same day, January 9, but Giuliano probably had no part in it. The bandit chieftain's visit was to a popular coffee bar in the center of Carini, a substantial rural town just in from the sea, to the north of Partinico.

The bar was full of people who habitually dropped in to listen to the 7:30 P.M. news on the radio. None of them much noticed two strangers in peasant dress who came in. But someone remembered that when they finished their coffee they stopped at the bar entrance, one on each side of it, carefully looking over the scene, as if they were searching for something or someone. A few minutes later, while the two continued to hold their positions, a car drove up, from which two others of a different sort alighted. The driver was noticeable for his pompadoured hair and elegant dress, set off by a wildly flowered tie. The other, more impressive in a subdued way, wore leggings, riding pants, and a rust colored jacket, under which was a turtleneck sweater. Rakishly aligned on his head sat a black beret.

Already having been spied, they made an auspicious entrance, saluting the crowd with a hearty "*Buona sera a tutti*" (Good evening to all). They ordered coffee, and while waiting for it to be prepared ate several creme pastries, sending others to the two men who still kept their vigil at the door. After drinking the tiny cups of strong sweet coffee, the elegant one ceremoniously extracted a note of an impressive denomination from a bulging wallet with which to pay the bill. He refused any change, instead instructing the bartender to extend a round of coffees to the by now hushed and attentive clientele. Then, pointing to his companion, he said "My friend here, Giuliano, has the pleasure of offering you coffee." And with another "*Buona sera a tutti*," they boarded the car and sped away in the darkness toward Montelepre. Only then did the two men in peasant dress depart—

quickly, in opposite directions. When a reporter for *L'Ora* wrote up the story, he ended on a romantic note. It seemed, he wrote, that Giuliano had a girlfriend in Carini and doubtless had spent several hours with her before he stopped in for his evening coffee.[10]

Mamma Giuliano's Troubles

No matter what reporters wrote, the woman most frequently on the bandit's mind was his mother. He was resentful and angry over the heartaches and troubles that his life caused her. Naturally, he did not see himself as responsible for them; instead, he blamed others, especially the police. His anger could almost overwhelm him when they moved against her, or other members of his family, for helping him. The police knew, of course, that family solidarity in Sicily was strong and that the Giulianos' support of their errant member was to be expected. Nonetheless, the authorities watched the family members closely and often appeared over eager to subject them to interrogations, searches, and arrests.

The bandit's mother and Mariannina drew the police's closest attention. Twice in 1946, they were arrested, held for a time, and released. They were suspected of having recruited men for Giuliano, an accusation that had substance, since the easiest way to the bandit was through them. In June 1947, the pair was taken into custody again. That time the police thought that they had been to see Giuliano and might be involved in negotiations regarding one of his recent abductions. Nothing came of the investigation, and they soon were released. Mariannina was arrested again in September, charged with complicity in her brother's plot to abduct a Palermo physician in 1946. In this instance, there was circumstantial evidence against her, and she would not be absolved of the charge until 1954.

It was next the mother's turn. She was arrested again in early February 1948. The charge, aggravated extortion, arose from allegations that she had forced her way into a partnership in a new business that was opened a few steps from the Giuliano home. According to the charges, the "King of Montelepre" was displeased because the original initiators of the business, a pasta factory, were strangers from Palermo. When he told them to abandon the effort, his uncle, Antonio Lombardo, from whom space for the enterprise was being rented, negotiated a compromise. The business could remain, but only on the condition that Maria Lombardo be made a full-fledged partner in it. The terms of the pact were accepted, although with reluctance by the Palermo entrepreneurs, since their new partner brought no capital of her own into the business. She was simply the mother of Giuliano, with whom, realism dictated, one had to get along to do business in Montelepre—just as in many other Sicilian communities the Mafia had to be appeased. Maria Lombardo was released from jail soon, although the charge was not dropped.[11]

A Promise of Freedom: Politics Again

In the late winter and spring of 1948, Giuliano took the troubles of his mother and sister with uncharacteristic equanimity. He believed that there was a way out of them, not only for his family but for himself too. The way out was the way of politics, which once more seemed to hold promise. Events, however bitter, stripped Giuliano of his illusions concerning politicians only slowly and perhaps never completely. The young bandit remained naive and impressionable, even if, as time passed, to decreasing degrees. A part of the problem was his monumental ego, fed by notoriety both at home and abroad. His head hardly could have not been turned when well-known politicians from both Palermo and Rome came to him, or sent emissaries, to solicit his support in elections. Their flattery and attention led him to exaggerate his importance. His value to them lay in his influence over a few thousand voters in, at most, a half dozen towns. He was important in building a regional electoral coalition, but he was only one among many and, in view of his outlaw status, of doubtful durability.

Yet, in spite of the overblown conception that he had of himself, Giuliano possessed a high degree of native astuteness and, at least on vital matters, seldom let his conceit overwhelm it. He dealt with politicians warily and always took care to keep his rear covered. In reality, he had almost no alternatives to dealing with them, since only they could grant him the lawful status that he sought.

The occasion for Giuliano's political activity in 1948 was the parliamentary elections. The first under the new Republican constitution, the April 18 elections were of prime importance to both the left and the right. Furthermore they were watched closely by the United States and the Soviet Union, which saw Italy as a major point of contention in the Cold War. In Sicily, the right and center, especially the Christian Democratic Party, were determined to recover from the defeat that had been dealt them by the left in the Regional Assembly elections of the previous year. It was to this end that they attempted to marshal all possible support, including Giuliano's.

Although the bandit still claimed to be a separatist, there was no party of that persuasion that he could conscientiously support. Varvaro's dissident group had disintegrated, and the regulars were led by men who had no more interest in Giuliano. Anyhow, the separatist party was of no use to him any longer. The minuscule number of deputies it might elect would scarcely be able to influence the government in his favor. His closest allies in politics were now the monarchists. Maybe he ought to have been angry at them, in view of the failure of his action at Portella della Ginestra to produce the liberation that had been offered in return for it. But his relations with prominent monarchists were close and not easily broken. Too, the party was small, particularly outside Sicily and the southern mainland, and its leaders were not in a position to dictate to the government. Giuliano apparently understood why they had been unable to help him.

In the 1948 elections, the monarchists were his first choice, but he did not limit his support to them alone. He was, in this way, like many other conservative and middle-of-the-road Italians in that year, who saw the elections as a struggle to keep the left from coming to power. While the conservatives maintained their party loyalties as usual, their main hope lay not in the victory of any single party, which was unlikely, but rather in a large vote for a broad range of centrist and rightist parties that then could form a strong coalition anticommunist government. In Sicily, as in most of the nation, the leader of the movement was the Christian Democratic Party, which, despite its reformist roots, was becoming increasingly conservative. This political climate of interparty cooperation on the right—on the other side the socialists and communists were running a common effort under the name of the Popular Democratic Front—brought Giuliano his best possibilities yet for access to high level government figures. For him, here was another chance—his most realistic ever—to win amnesty for himself and his men. The politicians were ready to deal and so was he.

The political figures with whom Giuliano dealt directly in the spring of 1948 included monarchists like Leone Marchesano and area bosses such as Santo Fleres, the noted mafioso and Liberal Party boss from Partinico. Santo Fleres, in particular, had close relations with the

Christian Democratic Party, with whom his party usually cooperated in the formation of a ruling coalition. It is a matter of some substance, and not easy to resolve, whether Giuliano's pact with the Catholic party was made only through men like Santo Fleres or, as many believe, was sealed in its final stage by a face-to-face encounter between him and a high party official.

Gaspare Pisciotta testified later that Giuliano met with notable politicians from more than one party, among whom he named Bernardo Mattarella, one of Sicily's leading Christian democrats. Other bandits also pointed their fingers at him, as did leftist activists. Although no one offered conclusive proof of the charges, the suspicion that Mattarella was involved, either directly or through intermediaries, was hard to dispel. Many suspected that even if he had not met personally with Giuliano he had authorized a promise of amnesty. It seemed doubtful that Giuliano would have entered the pact this time, unless he had assurances from some authoritative official that the promise was genuine. In the event the conservatives lost the election to the left, the band was assured again of expatriation to Brazil by the monarchists.[12]

There is every reason to believe that Giuliano worked hard to keep his part of the agreement. His area, it was certain, would vote heavily for the parties of the right. None other, in fact, was permitted to campaign there. A good indication of the difficulties encountered by the left in his country was contained in a report by Dr. Giuseppe Morina to the Popular Democratic Front directors.

Morina, a socialist, wrote that he was scheduled to speak at a rally in Montelepre in late afternoon of April 14, the last Sunday before the election. When he and his party arrived, they found that the posters announcing the event had been ripped down or else defaced by vulgar phrases. The Socialist Party office was closed, and subsequent inquiries to townspeople as to where the local party members might be found brought no satisfactory responses. Finally, and only by chance, they located the section secretary, alone, frightened, and all but hidden in the corner of a square. He told the visitors that the rally could not be held, no one would come to it, and to attempt it would be dangerous. Local leftists had been warned to stay in their homes. Asked who had made the threats, he would not say. Naming the person would do no good, and in any case, nothing could be done. Above all, the visitors should depart as discreetly as possible.

Concluding that the situation was hopeless, Morina and his party started to leave but, before reaching the edge of town, met a police sergeant. He assured them that they had the right to hold their rally, then with equal certainty warned them he could not guarantee their safety. There were many armed men in town who disliked the leftists. To protect the meeting, he would need at least 120 men; he had only 12. Anyhow, he added, even if the rally could be held, there would be no one at it except for the speakers and the military.[13]

That same afternoon, Mattarella spoke to a large crowd in Montelepre's central square. Only the Christian democrats, together with the monarchists and the National Bloc (of which the liberals were a part), were permitted by Giuliano to seek votes in Montelepre during the campaign. As to which party he really favored, there is little doubt but what he felt most kindly toward the monarchists. His family voted that way; however, many others among his supporters, including the families of some of his band members, voted Christian democratic.[14]

Publicly, Giuliano excoriated the communists and announced his support of the rightist parties in a series of letters to the press. In one, he accused Li Causi of "dirty politics," of cynically exploiting the peasants for his own political gain. He challenged the communist leader to tell the truth about how peasants were treated in the Soviet Union; to admit that they were not permitted to own land. In a timely letter that the conservative *Giornale di Sicilia* published on election day, he wrote: "I support all the parties of the right in order to combat communism." Giuliano was also to go on the radio on election day with a lengthy, prepared speech to urge a large anticommunist vote. Because of his caution, the broadcast was to emanate from the band's own transmitter. However, at the last moment, the equipment failed, and what surely would have been one of his moments of glory eluded him.[15]

On April 18, Montelepre and Giardinello once again heeded the call from the mountain and voted overwhelmingly for the Christian democrats and the monarchists, almost shutting out all other parties. Montelepre cast 1593 votes for Mattarella's party, 1034 for the monarchists. The National Bloc, which was third, received 49. Exactly 26 voters favored the Popular Democratic Front. The returns from Giardinello, a much smaller town, read 511 for the Christian democrats, 116 for the monarchists, just a scattering for other parties, and no votes for the leftist front. Neighboring towns, like Partinico and Monreale, also voted heavily for the various conservative parties, Piana degli Albanesi excepted; there, the leftists produced their usual impressive triumph.[16]

Nationally, the Christian Democratic Party victory, although not overwhelming, was even more impressive, since the party received almost 49 percent of the total vote and, crucially, a majority in the Chamber of Deputies. The Popular Democratic Front vote was a disappointing 31 percent of the total; in Sicily, it was just under 21 percent, down 8 points from the socialist-communist vote in the Regional Assembly elections of the previous year.

Giuliano had good reason to believe that all had gone well. The Christian Democratic Party, backed by the other conservative parties, could easily extend the promised pardon, even in the face of the howls of anger that would come from the left. And he expected a speedy fulfillment of the promise. In fact, he was forced to wait a good many weeks for the government's answer. When it came, it was delivered to him on an estate held in lease by noted Comporeale Mafia boss and Liberal Party politician, Vanni Sacco. There, two of Giuliano's political contacts gave him the answer he feared. Scelba, the Minister of the Interior, had rejected the agreement to grant amnesty. The only thing left, the pair told Giuliano, was refuge in Brazil on Prince Alliata's land.[17]

Giuliano had reason to feel betrayed and angry. He had held up his end of the bargain admirably, and an offer of exile was insulting to him. Anyhow, he wanted to remain in Sicily, not only because he was reluctant to leave his family as always, but also because his anger dictated retaliation against those who had betrayed him so shamelessly.

The Assassination

The first major victim of Giuliano's vengeance in the period following the elections was Santo Fleres. He was assassinated as he strolled with a friend in Partinico's main square a little before 10:00 P.M. on July 17, 1948. His two attackers fired on him with automatic weapons, then speedily departed in opposite directions. Nearby residents fearfully waited for a few minutes before coming out to investigate. In Mafia country, where even children who witnessed a crime were frequently slain, no one wanted to see, or be seen by, the assassins. When they came out, they found the prominent landowner bleeding from numerous bullet wounds but still alive. He died in the ambulance on the way to seek medical aid. His slaying occasioned much comment, for he was, as the Christian Democratic *Sicilia del Popolo* noted, "an eminent figure of that zone."[18] Indeed, he was. Santo Fleres was not a run-of-the-mill Mafia head but a "chief among chiefs." His funeral attracted a large crowd, among them many well-known mafiosi from various parts of the island.

There was no reason to believe that Giuliano had personally killed Santo Fleres. He was too cautious to take as much risk as an attack in the center of a substantial town like Partinico would entail, especially at an hour when many people were still up and about. Almost certainly, he entrusted his men with the killing or hired others to do it. According to a jury that heard the trial in 1955, the latter was true. In that case, a former member of the Labruzzo band, a Partinico area group that often cooperated with Giuliano, was judged guilty of the crime. The court declared in its verdict that the motive for the slaying lay in conflicts between some parts of the Mafia and youthful bandits in the area.[19]

The court's reasoning conformed to what was known locally in specific terms, that Santo Fleres was slain because of his close ties to politicians who had betrayed Giuliano. As true as that was, there seems to have been an additional, underlying current in the conflict between the two men, one that was ominous for Giuliano in the long run. This involved his general relations with both the Mafia and the politicians. He had worked intimately with the first and intermittently with the second, but, since he was a bandit, neither saw him as a permanent ally. For the ruling Christian Democratic Party, he had been useful during the April elections; otherwise, he was a gross embarrassment. They not only wanted to disassociate themselves from him, but they were also anxious to see him eliminated. No elections were anticipated soon in which his influence would be valuable. In any case, no one knew how much longer he could last. The politicians of the major parties had no further use of him. The only political friends he had left were among the monarchists, some of whom, like the Sicilian nobility of old, had long sheltered bandits.

With respect to the Mafia, it had rarely been a trustworthy ally of bandits. Its closeness to Giuliano over a considerable period of time was an aberration that arose from conditions peculiar to the immediate postwar years. In the past, these two kinds of criminals had seldom gotten along well with each other. Mafia groups had sometimes tolerated bandits and shared in their profits but usually not for long. Bandits were outlaws, a disturbance, unpredictable, uncontrollable, and notoriously disdainful of property rights. They were a threat to the kind of orderly society in which mafiosi, as quietly and unobtrusively as possible, built their power and prestige and from which they exacted their profits. Sooner or later, in normal times, they either eliminated bandits themselves or betrayed them to the police.

In 1943–1944, when Giuliano was becoming a force to be reckoned with in Montelepre, the Mafia was in a debilitated condition. If Mafia groups disapproved of his actions, there was little that they could do about them. In his own area, as elsewhere, where there was no scarcity of mafiosi, he quickly achieved dominance; there, with little choice, they did his bidding, shared his profits, and were soon absorbed into his structure of power. In his area, he built a degree of control and popular support that made him a "chief among chiefs." However, he was a bandit and not a mafioso, two categories that should not be confused. Neither Giuliano nor they made that mistake. He once told a reporter that while he worked with mafiosi, he had only disdain for their kind; they were, he said, "parasites." [20]

In spite of the Mafia's disapproval of bandits, its members found that cooperation with Giuliano brought tangible benefits. They worked closely with him, and he with them, in a broad range of matters. In abductions, they were often useful as intermediaries between the bandits and the families of the victims. They also provided the bandits with safe refuge on the lands that they controlled, informed them of police movements, and also protected them from the law in other ways. For all of these services, they were handsomely remunerated.

Nonetheless, the Mafia's alliance with bandits was pragmatic and temporary. A revitalized Mafia, in combination with an almost certain decline in the power of the bandits, was bound to produce a changed relationship. Once the Mafia rebuilt its power, it would not likely tolerate such a challenge to its prestige and control for very long. Too, the presence of bandits had another undesirable result. An upsurge of bandit activity, the killing of a policeman or something sensational like Portella della Ginestra, brought large numbers of troops to the area, and if the situation was critical enough, they might remain for considerable lengths of time. These forces potentially threatened the Mafia chiefs, too, especially when they were composed of *carabinieri* and regular army under the command of high-ranking officers. The Mafia chiefs could usually neutralize the low-ranking personnel who commanded the permanent local detachments, but outside troops, under prestigious commanders, were another matter. Anyhow, the

Mafia had an inherent distrust of any impartial and effective police power.

Various Mafia chiefs began to reassert the Mafia's traditional position on banditry well before any of them felt compelled to move against Giuliano. Of the many bands that had been formed in the years just after the war, few were left by the end of 1948. A surprising number of bandits were killed inexplicably. Others dropped from sight, their remains to be discovered months or even years later at the bottom of wells. Still others were apprehended all too easily. The police naturally claimed credit for their elimination, but people who lived in Mafia country knew better.

Sometime soon after the April 1948 elections, a portion of the Mafia, within which Santo Fleres was a respected figure, decided that the time had come to move against Giuliano, too. True, he had an impressive base of support and was a dependable ally, not commonly given to stupid acts. But Giuliano's mood in the months following the election possessed a quality that, arising from an impatience that bordered on desperation, made him a threat to some of the prestigious Mafia heads and their political allies.

Giuliano was now dealing with a Mafia that had become formidable. By 1948, five years after liberation, it had made a remarkable recovery. The entry of many of its chiefs into the ruling Christian Democratic Party ranks signalled its success. Giuliano's threatening insistence that the promise of amnesty be kept in the face of the government's refusal to grant it brought the bandit into conflict with his political ally, Santo Fleres. Forced to choose between Giuliano and his own powerful allies, the Partinico boss made a decision that was entirely in keeping with the pragmatic nature of his kind. He began to supply the authorities with information on Giuliano's movements and activities. The bandit learned of it through his own vast network of informers and had him killed.[21]

The killing of the prestigious mafioso was understandable and, from where Giuliano stood, necessary. In a society where raw power ruled, he could survive only if his own was accorded respect. Still, he could ill afford to risk the anger of the Mafia. In view of its strengthened condition, it was doubtful that he could long endure except by its leave. The threat to him, however, was not immediate, for he by no means lost all of his Mafia support as a result of the slaying. The Mafia was far from monolithic, and many of its groups continued to work profitably with him for yet a long time, some even until his death. Even so, it was a bad turn, and the time had come when the question of just how much longer he would last could be reasonably broached. Not long, thought some. At Santo Fleres's last rites, a policeman overheard an elderly mafioso to remark, "Giuliano has his days counted." [22]

CHAPTER SEVEN

A Mother's Last Visit

THE MONTHS FOLLOWING THE ELECTIONS of April 1948 and the killing of Santo Fleres were grim ones for Giuliano. They brought an end to a period during which his hopes for amnesty or pardon had been high. Now, there no longer was any reasonable chance that he ever again would play a role in Sicilian politics or that politicians might make any more major efforts to intercede on his behalf. Instead, it seemed, he was destined to remain a bandit, until either his freedom or his life should end.

One event of the summer of 1948 especially symbolized the turn that Giuliano was reaching in his life. He saw his mother for the last time. Giuliano loved her dearly, as indeed she loved him. Maria Lombardo Giuliano, then 58 years old, would outlive her bandit son by two decades. Maria Giuliano was a strong woman with considerable breadth of experience. She had emigrated as a child to America, where she lived in New York, before returning to Montelepre to meet the man who became her husband. He subsequently made another extended trip to the United States, and like so many other Sicilian women whose spouses sought work elsewhere, she headed the family during his absence.

The authorities portrayed Mamma Giuliano as a Sicilian Ma Barker; in the words of one police document, a "crafty, cynical, wicked, and money hungry woman, the chief instigator of her already criminally prone son." [1] What they found objectionable, of course, was her absolute devotion to her bandit son, cooperation with him when he asked for it, and a defense of him on all counts; in short, a partisanship without limits. They surely knew, however, that in a strong woman like Maria Lombardo anything other than blind filial devotion would have been an aberration, because, if Sicilian sons adore their mothers to a degree scarcely surpassed anywhere, the return of that adoration is no less striking.

Giuliano visited his mother almost at will at least until 1947. The location of their house at the edge of town, the rough terrain, the unobstructed view of it from the mountain, and the fear of the police to be outside their quarters after dark made such visits fairly safe; so also did the secret compartment in the house and an equally concealed tunnel that led from the house to the open countryside. Still, anxious lest he overburden his luck, he came only now and then. The door that opened onto the country was always left unlocked. There was no fear of intruders, since, Giulia, Giuliano's small dog, let the family know if anyone was around. When it was her master, Giulia would go into a state of frenzy, awakening everyone as she raced joyously from room to room.

On his visits, Giuliano had the chance to see his family, eat well, bathe, and sleep in a bed for a change. The women kept a vigil on the terrace while he slept. A little before dawn, they would awaken him, give him his refilled knapsack, bid him good-bye, and watch until they could see him no longer. If they heard no shots in the next few minutes, they assumed that he had gotten back to the safety of his mountain. It all seemed to be without serious risk. Only once, on the Christmas Eve of 1943, did he ever have to flee from the house. Even when Giuliano did not come down from the mountain, the family often knew that he was nearby. If he saw nothing suspicious—he had good military binoculars—he would signal with a mirror, bouncing the light off a window or them if they were outside. They worked out a code of their own, so that they could communicate with each other. Frequently, he signalled because he wanted something sent up to him.

After Portella della Ginestra, Giuliano's visits ended. Thenceforth, members of his family went to see him, at a time and location of his own choosing. The last time that he sent for his mother was in June 1948. Early that morning, a note was passed furtively to her from a boy who had come down from the mountain to peddle milk. In it, Giuliano asked his mother and Mariannina to meet him toward the middle of the day at a place in the countryside, some 4 or 5 kilometers distant. "Bring lunch," he wrote, "and we will eat together."

Maria Lombardo bought a cake and fish, prepared vegetables, took out two bottles of her best wine, and after carefully observing the *carabiniere* station from the vantage point of her terrace, quickly set off with Mariannina for the mountain. Actually, there was not much risk to Giuliano, for he knew the route that they would take and saw them coming from afar. Had they been followed, he would not have been there when they arrived. When they reached the spot, they found him waiting in the shade of an olive tree. He already had a fire going. They roasted the fish and had a long, leisurely visit. Her son ate more than usual, Mamma Giuliano happily noted, and even drank a little wine (he partook of alcoholic beverages sparingly). He enjoyed the cake immensely with his coffee, as she had known he would.

Turridu stood up when they finished eating, as he had done several times already, to look over the area carefully with his binoculars. Afterwards, they had a serious talk. He intended to continue his struggle, he told them, to force the government to grant him amnesty. "The men of the government," he said, "have to understand that I was not born a criminal, that I am not a son of criminals. They have to take into account that I and so many others who are with me find ourselves in this situation because of events above and beyond our control: the war, economic need, the bad advice of politicians." Giuliano expressed confidence that in time Rome would see the justice of his side. At the moment, he said, the politicians wanted him to emigrate, offering to put a ship or a plane at his disposal. But he did not trust them.

Giuliano's forceful words gave his mother hope. The thought that she might never see him again was not in her mind as she kissed him goodbye.[2]

A Foiled Plot

Emigration abroad would have held the best promise of a future for Giuliano, and in spite of what he had told his mother, he was giving consideration to such a move by mid-summer of 1948. He was much concerned about his safety then, for he knew that a portion of the Mafia was out to get him for his killing of Santo Fleres. He did not know, however, how extensive the efforts against him were. In reality, a Mafia association from the Madonie region of north central Sicily was cooperating with a police plot to entrap him through an offer to arrange his emigration.

The police had strong hopes for the success of the plot, which was set for August. Giuliano was told that a fishing boat would pick him up on Sicily's east coast to take him by night to Tunisia. All seemed to be in order, until the police received a message from one of their Mafia contacts cancelling it. Although they were given no explanation, they believed that one of the bandit's well placed friends, likely a Mafia boss or a prominent monarchist, had learned of the conspiracy and told him of it.[3] Thereafter, Giuliano felt less secure than ever. Word reached the outside in mid-September that he thought even his closest friends were plotting to poison him; he had acquired two German police dogs to which he gave portions of his food before he ate.[4]

Giuliano's depression also may have been motivated by the continuing difficulties of his family, which again were worsening. His mother had been rearrested on the extortion charge and was in prison in Trapani. In October, Mariannina was taken into custody again, also on old charges. For that matter, the entire Giuliano family would be either in prison or confinement before the year ended. Perhaps, the authorities were only trying to isolate the bandit from his supporters, but it was hard to avoid the conclusion that they were moved at least as much by spite. Giuliano certainly believed it to be that way. In December, he sent a letter to the monarchist press in which he asked plaintively if "because a mother is the mother of a bandit, because a sister, a father . . . are relatives of a bandit, for this alone ought they to be marched off to jail?"[5]

More Violence and More Repression

It may be assumed that the police were not trying to goad Giuliano into attacking them, since they had been given many lessons already in the folly of that tactic. Yet, that is what ensued. For over a year, from the Portella incident to the summer of 1948, Giuliano's violence against the police had been held to a low level. He did not forbid his men to fire on them, an occasional attack being necessary to keep them cowed, but as long as he maintained hopes of a deal with the politicians, he exercised a great deal of restraint. When, on May 1, 1948, he killed a *carabiniere,* he felt compelled to apologize publicly for his mistake. He had not intended to kill the trooper, he wrote in a letter to the press; he fired only because the soldier had one of the bandits in the sights of his rifle. To further show his remorse, he enclosed 50,000 lire for the dead man's mother.[6]

In early August, some three months later, a Montelepre barber also fell to Giuliano's band, an act for which no apology was forthcoming. Bernardo Frisella, the barber, was sitting in front of his house in late evening on the town's main street, in the company of his wife, his son, and a teenage girl, when machine guns spit fire from the roof of a nearby building. The boy fled to safety but the other three were hit, the barber and his wife fatally. The object of the attack was Frisella, who, Giuliano had learned, was a police informant.[7] Later in the same month, the band also killed a Giardinello farmer, who had loudly protested the presence of bandits on his land and threatened to "do them in."[8]

Giuliano was ready to resume his violence against the police, too, by early September, in reaction to his mother's imprisonment. On September 3, his bandits ambushed a contingent of troops on the outskirts of Partinico and killed three of them, a captain included. On a night in mid-October, they attacked the Montelepre police barracks, however, without injuring anyone, a result that they surely had anticipated. Few troops there had ventured outside their well-fortified quarters after the bedtime hour in several years, a practice that the bandits' frequent nighttime raids—the embarrassed police seldom reported them—were expected to accomplish. Only when the authorities were tipped off to the whereabouts of one bandit or another did they sometimes send out a patrol after darkness fell. On the night following the raid on the barracks, the outlaws struck again, this time seriously wounding three policemen near Giardinello.[9]

Giuliano's next major burst of activity against the police resulted from the death on November 25 of Giuseppe Passatempo, a veteran member of the band. He and Giuliano had passed the night in the former's house at the edge of Giardinello and were making their way toward the mountains in the normally safe hours just before dawn when they were ordered to halt by a small contingent of *carabinieri* in civilian dress. Passatempo, ever alert with his machine gun, immediately fired, hitting at least two of the policemen, one of whom soon died. In that same instant, Giuliano bolted for safety, and Passatempo, who had been hit by the first police fire, was struck again when he tried to follow his chief. He then took cover until he died. The police triumphantly announced his death, identifying him as one of Giuliano's inseparable companions.

Passatempo, a Montelepre native who died at age 27, had joined the band in September 1944, not many months after its founding. The long list of crimes for which he was charged included most of Giuliano's major actions. He had been a participant in more than two dozen kidnappings, several of them in the months immediately preceding his death, and he had one of the bloodiest reputations among

Giuliano's men. Any of the enemy that fell into his hands was likely to die, fellow band member Frank Mannino later said. But around Giuliano, whom he ardently admired, he was almost "angelic." Giuseppe was one of three of the boys in his family to be involved with the gang, and the second to die.[10]

Giuliano was much angered by the killing of Passatempo, if not more disturbed by his own close call. He took his revenge during the following days, first with a few bursts of machine gun fire against a building in Montelepre that housed a mobile police unit, then with an attack on a police vehicle. The latter target was a good one; three officers were aboard, including a colonel. All of the three were seriously wounded, although none was killed.[11]

The brazen attack on the officers—it happened down from Bellolampo almost within the city of Palermo—led the authorities to organize another large-scale effort to neutralize the bandits' base of support in Montelepre. On the night of December 16, troops descended on the town, ordered residents from their homes, gathered them in public places under gunpoint, and subjected them to prolonged interrogation. Numerous arrests followed. The action did not escape Giuliano's notice. That night, his men fired on troops barely outside the town and, on the next, attacked a police truck near Giardinello—at the same spot where Passatempo had died—killing one of its occupants and wounding three others. In another attack, a twenty-two-year-old soldier was gravely wounded in a shootout with the bandits near San Giuseppe Jato on December 23. He died the next day on Christmas Eve.[12]

Montelepre, Late 1948

For Montelepre residents, the mid-December roundup was part of an extremely grim period. Anytime Giuliano increased his attacks on the police, the already bad situation in the town worsened. Life there in such times was described by two journalists who went to Montelepre in late fall and early winter of 1948. Carlo Soresi of *Sicilia del Popolo* made three trips, one in each of the last three months of the year. *L'Ora* sent Enzo Perrone, who went at the end of December. Soresi took the train and got off at the stop called Montelepre–Lo Zucco, which in spite of its name lies far from where Montelepre actually clings to its mountain. Such apparent discrepancies were common to the region, since the railroad builders took advantage of the lower, smoother elevations for their routes, while the ancient founders of its towns typically chose a location on the top of a mountain or high on one of its slopes—valuable defensively when barbarians raided the coast.

Soresi, not finding any transportation, covered the remaining 10 kilometers to his destination on foot. Once he arrived in the town, as almost every reporter who went there discovered to his dismay, there frequently was no place to spend the night; that is, if the authorities permitted you to stay that long. Before an outsider could remain overnight, application had to be made to the police, complete with information on the supplicant's identity, purpose of visit, and intended duration of stay. By the time this hurdle was overcome, the visitor would likely find that the town's single hotel, a simple *locanda* of one room, was full already, its several beds taken by bus and truck drivers.

The appearance and atmosphere of the town were oppressive. Its entrances were guarded, and all who came or went were carefully checked. Numerous military trucks, armored cars, and other official vehicles could be seen; troops were everywhere. The jails were full. If the town appeared bustling during the day, although in an abnormal way, the scene was radically different after seven o'clock in the evening. Then, the townspeople were forbidden to leave their dwellings, doors and windows were barred, the troops took cover. The town was eerily silent, except when the firing of automatic weapons or the explosion of hand grenades let the residents know that the bandits had come down from the mountain to harass the police.

The poverty and misery of Montelepre seldom failed to impress a stranger, and conditions in 1948 were growing worse. The streets were torn up by the constant passing of heavy military vehicles. The town had only one school, which was hardly functioning. It had a building, one teacher, and a few students, in a town of 5000; but there were no desks, no toilet, and despite the winter bouts of cold weather, no heat. Many of the town's residents were practically destitute. Public employees went months without pay. Farmers could cultivate their plots or care for their flocks only with extreme difficulty. If they attended their land daily, returning home at night, they likely would be accused by the police of aiding the bandits. Many of them, finding no other recourse, temporarily left their families to live on their plots, but that put them in even worse stead with the police.

Most pathetic were the families of the men, boys, and women who had been jailed or sent off to confinement. Losing their main bread-winners in this way meant living in utter misery. Every week, the dreaded town confinement commission met again. Commonly, another dozen or two would be sent off to confinement for three, four, or five years. Most of Montelepre's confinees, Giuliano's brother included (his father too by year's end), were sent to Ustica, a small island some 65 kilometers off Sicily's northern coast. Frequently used as a place of confinement—there was little chance of escaping from it—often a majority of the small island's residents were there under sentence.

Few of Montelepre's people would answer reporters' questions on anything related to Giuliano. Those who would talk led Soresi to believe that their toleration of the harsh conditions would reach a breaking point before long, and in a way that was dangerous to Giuliano. Until recently, they would have pardoned him for almost anything, but suffering and fear of confinement were beginning to erode their loyalty to him. They were beginning to doubt that the troubles of one man were worth the misery of an entire town. The day might not be far off when his capture would occasion more relief than sorrow. Ominously, the police were receiving more and more anonymous letters that furnished bits of information on his activities and hiding places.

One man who did talk freely with Soresi said what others were afraid to say. Montelepre had two sets of bosses, the police and the bandits. The first were engaging in hard, dangerous, even heroic work. They wanted the townspeople to become their collaborators, to break their ties with the outlaws. If they would not, they were threatened with confinement. He illustrated this dire situation with his own story. Like others there, he had his own "postage stamp" of land outside the town, to which he had to go daily to care for his plantings, especially during the summer. He was there one day when three men came up whom he knew to be Giuliano's. They asked for bread and matches. "Was I to refuse them?" he asked. "Was I supposed to go to the police and tell them?" If he did not, and they learned of his contact with the bandits, he was certain to be sentenced to confinement. If he refused the bandits or informed on them, his fate could be worse—burning the shed on his land, destroying crops and groves, and almost surely death. Death or confinement, he sadly concluded, were the choices offered to the people of Montelepre.[13]

The reporters, like all other visitors to Montelepre in those times, went to look at Giuliano's home. It was, they saw, the town's finest residence. It had not always been so, only since their son became a bandit had the Giulianos remodeled and enlarged the building. The addition of certain Arabic architectural features to it had made it resemble a fortress somewhat. By late December 1948, the Giulianos, the bandit apart, were all in the clutches of the law, but the house was not empty. In fact, one of the things that made the sight especially interesting to outsiders was its new occupants. The public security police had temporarily appropriated the structure for use as a command post. When the bandit descended at night to attack the troops, he sometimes had to direct fire at his own house.[14]

Resignations from the Band

Meanwhile, among Giuliano's men, things were not going well either. True, money was plentiful—extortions and abductions saw to that—and the police were still manageable. But conditions were not like they had been in the old days. The once bright hopes of independence, American help, or salvation under the anticommunist banner had vanished. Any reasonable hopes for amnesty had also evaporated. Some Mafia families had passed to the enemy, and others were likely to follow them; it was to be wondered if the townspeople could afford to remain faithful much longer. In the midst of this gloom came the death of Passatempo, which severely shook the men. He was a part of the core of the band from which losses had been few, and they suspected that someone in Giardinello had betrayed him and Giuliano. What kind of future was there for the band? This was the question asked by several of Giuliano's most faithful comrades in the fall of 1948.

The men finally told Giuliano that the time had come to go abroad, as they had often talked of doing. At the least, those who wanted to leave should be permitted to do so. Giuliano angrily rebuffed their proposals at first. True, he himself had thought of emigrating, but he frequently changed his mind on the matter. He had told his mother earlier that same year: "Here, my story began; here, it ought to finish."[15] He now urged his men to stay with him and fight, to raise the level of the war and force the authorities to recognize the justice of their struggle. He spoke to them of larger scale assaults, blowing up railroad bridges, and the like. As plainly as they dared, they turned him down. Seeing their firm resolve, he decided to cooperate with them.[16]

Seven wanted to leave, and to finance their venture a wealthy landowner was abducted. This time, the ransom was divided equally among all, unlike customarily happened, when Giuliano received the lion's share. Fake identification papers were obtained and, to transport the men from a point near Castellammare del Golfo to Tunisia, a motorized fishing boat was hired. When they sailed, on December 7, Giuliano and the remaining men provided cover by holding the nearby maritime police post under fire until the boat was safely out to sea.[17]

Giuliano was saddened by the resignations, and not merely because he was left with a much decimated band, for new recruits were easy to find. These men were among his most trusted companions. The core of the departing group was Antonio Terranova and his squad, whose skill in kidnapping had proved their worth time and again. Frank Mannino was among them. Antonio Cucinella and Francesco Pisciotta also departed, both of them having been with him since he freed them from the Monreale jail in 1944. Gaspare Pisciotta was among the few who did not leave.

For the seven, it promised to be the beginning of quite an adventure. They were all under 30 years old. Their plans were not well worked out, at least not any further than Tunisia. They talked of going on to Argentina and then to the United States. None of the group was to ever reach the New World, as far as is publicly known with certainty, although one may have, eventually. Some got into trouble in Tunisia within a couple of months of their landing when they ran over a native and, identified by Interpol, were returned to Sicily under arrest. After that, the Tunisian authorities, afraid that Giuliano might be transferring his operations to their land, became especially vigilant.

The remaining three looked for safer ground in Algeria, where they decided to enlist in the French Foreign Legion. Asked why they wanted to join that famed service, they replied that it was from a thirst for adventure. That being the main question asked, they were sent to Sidi Bel Abbes in far western Algeria for basic training. At the end of about three months, Mannino and Rosario Candela were turned out, told that they had not measured up. The harsh discipline had been their undoing, said Mannino. The other one, Francesco Palma Abate was accepted into the legion and later sent to French Indochina for service against Ho Chi Minh's communist insurgents. He was the only one of the seven who dropped from sight. Mannino and Candela would remain a part of Giuliano's story.[18]

A Lonely Life

Giuliano's cooperation with Terranova and the others who left was suggestive of how he felt toward them. He respected them, treated them well, and demanded their obedience. He held them to strict standards in their relations with the opposite sex, once whipping his closest friend, the rakish Pisciotta, for improper conduct with a girl of good reputation. His men respected, trusted, and liked him. How relaxed he might be with them varied with circumstances. In good times, as in the early days, he passed a great deal of time with them or at least was accessible to them. Now and then, either alone or in the company of one or more of them, he engaged in an act of public daring that made its way into popular fancy.

He was in Montelepre for Christmas in 1946; he boldly masqueraded as a king in the 1947 carnival there. He went into Palermo for diversion on quite a number of occasions, sometimes on a motorcycle in the company of members of his band. He would go to some of the city's best restaurants, leaving a "Giuliano was here" note on his table if he felt especially bold. His favorite disguise for such trips was an army captain's uniform.[19] Of course, such larks were limited to times when he knew that the police had relaxed their efforts against him. Gross imprudence was not characteristic of him, especially past the midpoint of his career.

As his caution increased, especially during the last year of his life, he was wary of even his own men. He kept them divided into three or four squads, each independent of the others except for his central authority. Other than when an important matter dictated a meeting with a squad or, more often, just its leader, he spent most of his time alone or in the company of only one comrade. Orders were given through intermediaries and only at the last moment, so that any possible traitors among the men would not have time to inform the police of the planned event. If a meeting was necessary, he chose the place carefully, one that he could see beforehand from a safely distant location. In this way, he could know if the men were being followed when they came or if a trap was being prepared for him at the meeting site. Frequently, the designated meeting place would not be the actual one; the men would find there only a peasant or a boy who then would lead them to Giuliano at still another location.

As to where Giuliano spent his nights, that was a matter about which he had been secretive since he became a bandit. His mother recalled that one day his older brother innocently asked him where he would go for the night. Giuliano gave him a long, mean look before finally telling him that he would let the question pass only because it was asked by his brother. None of his men, he said, dared ask him where he slept, even those he trusted the most. In actuality, bedtime might find him almost anywhere. He did occasionally sleep in the house of one friend or another, or with a family of trust, or at home as long as that was possible. More often, nightfall found him alone in a cave, preferably one with two exits, an abandoned house or barn, or in good weather, out in the open under an olive tree. He seldom stayed for long in one place. During the daylight hours, and at night, too, he often was on the move, walking for hours on end.[20]

The Scandalous Cyliakus

Late 1948 was as bad a time as Giuliano had yet undergone, but in the midst of it, a surprise visit by an exotic woman journalist, temporarily dispelled some of the gloom.

Giuliano had never had much experience with women of his own age. He was not unique in this respect, since relations in Sicily between unmarried men and women, by custom, were strictly defined and closely monitored. Families guarded the chastity of their young unmarried women, and any violation of it without an immediate offer of marriage would produce a violent reaction by the father and brothers of the offended girl. The custom was so ingrained that, in a cruel turnabout of it, a rejected suitor would sometimes abduct the object of his affection, spend the night with her, and then let the community know of it. After that, there was little else to do than for the girl's family to consent to the marriage, a legal union with even an unwanted mate being considered preferable to the shame of having an unmarriageable former virgin on their hands. As to married women, their roles were equally defined by custom, as well as by their hard work and many children.

On the day following the death of Passatempo, Maria Cyliakus came into Giuliano's old-fashioned world. She was 32 years old, bold,

Swedish, liberated, spirited, "the Greta Garbo of the bandits."[21] The name Cyliakus came from her estranged Greek industrialist husband. She worked for a time on a small newspaper in Stockholm and, four months prior to her arrival in Montelepre, had come to Rome as a translator for the Cuban legation. Having become intrigued by Giuliano, after reading one of Stern's articles on him, she decided that she, too, would interview the bandit. Tall, well proportioned, with copper colored hair and striking gray eyes, Cyliakus was perhaps more interesting than pretty, characterized by a vibrant personality and filled with a nervous, almost virile, energy that Sicilian men found exciting. She spoke Italian well, albeit with an accent that natives thought exceptionally queer.

Unlike Stern who had both a ploy to get to Giuliano and a jeep, Cyliakus had neither. She went first to Palermo, where she tried unsuccessfully to contact him for two weeks, then to Montelepre. There, she, too, found the people closemouthed. That, she supposed, was the law of the mountains. Finally, a friendly *carabiniere* accompanied her to the bandit's father, who had not yet followed the other members of the family into jail or confinement, although he soon would. His manner was civil until he found out that she was a journalist. He suspected then that she was an agent of the police and would talk to her no more.

Cyliakus, undaunted, donned trousers and a heavy sweater, packed some toilet articles and her camera in a straw bag, and, armed with a map, headed up the mountain. After she had wandered for several hours, a sentry ordered her to put her hands into the air. Momentarily alarmed, but still in control, she could but see that the boy before her was strikingly handsome. She described him as very masculine, with an open, friendly face, dark hair and eyes, and a sensuous mouth— and armed with a machine gun. He inspected her bag. She asked him if her message had arrived. The boy thought for some seconds, then, with a quiver of excitement in his voice, inquired: "Are you Giuliano's lover?" She admitted that she was not, but sharply remembering her mission, asked him: "Does Giuliano have a lover?" "We don't know," the boy answered, "but we think so."

The boy then told Cyliakus that he would escort her to the "general headquarters" at Lo Zucco. Along the way—it was now dark—additional men joined the two, none of whom, to her disappointment, would admit that he was a bandit. She had almost decided that she was in the hands of the police when, during a brief stop, the men confessed to being outlaws after all. Giuliano was nearby, they told her; she then learned that he was one of the men with whom she had been talking. Speaking in a tranquil, though decisive voice, the brigand chieftain questioned her intently, asking her among other things the names of persons in Sweden who knew her, so as, he said, to send telegrams there to verify her story. The police, he explained, had been sending spies against him, even women, posing as journalists.

Cyliakus had been "captured" about 5:30 P.M.; it was 10:00 before the party stopped for any length of time. Their resting place was one of those abandoned, half-destroyed farm houses so common in Europe after the war—a squalid place, with straw on the floor. In it were seven or eight more men, ranging from teenagers to around 40, some dressed like bandits, some as simple peasants. Soon, a man brought in a large basket filled with tomatoes, onions, lemons, oranges, bread, wine, oil, and spaghetti. They ate, then resumed their journey, stopping to sleep only after midnight, in the cold of a herdsman's shelter made of brush and straw. Up again before daylight, they covered another long distance, finally halting near a highway, where, Giuliano told her, they planned to attack a police force when it passed. The Swedish adventurer was getting a rare view of Giuliano and his band, the likes of which few outsiders ever saw.

She remained with them for over twenty-four hours and later wrote that she witnessed the attack on the police; she did not describe the action. What clearly interested her more was Giuliano himself, with whose charms she was quickly smitten. Nothing like the Sicilian gangster of American films, he was so clean-cut, masculine, and handsome that any Hollywood producer would see great possibilities in him, she thought. She described him as a man of about 5 feet, 6 inches tall, with a ready smile, an open countenance, and strong hands. His nails were well manicured; he affected a long fingernail; and he wore a diamond ring. He loved to have his photograph taken and had a motion-picture camera of his own. She was permitted to look into his knapsack, his only baggage, and found soap, razor, blades, mirror, toothbrush, toothpaste, a pocket knife, and three white handkerchiefs, mixed in with a few rounds of ammunition and hand grenades.

Giuliano told her a version of the story of his life that was exactly what she wanted to hear. It was a chronicle of hardship, poverty, tragedy, betrayal, and despair, but also of a simple faith in Divine Justice. That he was alive and free after five years of struggle was a sign, he said, that God favored him. He assured her that he never killed unjustly nor, unlike the police, did he use torture. When he "arrested" someone, he interrogated him, gave him a chance to answer the charges, and if a sentence of death was deemed just and necessary, to pray before he was shot. He did not hate the police, especially not the *carabinieri,* who were only doing their duty. He and his men took nothing from the poor, treated the rich with respect, and always honored women. In answer to the query as to what he did if the rich did not pay up, he replied that they always paid.

The bandit took leave of his visitor in the evening. He left her at a granary, telling her to spend the night there and, at dawn, to go back to Montelepre. She shook hands all around, and as he and his men walked off into the darkness, he called back to her not to forget them. One supposes that she never did. The meeting with the famous brigand made her an instant, if temporary, journalistic success over much of Europe, and in Italy, her story was published by the popular weekly magazine *Oggi* (Today) early in 1949.

The police took her article as an insult, finding themselves depicted as persecuting a Robin Hood. When she reappeared in Montelepre in March, in hope of a second interview with Giuliano, they took her into custody. Her reaction was indignant and, the police said, violent. She was transferred to Palermo, where she continued to be equally difficult to handle, hurling "grave insults" at the officials present and the Italian police in general. They said she became so overwrought that she smashed a window; she said they pushed her into it. However it was, she cut her hand in the fray and tried to escape when they took her to a hospital for treatment.

Cyliakus was charged with assault on the police, as well as the unauthorized entry into a "war zone." They threatened to prosecute her additionally for participation in an armed attack on the police, based upon her claims that she was with Giuliano in one of his actions. But, wanting to be free of the volatile woman as quickly as possible, the authorities quickly brought her to trial on only the lesser charges. Giuliano, in the meantime, had demanded her release in a letter to the press and accused the state of trampling upon standards of journalistic freedom that the whole world regarded as inviolate. It had also been learned in the meantime that Cyliakus was known to the police in Rome, who twice had questioned her for associating with persons of suspicious character.

At her trial, Cyliakus was found guilty and sentenced to jail for 4 months and 20 days. The sentence, however, was suspended for five years on the condition of good behavior. The court ordered her immediate expulsion from Italy. She left Palermo under escort on March 24 and, after stopping briefly in Rome to reclaim her personal belongings and her fox terrier, she was taken to the French border. As soon as she arrived in Paris, she granted an interview. In it, she spoke of her adventures with Giuliano and stated her admiration for Sicilians, whom she hoped to visit again.[22] With that, the Swedish firebrand mostly fell from the Italian view, although one small news item later reported her arrest in Paris for creating a disturbance.

Many people wanted to link Cyliakus and Giuliano romantically, which she herself had encouraged in her Paris interview, when she pointedly asserted that she had spent the night with him. Of course, in a manner of speaking she had but not as she insinuated. All that passed between the two, Frank Mannino said, was friendly conversation. The woman was treated with respect, as Giuliano treated all women, and guarded around the clock, lest she be in league with the authorities.[23] In another, more personal way, Cyliakus revealed the true nature of Giuliano's relationship with her. When she was detained by the police, she had with her photographs from her earlier visit, among them a picture of herself on which she had inscribed: "To Turridu Giuliano, who has more fear of me, a woman, than everybody else, including the entire police force."[24]

Cyliakus had asked the bandit about his experiences with the opposite sex. The stories of his love affairs were all without foundation, he answered. There, on the mountain, he wanted nothing to do with women nor did he trust them, and as to girls of dubious reputation, he had no desire for them. He confessed that he once had a girlfriend, when he was 18, but after becoming an outlaw he sent word to her that he would not see her any more; a decision, he added, that was for her own sake.

The girl that Giuliano mentioned was Mariuccia Bono, who in 1946 went to the United States, where her father was living already. Beset by a homesickness that would not go away, she returned to Montelepre early in 1949 and later married a *carabiniere*. Mariuccia, said to be very pretty, was the only serious girlfriend Giuliano ever had, although stories of alleged love affairs continued to be talked about. A rumor of his involvement with a young woman of Carini was especially persistent, so much so that the police investigated it in hopes of ambushing the bandit when he came calling. At one point, they thought that they had identified the woman, watched her house closely, and on a tip raided it, but he was not there.[25] Another allegation, that he had a child in Montelepre, whose mother later married another, was equally persistent but based, it seems, only upon physical likeness.

What Giuliano told Cyliakus about his love affairs appears to be mostly true. His sister corroborated it as did Frank Mannino. Mariannina noted that he did not like to talk about such matters and added that he had a certain diffidence toward women, as if they did not mean much to him. Mannino said that while Giuliano did engage in an affair or two, there was never any doubt that the only women who meant a lot to him were his mother and sister.[26]

If the known record does not sustain the romantic's image of the bandit as a Latin lover neither does it lend factual support for an accusation that the police levelled at him. They tried to make the public believe that in affairs of the heart and flesh their adversary was more inclined toward his own kind than toward the fairer one.[27] They offered no proof, other than his rejection of the women whom they sent into the mountains in efforts to trap him. Maybe, it was anger over their failures as well as a desire to puncture his virile image that caused them to make the allegation. Whatever their motivation, it produced no noticeable effect. It was the wrong part of the world to try to discredit as strong a man as Giuliano in that way. Sicilian culture—that of the Mediterranean area in general, for that matter, as well as much of the rest of the world—allowed a higher degree of freedom to male closeness and sexual activity between males, especially among boys and unmarried young men, than northern Europe and Anglo-America. Unless carried on in public in an offensive manner, such conduct was not cause for much comment; instead, in a society that was permissive toward male sexual behavior and severely restrictive toward female behavior, it was expected.

Cyliakus was not the last of the journalists, foreign or domestic, to try to interview Giuliano. As time passed, more and more of them sought to profit from his ever-growing fame. Of them, the Italian Jacopo Rizza succeeded in getting to see the bandit late in 1949. He subsequently presented the most revealing picture of him that any produced.[28] The others, almost all of whom were women, failed in their missions. Either Giuliano did not want to see them, or the authorities ordered them out first.

CHAPTER EIGHT

Bellolampo!

A Still Dangerous Giuliano

The first two-thirds or so of 1949 formed the last period in which Giuliano could operate with any ease. Already, early in the year, some observers were wondering whether his career was about over. In view of the recent desertions, in addition to deaths and arrests, he must have had only three or four men left, one reporter concluded.[1]

In fact, it did seem that the campaign against the bandits was on the upswing. Passatempo had been killed, and most of those who had fled to Tunisia had been arrested and brought back. The police soon announced the capture of another. Tommaso Di Maggio, also a part of the famous Monreale jail break, was taken into custody in Montelepre in February. The police, acting on a tip, surrounded his home and found him ignominiously hiding under a pile of straw.[2] The newly found ability of the authorities to secure inside information, as had happened in both the death of Passatempo and the arrest of Di Maggio, among other cases, underscored Giuliano's difficulties. It was known already that some mafiosi were working against him; now, apparently, some of his fellow townspeople were abandoning him, too.

Yet, the tendency to count Giuliano out was premature. The men whom he had at his call were much more numerous than the mere three or four that some thought he had left. Cyliakus had seen from twenty-five to thirty bandits, in addition to a score of other men who were doing his bidding. As always, it was difficult to say how many men the bandit had, for the figure mostly depended on how many he needed. As long as he was active, he was capable of raising as many men as he desired.

Even if Montelepre and surrounding towns had not furnished Giuliano with an ample supply of bandits, he could have found plenty by letting it be known that he was willing to accept recruits from outside Sicily. Quite a few came looking for him without such a call. In one instance, in late 1946, he enlisted three men from Milan in his band but soon dismissed them. They subsequently cooperated with the police and in 1953 testified against some of the band's surviving members.[3]

A steady trickle of other continentals followed, especially in 1948 and 1949 after Giuliano became well known, but none of them succeeded in getting into the band. Press reports indicated that most were boys from 16 to 18 years old. Some said they wanted to become bandits, while others only yearned to meet Giuliano. One stole money from his mother to make the trip; another financed his from his employer's cashbox. A few were in Montelepre or wandering around Giuliano's mountain when they were arrested; seventeen-year-old Albert of Paris only got as far as the Palermo airport. Gino, of Venice, who at eighteen should have known better, was swindled by a Palermo sharpster before his journey ended with his arrest in Partinico. The helpful fellow told him that he needed a pistol if he was to be a bandit, sold one to him, and then showed him where to hide it until he needed it. Of course, when Gino returned to pick up his weapon, it was gone. Such admirers of Giuliano continued to come until at least the end of 1949. Albert was one of the last.

Early in 1949, Giuliano threatened to use his still potent strength to make the year a violent one, unless the government heeded his warning to end its repressive policies in Montelepre. In a letter to seven members of the Chamber of Deputies, he wrote: "Remember that blood demands blood. . . . To avoid new battles, I beg you to restore peace to our families."[4] A perusal of the addressees suggests that the bandit was calling in debts. All seven were prominent figures with whom he had cooperated in one venture or another. One monarchist (Leone Marchesano), two liberals, and four Christian democrats were on the list. Among the last named, Bernardo Mattarella stood out. All came from Palermo province, except for Calogero Volpe, a Christian democrat from Caltanisetta who was a political ally of Calogero Vizzini. The leftist deputies from the region did not receive the letter nor, for that matter, did some nine other conservatives. The list was clearly drawn up with some discrimination. One would like to know the bandit's thoughts as he composed the list, perhaps, ticking off what each one on it owed him.

The threats of Giuliano did not mean that he intended to wage constant war. He preferred occasional surprise attacks that kept the forces off balance, perhaps, with a rash of action now and then to show them what he was capable of doing, if he really put his heart to it. His activities followed this pattern through the early and middle parts of 1949, at least insofar as press reports and available police records indicated. The absence in the newspapers of reports of incidents did not always mean that such were not taking place, however. The authorities generally manipulated the news with considerable skill, even at times forbidding the press to publish anything about the campaign against Giuliano without their permission. Nonetheless, it appears that when anything of real significance occurred at least some word of it got out, no matter how embarrassing it was to the state. Giuliano's chronic complaint was about the underreporting of police casualties. If he killed four of the state's men, the press reported two, he complained.

In late February, Giuliano's outlaws slipped into Montelepre and boldly engaged the police in a brief battle in the center of town in broad daylight. Soon thereafter, in early March, the police sent a large force into the mountains when an unexpected snowfall hit the area. They hoped to track the bandits down but found nothing. In April, Giuliano sprang one of those carefully prepared ambushes that the authorities feared so much. He saw his opportunity when he learned that almost 1000 troops had been sent to Alcamo in the belief that he would be passing through there. In fact, that had been his intention, but now he went north instead.

Near Torretta, on March 7, he baited his trap. He sent an anonymous letter to the Torretta police, telling them that outlaws were holed up nearby in a cave. A little after midnight, a force of ten men searched the cave and found nothing, but as they returned in their truck they were ambushed on a curve just before reaching home. Hurling hand grenades and firing weapons from three different positions behind trees and boulders, the bandits put the force under a withering attack that left one dead and nine wounded. In a way, the troops were lucky. Just beyond the place where they were attacked lay a land mine that their passing would have detonated. When, a few days later, Giuliano reappeared in the Torretta area, the authorities launched one of their most ambitious operations yet. Combining every policeman, *carabiniere,* and soldier available, they sent a force into the Torretta-Bellolampo area that numbered in the thousands. Every square meter of the area was checked and 800 interrogations conducted. The results were a meager thirty persons charged with "favoring" the bandits.[5]

Another of Giuliano's letters appeared in the press on April 20. In it, he lamented the "tormented situation" that his family was undergoing and threatened to initiate a new campaign against the state.[6] The editors of the newspaper opined that the bandit was bluffing, but in reality, he was deadly serious. For their part, the police knew better than to take the threats lightly. They were especially vigilant on May 1 when they watched all roads and dispatched extra guards to May Day celebrations. Giuliano let the day pass without incident; instead, he started his raids just before dusk on May 2 and in something of a spectacular manner.

On that Monday evening, Lieutenant Benedetto Saccodato was leading his mobile column of eight men back to its headquarters in the state-occupied home of the Giuliano family. Ever alert to attack, the force was divided into three groups, marching about 50 meters apart. Like in almost all Italian towns in the evening, the streets were full of people. The atmosphere was convivial, not a likely setting for an ambush. But Giuliano had sneaked in his raiders, who were ready to attack at the most dramatic moment. That moment came just as the first contingent of the patrol reached Giuliano's house. From behind a low wall directly in front of the house, an unknown number of men opened fire. In that same instant, another group, on a higher position, fired at the building to discourage a reaction from those inside. One policeman was killed and two wounded before the bandits hastily took their leave. The authorities reacted in a predictable way. They sent in more troops to reinforce the many already there and that same night the search began, but it was without significant results.

The authorities were especially disturbed by the ease with which the outlaws had taken up fixed positions so near the mobile unit's headquarters. They surely were seen by quite a few of the townspeople who were about at the time. Some of them must have walked with them, talked with them. The police strongly suspected that the bandits had slipped in, dressed as peasants, in the company of peasants. Their search for information, Chief Inspector Ciro Verdiani reported to his superiors, met a "wall of silence."[7]

More reinforcements continued to arrive until the number of troops in Montelepre alone totalled close to 1200. A second attack occurred near Carini, on May 6, when the bandits attacked a troop convoy. One soldier was killed and two wounded. Shortly thereafter, a small patrol came upon a party of bandits who took refuge in a cave. Additional troops were sent, and a 45-minute battle ensued. By the time the three outlaws left through the cave's rear exit, seven on the government's side had been wounded.[8]

Alarmed by these attacks, the authorities imposed a state of siege on Montelepre as harsh as ever before. Early on May 17, every house was checked. All male inhabitants over age 16 were taken into custody, placed in chains, and gathered in Prince of Piedmont Square, where they were subjected to interrogation, physical abuse, and dire threats. Many were forced to strip naked, a humiliating fate from which Padre Di Bella was narrowly rescued by the benevolent intervention of an influential citizen. Some two dozen persons were arrested and sent to Palermo. All business establishments, including food stores, already had been ordered closed for a period of five days as extra punishment.[9]

On May 20, following two more attacks and several additional government casualties, the Minister of the Interior declared from Rome that Giuliano was being pursued so relentlessly that he could not "but fall into the net." There were 6000 men after him, Scelba said, and on his head now was a reward of 20 million lire.[10]

By early June, even harsher restrictions had been imposed on Montelepre and Giardinello. Only persons who could prove that they urgently needed to go outside the towns to care for their fields and animals were being permitted to leave and return. Even then, permission had to be obtained daily. Not infrequently, it was being denied; some persons were being arrested when they went to ask for it. On June 7, fifteen additional persons were arrested in another house-to-house search. At dusk that same day, the *carabiniere* station at Giardinello was attacked. On June 28, it again was the turn of the mobile unit that occupied Giuliano's house.[11]

Meanwhile, the police reported the arrests of six bandits during May and June. The best known was Pietro Licari, who was associated with both Partinico's Labruzzo band and Giuliano's. Acting on a tip, the police found him in a secret compartment underneath the floor of his home in Terrasini, along with his pregnant wife and their infant son.[12]

In spite of some recent police success, the major initiative was still with Giuliano, as was evinced by his ambush of a police truck in a mountain pass near San Giuseppe Jato on July 2. Five of the troops riding in it were killed.[13] More shocking, however, was the assassination of a locally prominent politician about a week later. Giuliano had killed so many members of the public forces that announcements of additional deaths were ever anticipated, but the slaying of Leonardo Renda, the secretary of the Alcamo Christian democrats and town clerk, was big news.

Renda's position had been precarious ever since the previous summer when the politicians betrayed Giuliano. The town clerk was not so prominent that he could be blamed for the failure of the government to grant amnesty. Instead, he was in danger because he was an intimate friend of Bernardo Mattarella, whom Giuliano did blame. In spite of his uneasy situation, Renda hardly could avoid the bandits. Not only was Alcamo as much a part of Giuliano's territory as any other town outside of Montelepre and Giardinello, but more critically, Renda was the *gabelloto* of a rural estate that the bandits frequented.

In the end, Renda decided to cooperate with the police against the bandits. When, in the spring of 1949, a large group of them came to celebrate the Maundy Thursday before Easter at the farm he held in lease, he feasted them well, but at the same time sent word to the police that they were there. All might have gone well for him were it not for that sixth sense that outlaws who last very long seem to develop. Feeling that something was not in place, they quickly took their leave, though not to go far. The next morning just before dawn, they watched a force of 300 soldiers encircle the place where they had intended to spend the night.

Aware now of his danger more than ever, Renda used his connections to obtain a detachment of *carabinieri* for the rural district where the farm lay, but it did him no good. On July 8, about four months after the Easter incident, he was on the farm when four armed men appeared who identified themselves as plainclothes police agents. They checked identification cards and, alleging that Renda's was not in order, asked him to accompany them to the station. His bullet ridden body was found the next day. Giuseppe Cucinella, one of Giuliano's squad leaders, was later identified as the head of the party that killed him.[14]

Giuliano struck again on the day that Renda's body was discovered, firing this time on a police truck as it travelled near San Giuseppe Jato. Such incidents were so common that they often were not reported publicly, unless they produced casualties. They were not hard to conceal, since most police vehicles in those times had bullet smashed windshields all the time, anyway. The police had quit replacing them, which not only saved scarce funds but also reduced the number of embarrassing questions.[15]

As if he was not subjecting the police to strong pressure already, in mid-July Giuliano threatened to launch an offensive against them. In a letter to the press, he wrote: "The peace and prosperity of Sicily will flourish when my loved ones and the people who suffer in prison are liberated and I seek my freedom abroad if they do not want me here in Italy. . . . I will give them [the authorities] another 15 days . . . and if by the first of August there have been no positive results, I will immediately go on the attack."[16] Giuliano had made his threats many times and often followed them up, too; this time, however, the police hardly could have known how determined he was. They would not forget soon August 1949.

A Curious Meeting

In the midst of Giuliano's summer offensive, and just before its most disastrous episode, a strange conference was held. The head of the antibandit campaign met the famous desperado face to face. The meeting was arranged by the former, Chief Inspector Verdiani, who, as he later tried to explain it, wanted to offer the bandit a bargain. His mother would be released from prison, if he would stop attacking the police; safe passage abroad would also be guaranteed him. That would be a way to bring the long story to an end, the commander reasoned. Still, he also had in mind, if contact with Giuliano was made and his confidence won, more decisive possibilities might open up. Anxious to make his proposition to Giuliano personally, Verdiani found a way.

At the time, the Palermo police had in custody a mafioso, who, Verdiani was sure, could get in touch with the bandit. The man was Ignazio Miceli, who had been caught in a roundup in early June. It was not the first time that he had been brought in; the authorities had long known that he was linked to Giuliano. Miceli was no petty mafioso. Based in Monreale, a historic Mafia center, he was the head of one of the island's most prestigious Mafia associations, perhaps the leading one at the time. Born on New Year's Day 1889, Miceli was an impressive man, intelligent, cunning, and subtle. Verdiani promised him release from jail in return for his help. The bargain was concluded, the necessary arrangements made, and in mid-August Verdiani and Giuliano had their first meeting. Neither ever revealed publicly what transpired in it, but as would be obvious very soon, it was without good result. Giuliano was wary and not yet desperate enough to deal.[17]

Death on the Curves of Bellolampo

In that same month, Giuliano attacked the state's forces, first near Alcamo on August 6, then in and around Partinico on August 10 and 17. Stories related that he was in the Alcamo area to abduct none other than Bernardo Mattarella, then the Assistant Secretary of Transportation, who Giuliano believed would be travelling down the Alcamo–Calatafimi highway. Whether the stories were true, however, was disputed. Nonetheless, even if they were untrue, Giuliano had entertained hopes of kidnapping the man whom he held responsible for the false promise of amnesty.[18] Another well-known figure for whom he held enmity was Calogero Vizzini, a part of the old-line Mafia that, along with the politicians, had betrayed him. The bandit, it was alleged, also had plans to abduct him; and, when the old Mafia boss learned of it, he took refuge in his Palermo hotel suite. Two men were said to have guarded him in his room, while others were in the corridor and the streets adjacent to the hotel.[19]

A successful abduction of either Mattarella or Vizzini—or Verdiani, had Giuliano been of such a mind—would have impressively capped the bandit chief's career, but as it turned out, his last major action was something less sensational. Nevertheless, the attack at Bellolampo on August 19, 1949, was impressive enough.

The police post at Bellolampo had often been the scene of Giuliano's attacks, largely because of its strategic location. It guarded, as it were, Palermo's access to Montelepre. To go to Montelepre in those days, when the capital city was much less spread out than it later became, one travelled for a few kilometers through open fields before reaching the extreme edge of the small coastal basin where Palermo lies. There, almost of a sudden, rises a solid wall of mountain, up on whose pine-tree–covered side snakes a highway so precipitous that it seems it might lose its hold at any moment and fall backward toward the city. At its top, almost as suddenly, the forest ends and a vista opens of fields of pasture on a highly accidented upland plain. Just above the tree line, and just after the last of the hairpin turns, starkly stood the

Bellolampo station, an isolated two-story structure on the road's left flank. From there, the distance on to Montelepre was less than 20 kilometers. Along this road, troops from Palermo usually came in answer to calls that there was trouble in Montelepre. For Giuliano, Bellolampo was where his country started.

In the early evening of August 19, the bandits opened fire with several bursts against the station walls. Such incidents occurred so frequently that the men on duty could have assumed that the outlaws were merely passing by and unable to resist the temptation to fire a few intimidating rounds. But, since they lived in fear of being overwhelmed by them, they waited a few minutes, then sent out one of their number in civilian dress to ride his bicycle down to Palermo to tell the central command that the bandits were in the area. The concealed desperadoes were watching, having anticipated such a move, and they doubtless smiled as the soldier hurriedly pedalled by.

Down in Palermo, Chief Inspector Verdiani could have sent word to Torretta, Carini, or Montelepre to send over a small party to investigate the incident, but he chose a bolder course. He had been under fire almost from the day he arrived, seven months earlier, for his failure to eliminate Giuliano, and at that moment Colonel Ugo Luca of the *carabinieri* was in the city, sent down by Rome to look into the faltering campaign against the bandits. Thus, it seemed to be the opportune moment for the inspector to demonstrate his decisiveness. He immediately ordered the assembling of a large force, complete with two armored cars, eight transport trucks, and several automobiles. In one of the automobiles rode the inspector himself and another high-ranking officer, in addition to Colonel Luca who had been invited to go along.

The impressive force arrived at Bellolampo without incident, and its search of the area yielded nothing. Deciding that the earlier firing had been only of a casual nature, Verdiani ordered the force to return to the city. By then, Giuliano had prepared his surprise: seven explosive charges, implanted in the roadway about a kilometer from where the vehicles had stopped. As the convoy passed, the charges were detonated by remote control, one of which went off directly under the automobile in which Verdiani and the distinguished visitor had ridden up; fortunately for them, they were returning in another. Even so, they came under heavy fire from the bandits as they careened down the winding road in the attempt to escape with their lives.

The Bellolampo attack was a costly one. Casualties totalled more than two dozen, eight of which were fatalities. It could have been much worse. Its organizer later bragged in a letter that *L'Ora* published on September 2: "Had I wanted to, I could have destroyed the entire column." More than 1000 men were sent to search for the outlaws, with no more success than usual. All they found were a few beer bottles and a pack of playing cards where the assailants had coolly entertained themselves while waiting for the force's arrival. Those who suffered most were the alleged supporters of the bandits, over a hundred of whom were taken into custody. Before month's end, the bandits killed two more *carabinieri* in an attack near San Cipirello.[20]

The Replacement of Verdiani

The disaster at Bellolampo resulted in the immediate removal of Verdiani as the head of the antibandit campaign. Even before then, his substitution was under consideration; Bellolampo made any further discussion unnecessary. Already in July, a high-level recommendation for the reorganization of the campaign had been made to the Minister of the Interior. There was a need, General F. Di Giorgis had told Scelba, to give it a new direction, perhaps entrusting its direction to an expert in intelligence and antiguerrilla warfare. Furthermore, an excellent man was available for the task, the general advised, Colonel Ugo Luca, the commander of the *carabinieri* in Lazio, the region in which Rome lies.[21] Thus, Luca's visit to Sicily was not only a fact finding mission but also a view of a possible new assignment; and before August ended, the job was his. At the same time, the General Inspectorate of Public Security in Sicily, which Verdiani had headed, was suppressed and replaced by the Command of the Forces for the Repression of Banditry (CFRB), with Luca at its head. The reorganization transferred the direction of the campaign from the civilian-oriented public security police, under which the Inspectorate had been established in 1945 specifically to eradicate banditry, to the *carabinieri*, a part of the army. However, the men and officers were still to come from both forces, as was the case in the inspectorate.

It was to be wondered if the men from the two rival forces would work together under the new command any better than they had under the old. They had fought over scarce material resources, and each had its own sources of information, which it often withheld from the other, even at the risk of endangering lives. The *carabinieri* were especially resentful, believing themselves to be superior in training, ability, and prestige—a haughty attitude that rankled the public security police. In fact, the *carabinieri* did bear the brunt of the war against the bandits, from its beginning to its end. Of the approximately 120 agents of the law whose lives Giuliano and his bandits took, 87 belonged to *carabinieri*.[22]

When it was suppressed, the General Inspectorate had had five commanders in its four year history. The only one who lasted very long was the first, Ettore Messana. He held the post from October 1945 until the summer of 1947, when he was relieved not long after the Portella della Ginestra disaster. Four others followed him in quick succession. One lasted fewer than two months. The three others, the last of whom was Verdiani, held the post for from seven to nine months each. The left accused all of them, especially Messana and Verdiani, of working with the Mafia. As a matter of fact, in view of the ineffectiveness of most official efforts, winning the cooperation of various Mafia associations was the most potent tactic that the police developed in the war against the bandits. It was one that Luca, too, would not overlook.

Following his dismissal, Verdiani went to Rome to command the police along Italy's northern border. But, having an established line to Giuliano through Miceli, and easy access to high officials of justice in both Palermo and Rome, he saw possibilities in negotiating with the bandit yet. He might be able to vindicate himself, his extinct command, and the public security police, thereby cutting down to size Luca and his haughty *carabinieri*. So resentful was he that when he left Palermo he took all of his files with him, leaving no information for the new command. Especially of his contact with Giuliano, he told Luca nothing.[23]

CHAPTER NINE

Colonel Ugo Luca

IN COLONEL LUCA OF THE *CARABINIERI*, Giuliano met a more formidable agent of the state than he had yet faced, as he soon realized. The struggle between them would be much like the classic tale of the successful outlaw who meets the determined lawman. The outcome in this instance would also conform to the classic one, for, no matter how dangerous their profession may be, lawmen usually outlive bandits by several decades.

Of course, this particular story was set in Sicily of 1949 and 1950 and not the American West of the 1880s. It did not end in a shootout on main street at high noon. If it had, bringing Giuliano's story to a conclusion would be an easy task. In actuality, it is a difficult one, for the bandit died not in public view but rather in that murky underworld of Sicilian life from which truth emerged only with extreme difficulty and sometimes not at all. When it did, it was only partial and then often so intermingled with falsehood that the separation of one from the other was severely difficult.

Ugo Luca was already into late middle age when he took command of the antibandit campaign on August 27, 1949. In the next spring, he would become fifty-eight, too old to win his long-sought promotion to brigadier general except for extraordinary merit. His pursuit of this honor, the outcome of which now rested almost wholly on success against Giuliano, was waged with the same dogged determination that already characterized his life. Of humble origin, he had gone to sea as a cabin boy and later entered the army as a simple recruit. He fought in various of Italy's conflicts, including the Civil War in Spain and World War II, until 1943, when he temporarily left active service. Long before then, he had established a reputation for skill in intelligence work that led the press to call him the "Italian Lawrence"; even if the short, balding man with the quiet, almost apologetic manner did not much look the part.

Luca's second in command was Captain Antonio Perenze, a seasoned campaigner who had fought brigands in Libya and Ethiopia when they were Italian colonies. A large, fleshy man with a carefully trimmed mustache, he was some 20 years younger than Luca.[1]

Luca found the men in his command demoralized and disorganized. To try to boost their spirits, he gave demonstrations of his courage during his first few days in the post by travelling through Giuliano's territory only with a light escort, then later with none at all. His plan of reorganization included abandoning the large-scale military operations that Verdiani had employed, in their stead permanently dispersing his men in small contingents throughout the region that the bandits inhabited. He identified as the bandits' area twenty contiguous communes, stretching from Castellammare del Golfo to Termini Imerese along the northern coast and as deep into the interior as Contessa Entellina. Within it, seventy zones were marked off, and a squadron of twenty men assigned to each one. Each squadron was given radio communications equipment to keep in touch with the others. The squadrons were divided further into subgroups of three or four men. In all, Luca had approximately 2000 men and four dozen officers in his command, some 500 more than Verdiani normally had been allowed. At least three-quarters of them were *carabinieri*.

Within that region Luca planned to "isolate and neutralize" the outlaws by establishing a less obvious but more pervasive police presence.[2] Many of his men dressed like the herdsmen, peasants, rural guards, and others who normally were seen in the countryside, and they were told to cultivate friendly relations with the populace. Unlike former times, when troops barricaded themselves in their barracks at the first sign of darkness, they now remained in the field for days on end, sleeping in caves, abandoned buildings, or in the open, as the bandits did. What the commander was trying to accomplish in this first phase of his work was prove to the people that the police were more permanent and ultimately more powerful than the bandits. Luca also hoped to penetrate the band, as Messana had once been successful in doing.

These tactics were not wholly new, since Luca's predecessors had attempted one version or another of them at various times. What was new was a greater consistency and firmness of purpose. The change, in any event, was not lost on the Mafia groups. Having agents of that tough, experienced mainland army colonel in their midst was a threat to their power, too. It was said that not long after Luca's arrival a

Mafia council decreed the elimination of the bandits.[3] Not only does the allegation have the ring of truth about it, but it also is evident that Luca did not fulfill his mission solely on his own.

From late August, the public knew little of what the police were doing. Luca preferred to work in secrecy, keeping most police actions, even major accomplishments, out of the public eye. This was his style but it also was an attempt to throw Giuliano off balance, to erect a wall of silence around him, and to arouse in him feelings of mistrust and insecurity.[4] A reporter from Palermo's Christian Democratic Party organ went to Montelepre in early September to see what he could learn firsthand. He learned little. The police would not answer any questions on their activities. Neither Padre Di Bella nor the mayor would talk. No one would talk. Lunchtime came, and in the company of two foreign journalists, both of whom had come from London to visit Montelepre, he looked for a place to eat. The town had no restaurant, the three learned, although there was a private residence that furnished meals to travellers; but the owner could provide food only with permission from the authorities.[5]

Only gradually did Giuliano realize the threat that Luca posed to him. At first, he clearly intended to continue his war, as he indicated in manifestos that he affixed to walls in Palermo in early September. He threatened to go on the attack again unless the government made concessions. He again invited men to enroll in his forces. His most impassioned appeal was directed to the *carabinieri* in the name of his own imprisoned mother:

> If you yourselves love your mammas and your country, refuse to fight in this fratricidal war. . . . Do not be deceived by the propaganda of the press and your superiors, who call their war "a war against delinquency," because the war that they make against me should be called "a war against motherhood." Perhaps the reason for my success against this vast effort is due not only to my expertness but also to the Divine Hand whose aim is only one: To rein in those false prophets who want to destroy the greatest love that He defends for us, the most precious thing of our lives, our mammas.

In the same series of manifestos—there were three in all—he asked: "Of the two, who is the bloodiest: The government that hunts me like a wild beast, or I who defend myself?" To Luca, he threatened: "He who seeks me seeks death."[6]

The bandit followed his threats with an attack on a squadron headquarters at Poggioreale, located about midway between Montelepre and the southern coast. No police casualties were suffered. Luca believed that the outlaws were outside their usual zone because his efforts were beginning to be effective. In fact, in late September and early October, the capture of several bandits, one by one, indicated the beginning of success, even though none of them was among Giuliano's best-known henchmen. Also augering well for the campaign was the decisive reaction of the San Giuseppe Jato squadron when it was attacked. This time, the police not only repulsed the outlaws but chased them toward the coast, where, in a night battle near Balestrate, they killed two of them and captured a third. The San Giuseppe Jato attack was the last armed action against the police that the bandits initiated. In the month and a half since Luca had assumed command, Giuliano's men had not killed a single member of the state's forces.[7]

On the night of October 13, Luca's first spectacular accomplishment took place when Giuseppe Cucinella, Giuliano's most active squad leader, was captured. The colonel did not try to conceal his success this time. He hardly could have done so, since it happened in a wild battle in one of Palermo's residential neighborhoods. According to the commander, he had set up a secret service operation to try to learn where the bandits were habitually hiding out. Although he did not explain what his operation consisted of, it was believed that he gained the cooperation of Mafia elements who funnelled information to him. Giuliano speculated that the betrayal came from Cucinella's abduction enterprises in an area where the Mafia collected protection money.[8]

Luca learned that Cucinella and his men were in Palermo in a house that the squad leader rented. Normally occupying it were his 20-year-old girlfriend and her mother. The police surrounded the house after midnight, and when one of them cautiously knocked on the door to see what kind of reaction might be forthcoming, a window was opened from the inside and a hand grenade was thrown out. A hard battle ensued, in the midst of which a man who tried to escape was overpowered and wounded. The others, eight men and the two women, soon surrendered. The one who had tried to get away was Cucinella. On him, the police found several hand grenades, two automatic pistols, and about 1 million lire. The house, they said, was a genuine arsenal.[9]

For Giuliano, the capture of Cucinella and the main portion of his band was a setback of no small proportion. With Terranova in jail awaiting trial, Cucinella had become the major fund raiser. On the head of the boyish looking but fearsome outlaw were eighteen homicides, in addition to dozens of lesser crimes. After formal proceedings ran their course in later years, he was judged to be a schizophrenic and committed to an insane asylum.

Following this success, Luca expanded his secret service operation, setting up a special center in Palermo to coordinate its efforts. He also placed the seaports and air facilities of western Sicily under close vigilance, especially Mazara del Vallo, the preferred location of clandestine departures for Tunisia. He suspected that Giuliano and some of his men might be thinking of voluntary exile. From mid-October on through early December, twenty-five more men who had been in the band at one time or another were taken into custody, in addition to several dozen informers and supporters. And near Camporeale on December 9, one of the last armed clashes between Giuliano's men and the police occurred. Vincenzo Sappupo was killed in it. He was the last member of the state's forces to die at the hands of Giuliano's band, and the state's only fatality while Luca was in command.[10]

The Rizza Interview

Shortly thereafter, the bandit granted his third and last interview. This time, the journalist was the Italian Jacopo Rizza, accompanied by a photographer and a motion picture cameraman. The three came in the employ of *Oggi*, the same magazine that had published the Cyliakus interview. Rizza told a long story of how he found Giuliano entirely on his own, but it is virtually certain that he had the help of Verdiani who was still in contact with the bandit.[11] Helping to arrange the interview was a way for the resentful former commander to embarrass his successor. It would not reflect well on Luca that a trio of mainland reporters could locate the outlaw when neither he nor any of his 2000 agents had any clear idea of his whereabouts. The interview took place near Salemi at an abandoned house, to which the journalist and his assistants were directed the night before to await Giuliano's coming. Promptly at 8:00 A.M., a tall, brunette, mustachioed, thin-faced young man dressed in horseman's clothing opened the door. That was Gaspare Pisciotta. Just back of him was Giuliano.

The bandit chief, dressed in the same fashion as Pisciotta, looked a little older than his 27 years, Rizza thought. He wore a frown and had deep-set eyes that appeared a bit fixed and glassy. He moved with a certain boldness, even arrogance, and used gestures sparingly when he talked. He often stood with his thumbs in the loops of his trousers, a pose that set off his striking belt buckle. Large, artistically worked in gold, and clearly costly, it was the bandit's special sign. The star in the center, Giuliano explained, stood for fortune, the eagle on the left for intelligence, the lion on the right for strength. Rizza saw that Gaspare also wore one of the same design, except, where in Giuliano's there was the star, in his there was a small picture of Giuliano. Gaspare, the bandit told Rizza, was his one and only real lieutenant. Others had been described that way, but they actually were only squad captains, like the recently captured Cucinella, who, he added, had been one of his best men.

Rizza talked with Giuliano for over six hours, first within the rustic house, then outside. No guards were in sight, although peasants could be seen in the fields around. They would let Giuliano know if anyone was coming, Pisciotta said. Giuliano explained that he moved often and had come to Salemi only for the interview. Pisciotta alone knew of his movements. Rizza had the impression that his host was intelligent. He explained things well and watched closely to see if the journalist understood his Sicilian dialect. No questions seemed to surprise him, although on some matters, like Portella della Ginestra, the answers were less than complete.

While Giuliano told Rizza the story of his early years as an outlaw, the two photojournalists were filming and taking pictures. An avid photography buff himself, the bandit showed them his own Leica and said that he also had both a motion-picture camera and a projection machine. He planned to make a film, he added, to sell to the Americans. Gaspare, who was there all the while, said little on his own and usually replied to questions in monosyllables.

Giuliano talked easily of his difficulties. Luca was the only policeman who had ever pursued him intelligently, particularly in the astute manner in which he moved his small squadrons. The colonel's tactics were much like his own. A large force could be seen easily, but one divided into patrols of three or four could slip up on you before you knew they were around, Giuliano said. They were likely to get some of his men, he conceded, but not him. He would never be taken alive, for at that point his life would be worth nothing to him. He had a plan to kill Luca, but his family's lawyer, telling him there was a good chance his mother soon would be released, was advising him to remain calm.

What happened to his mother in the future, Giuliano made clear, would determine his own actions. If things worked out well for her, he would go abroad. It would be easy for him to leave Italy secretly with false documents, but before he did, he would also have to organize the expatriation of his "boys." That would cost a fair sum of money. Sciortino's leaving had cost 500,000 lire; the price of getting a cousin to Switzerland had been 100,000 lire. But, Giuliano wistfully added, he could do nothing until his mother was free.

Rizza wasted no time in getting his story into print. After all, it was a sensational piece, more so at that point than either Stern's or Cyliakus's had been. *Oggi* serialized it with lavish displays of pictures in three consecutive issues beginning December 22 (the film that was made has been presumed lost). To say that the publication of the interview angered the authorities is an understatement. Controversy between them and the press erupted in attacks and counterattacks from the day the first installment appeared. Rizza and the two others, together with *Oggi*'s editor, were quickly charged with encouraging criminality by romanticizing the bandits and exaggerating their effectiveness. Rizza had portrayed the bandit chieftain, the charge read, "as a nice young man, if, albeit, a bit lively." To some observers, the whole affair was a farce, and at the trial, the jury took fewer than 15 minutes to absolve the defendants.[12]

Marotta and De Maria

Not long after the interview, Luca reported to his superiors that his plan was working.[13] The bandits were doing nothing and the people were enjoying an uncommon peace. Even so, there was a need to maintain vigilance at all points, especially in Palermo, where he believed Giuliano was hiding. Luca was sure that his campaign would soon result in the outlaw chieftain's elimination. Yet, it was evident that he still did not know where Giuliano was nor how he was going to find him.

The commander was searching for his foe in the wrong place. Giuliano was spending most of his time away from his usual haunts, normally returning to his native region only when he needed to see a vital contact. Other than for Pisciotta, he rarely, if ever, dealt personally with his band members, now barely more than a half dozen and almost as invisible as he. As to the cardinal question of where the head bandit was, he was in the hands of a small coterie of Mafia groups, as, in the main, he had been for some time. A few of his Mafia friends, like Miceli of Monreale and Domenico Albano of Borgetto, were in his own area, while the others lived far to the south of it, in and around the city of Castelvetrano, just in from the island's southwestern coast. In this latter area the Mafia was hiding him. The bandit had lost the independence that had been so important in keeping him alive and free for over six years.

In the south, he moved frequently among the town houses, rural properties, and other locations that sheltered him. Mid-December found him and Gaspare on a farm of Giuseppe Marotta of Partanna, a town a few kilometers to Castelvetrano's northeast. Their host was a dealer in citrus fruits and, like most others who traded in agricultural produce in western Sicily, a mafioso. When Marotta later was forced to tell his story in court, he claimed that the pair had come to his farm unannounced, for reasons unknown to him. In that regard, his story was similar to that of almost all others who were found to be dealing with the bandit. The instance that the police knew about was the first time they had ever seen him, and his sudden appearance a complete surprise. Marotta did not want to keep the two bandits on his farm; instead, he decided to place them with a friend in the center of Castelvetrano. Thus, Giuliano and his comrade arrived at the home of a youthful, timorous, studious law-school graduate named Gregorio De Maria.

De Maria lived a retiring life for a young man. He did not practice his profession, instead doing some notarial work and taking care of his family's small farm near the city. His home was a two-story structure opening directly onto Via Mannone, one of the city's two principal streets. Beside it was a courtyard, enclosed by a wall on the street side and by adjacent buildings on the other sides. De Maria lived there with his widowed mother and a female servant. Although De Maria had a Mafia friend in Marotta, whom he had known since they both were boys, he was not a mafioso. Indeed, in appearance, bearing, and style of life, he was the antithesis of that breed. All in all, his house seemed to Marotta to be an ideal place to shelter Giuliano.

The hour was late and De Maria's house quiet on December 18 when Marotta arrived with the bandits. Awakened by the knocking, De Maria opened a window and saw his old friend "Pino" Marotta, who said that he had two friends with him who badly needed temporary shelter. When they came in, the barely awake De Maria was shocked into full consciousness, rent by a terror that he was hardly capable of describing, he later said. What he saw before him were two young men whose raincoats did not fully conceal the pistols and submachine guns they carried. He knew who they were, his initial suspicion confirmed by a glance at Giuliano's famous belt buckle. Before De Maria had either the chance or the courage to say no, the world famous desperado and his friend were lodged in his spare upstairs bedroom.

At the door when Marotta left, De Maria acidly asked why he had put him in such a predicament. He replied that he was unable to keep the bandits in his own home, being in an even worse position himself. Anyhow, he assured his friend, the pair would be there only temporarily. They did leave less than a week later but shortly returned.[14]

Going to Meet Verdiani

The matter that occasioned Giuliano and Gaspare's brief absence from De Maria's house in late December was an important one. They went to meet Ciro Verdiani, who came down from Rome to confer with Giuliano. Some months had passed since their August meeting, but the two men had remained in contact. Verdiani still hoped to pursue his plan; Giuliano, now pressed hard by Luca, was more open to negotiations. When Giuliano's lawyer informed him that there was a good chance of getting the charges against his mother dropped, he began to consider more seriously than ever before the possibility of foreign exile. By way of Miceli, he sent word to Verdiani that he wanted to talk with him again. Following further communications, the two agreed to meet at Marotta's farm on the night of December 23.

On that night, Marotta accompanied the two bandits to the farm; Giuliano sent a car to pick up Verdiani in Marsala, where he had stopped at a hotel; Ignazio Miceli, his nephew Antonino, and Domenico Albano drove down together to be there, too. When Verdiani arrived, he and the man who had tried to blow him up just months before embraced and kissed like old friends. The distinguished visitor from the capital brought liqueur and a sweet (*panettone*)—they were in the Christmas season—and the atmosphere in the farmhouse was festive.

The two chief conspirators, together with Miceli, arrived at an agreement. Giuliano would go into exile with the government's help, and his mother would be released from prison.[15] Subsequently, Verdiani lay out his plan before officials of the Ministry of the Interior; he later said that they told him to drop the matter immediately, to let Luca take care of Giuliano.[16] His statement, however, was only to protect the officials of the ministry. In reality, they did not order him to desist but, according to reliable evidence, placed at least 80 million lire at his disposal to execute the plot.[17] The plan, after all, had a good chance of success. It already involved not only Verdiani and Giuliano, through Miceli and Albano but, crucially, the prosecutor general in Palermo, Emanuele Pili, as well. Pili was an essential party to the conspiracy, since he would have a major voice in deciding the cases of the Giuliano family members. In fact, he was so intimately involved in it that he met personally with Giuliano during the course of the negotiations, although where and exactly when were not revealed.[18] If this appears confusing, even implausible, it need only be recalled that Luca and his *carabinieri,* on the one hand, and the public security police and officials of justice in both Rome and Palermo, on the other, were often at loggerheads, even to the point of trying to undermine the actions of each other.

Barely ten days after the conference at Marotta's farmhouse, the state took an important step toward meeting the major condition that Giuliano had imposed. On January 3, it dropped the serious charges against Maria Lombardo and a few days later found her guilty of lesser ones, carrying penalties that, with favorable consideration, her year and a half of incarceration could be construed already to have erased. She was released on January 21. *L'Unità*'s reporter wrote that the proceedings were cut and dried. The family's chief lawyer, Liberal Party politician Romano Battaglia, was uncharacteristically brief and to the point, as if he had no real need to convince anyone of anything. When at the end of his short defense he was asked by the judges what effect a favorable decision might have on Giuliano, he replied that it would surely be beneficial, although he was not at liberty to divulge whether the bandit would turn himself in or go abroad.[19]

Giuliano was ecstatic over his mother's release—she returned to Montelepre to reclaim the family home from the authorities—and he quickly penned a letter to the press. In it, he congratulated his lawyers and the judges, but deplored his mother's conviction on even the minor charges. He then digressed, as he usually did, to argue various aspects of his own case. Returning to a theme that he had neglected for a while, he denounced the pitiful conditions of Sicily's masses and wondered rhetorically why only the poor became bandits. He closed on a point close to his heart, imploring his readers to remember that "we are all sinners on this earth, and thus, none being blameless, all are worthy of pardon."[20]

If Giuliano was happy with his mother's release, Verdiani was scarcely less pleased by his own accomplishments. His plan appeared to be moving along smoothly. All he needed, he thought, was to convince Giuliano of his absolute sincerity. On January 30, he replied to a recent letter in which Giuliano had inquired further into the government's possible financial aid for his expatriation. Opening with a reference to the satisfaction that Giuliano must feel over his mother's freedom, Verdiani suggested that the time had come to dispose of Mariannina's legal troubles as well. Then, turning quickly to the money question, he wrote:

> Tell me how large your financial needs will be and I will be able to turn the necessary sums over to you at the moment we meet for your departure. I believe that the sooner you decide to go the better it will be for everyone. . . . I thank you for the greetings that we affectionately exchange but that which will make me the happiest of all will be when I salute you and your men, as you stand together on the bridge of a ship.[21]

Perhaps, Verdiani thought that such promises might immediately entice Giuliano. If so, he underestimated the fugitive's caution. The bandit had decided that exile was the only course left for him, but he wanted to be very careful about the conditions under which he might attempt it. Reportedly, he told Verdiani that he would accept his arrangements if he would loan him one of his young grandsons to take with him, the boy to be returned when the bandit was safely in exile.[22] The negotiations temporarily faltered at this point but were not broken off.

At De Maria's House

Meanwhile, Giuliano remained with De Maria. In fact, the house on Via Mannone was to be his place of refuge during the greater part of the period of life that was left to him. He and Pisciotta returned there immediately after the meeting with Verdiani. Gaspare left in February, but Giuliano stayed on until May, except for an absence of two weeks in March. When they came back the first time in late December, their reluctant host finally gathered enough courage to ask Giuliano if he was comfortable, hoping to then be able to tell him that it was unsafe for him to stay any longer. His needs were being well cared for and he would like to remain for another three to four weeks, the bandit replied. His house did not offer much security, De Maria protested; the servant girl, for instance, might be indiscreet when talking to neighbors. That had already been taken care of, the bandit assured him. She had been told by Pino that the two men were relatives of his involved in a family vendetta and that the most severe silence was expected of her. In reality, the maid probably saw very little of the two men. They rarely came down to the street level, except after dark; she was told not go to the upper floor, so as not to bother them. As for De Maria's "poor mamma," he was forced to tell her the same lie.

Thrown together by strange circumstances, the thirty-two-year-old intellectual and the twenty-seven-year-old legendary bandit discovered that they had more in common than one might imagine, and in a manner of speaking, they became friends. They spent many hours in conversation, and De Maria, who had studied in both Palermo and Rome, placed his substantial collection of books at Giuliano's disposal. Upon learning that the bandit loved photography, he also taught him to develop and print his own pictures. He gave him Italian exercises, so that he could improve his writing, and corrected them after they were completed. His progress was impressive, De Maria said.

Although their conversations ranged widely in content, Giuliano was most interested in those that turned on ideas, morality, and science. De Maria was the first genuine intellectual with whom he had ever spent any considerable amount of time. He particularly liked to hear him expound philosophically on the questions of good and evil and redemption. He once told him that if he had known him earlier his destiny might have been different. The bandit looked at books by Kant, Descartes, and Shakespeare, among others, and asked De Maria questions about them. He also told him of his own pet notion of a perpetual motion machine that in the past had helped him pass many a hour as he sat alone atop some mountain, breaking his train of thought only now and then to see if the police were coming.[23]

There is little doubt that Giuliano's native intellectual ability was considerable. Of course, when he became a fugitive he was scarcely literate but, soon drawn into the currents of politicians and ideas, he became aware of his backwardness and tried to improve himself. More than once, the police found discarded notebooks in which he had done English exercises. They also found reading material that he left behind.

His preferred reading consisted of newspapers, magazines, and novels of romance and chivalry. One of his favorite authors was Emilio Salgari, a fabulously popular but tragic Italian writer from Verona who died by his own hand in 1911 at the age of forty-eight.[24] His first novel, *La tigre di Malesia* (The Tiger of Malaysia), the story of a pirate, established the pattern for the more than 100 that followed. Their settings ranged widely, from the savage gauchos of the Argentine pampas to the horrors of the icy wastes of Siberia, by way of Caribbean raiders and African cannibals, among other routes. His most popular character, Sandokan, would be portrayed, in later times, in both movies and television.

Once, a peasant happened upon some of Giuliano's books in a cave near Borgetto, among them three of Salgari's. Two, with marginal notes in the bandit's handwriting, were *Briganti del Riff* (Brigands of the Riff) and *Il re della montagna* (The King of the Mountain). One wonders if the character of some of the bandit's ideas might not have been shaped by such reading. In 1948, he offered to surrender if the government would grant him amnesty, in order to do penance in China by freeing Catholic missionaries from their communist tormenters.[25] It was the kind of thing that Salgari, had he lived to old age, might have found to be a prime subject for his last adventure tale.

It is always interesting to speculate on what a man like Giuliano might have been if certain aspects of his formative years had been different, or to wonder what he might have become if he had reached exile in America. He envisioned himself in many grandiose ways: at the head of a liberating army, occupying a cabinet post in the Sicilian republic, saving his homeland from the reds, and so on. But toward the end of his life, his aims moderated. He told Rizza, for instance, that he would like to study engineering in America. In the end, one does not know what Giuliano would have become, if he had been privileged to grow into old age in Detroit, Pittsburgh, or Kansas City. It is hard to picture him under those circumstances. He never really pictured that kind of an end to his life. Rather, the one closest to his heart was suggested by the epitaph that he once wrote for himself in his ever present notebook: "Here lies Giuliano, Hero of Sicily."[26]

While at De Maria's, Giuliano did not spend all of his time in his room. He went out frequently in the evening, returning after a few hours of absence; and there were also the longer periods when he was gone. His host professed to not knowing where his guest went— De Maria was not a mafioso but he knew to keep his mouth closed. It is evident, as Pisciotta admitted, that the house on Via Mannone was not the bandit's only place of refuge in and around Castelvetrano. There were at least three or four other places that he frequented, Marotta's residence among them. Weighty circumstantial evidence suggests that some of his calls were on a widely known but secretive Castelvetrano mafioso known as "the American." Actually, he was Nicola Piccione, an area native who had emigrated to the United States to return, years later, a wealthy man. His home was one of the city's most luxurious "palaces." Marotta was closely linked to him, and once when he was in trouble with the law, Piccione's daughter supplied him with an alibi.[27] Said to have been equally as formidable as her father, she told the authorities that she and Pino were out hunting wild game when the crime occurred. It is likely that while Giuliano was in Castelvetrano, he was in Piccione's hands. However, in the mysterious events that were to come, "the American" would continue to remain in the shadows.

The months in Castelvetrano were unique for Giuliano. Such an extended exposure to urban life was rare for him. While Castelvetrano was hardly a metropolis, it was an attractive provincial city of approximately 40,000 people. Of probable origin in ancient Greek times and resembling North Africa in appearance, it sits at an altitude of about 200 meters on hills that overlook what is known locally as the African Sea. Giuliano seemed to enjoy it and feel reasonably secure there. At least as residents would claim to recall, he was seen more about town than one would have expected, although only later did they learn that the stranger they had seen was he.

Narrowing the Gap

In Castelvetrano, Giuliano was cut off from his remaining band members more than ever, having contact with them only through Pisciotta or by way of a trusted mafioso. He did not know how closely Luca was pursuing his men nor—as they fell one by one, silently, for the most part—how close he was getting to him. When 1950 began, six bandits were still nominally under his command. One of these, Salvatore Pecoraro, was killed in the first month of the year, betrayed to the police by one of his protectors. Contrary to the official press release, which stated that he had died in a gun battle at Bellolampo, he was taken peacefully through deception, then murdered by *carabinieri*, who wanted to protect the identity of their informant.[28]

The incident underscored the highly secretive nature of Luca's enterprise. As yet, however, he had not succeeded in penetrating the inner network of Giuliano's protection. Through bribes, threats, and physical abuse, he could secure the collaboration of many of the landowners and rural workers who served the bandits, but they no longer saw Giuliano nor had any real knowledge of where he was. The major breakthrough came when Giovanni Lo Bianco, a veteran in the antibandit campaign, asked a prestigious Palermo Mafia chief for help in locating Giuliano. The high mafioso answered that while he knew nothing of the matter himself he could provide the name of a person who might be helpful. He suggested Benedetto Minasola of Monreale.

Minasola was known to the police already. He had been taken into custody for questioning several times in past years but had always been released. The one-time simple sheepherder was neither a mafioso nor a bandit, strictly speaking, but he had long been part of Giuliano's inner circle, serving as the bandit's treasurer and sharing generously in his earnings. He had gained control of Villa Carolina, a Monreale estate where the persons abducted by Giuliano were frequently held. Now in his fifties, his shrewdness, energy, and decisiveness concealed by the appearance of a modest country man, Minasola was asked to betray his benefactor.

Lo Bianco had two meetings with Minasola and threatened him with both confinement and formal charges before he admitted that he might be able to help. He added, however, that he alone could do nothing; he would have to have the cooperation of Don Ignazio Miceli, with whom he promised to talk. Two weeks later, when he came back to Palermo to report—the two met secretly in Lo Bianco's father's photographic studio—he informed the officer that the Mafia boss wanted nothing to do with the plot but that he had not forbidden him to participate in it. Don Ignazio had given his permission for the plan to proceed—up to a point. He told his nephew Antonino ("Nino," for short) to go along with it, too. Lo Bianco then learned from Minasola that Giuliano had moved to the Castelvetrano area, while his men were mostly around Castellammare del Golfo.

One of Giuliano's last walls of protection was developing cracks, although not as seriously as external appearances suggested. For while Ignazio Miceli was seeming to cooperate with Luca's forces, he continued to be the key link between the bandit and Verdiani. He had one foot in Verdiani's camp and the other in Luca's.

When Lo Bianco talked to Nino, he asked him to consign Giuliano to him. That might not be possible, the elegant young mafioso evasively answered; instead, he could have a couple of Giuliano's men. He met further protestations with "From one thing another is born." But he did not promise to ever deliver Giuliano. The first two bandits whom young Miceli got the chance to turn in were Frank Mannino and Rosario Candela, who had rejoined the band following their return from North Africa the previous June. They, and Giuliano, too, fell for a maneuver that Nino and Minasola executed. Giuliano was raising money in those times almost exclusively through extortion requests, since abductions could no longer be prudently attempted, and Minasola suggested the owner of a vast Monreale estate as a victim. Giuliano wrote the letter, which was duly delivered. But the police, informing the owner that they had learned of the request, forbade him to pay on it and guaranteed him protection. They assumed that Giuliano would send some of his men to punish the landowner for his failure to pay, and to encourage the bandits to act more boldly, they temporarily withdrew their squadrons from the Monreale area.[29]

Giuliano reacted as had been anticipated. He sent two men, Mannino and Candela, to investigate. Minasola alerted Lo Bianco. It had been thought that the two would come directly to Monreale, but beset by homesickness, they went by Montelepre, in spite of the heavy concentration of forces still there. On Sagana, on March 12, a squadron of *carabinieri* spotted them and, in a fierce 20-minute battle, Candela was killed.[30]

When the police searched the effects of the twenty-seven-year-old deceased bandit, they found, in addition to hand grenades and ample ammunition for his automatic pistol and submachine gun, a little printed incantation in one of his pockets. Bearing the statement that it had been discovered in the tomb of Christ and thereafter preserved in a small silver box by the Holy Father and the Christian emperors and empresses, it promised that by the recitation of its words the body of the bearer would be sealed from penetration by the weapons of his enemies. Although the sophisticated press claimed to think it a strange piece of esoterica, it was the kind of thing that bandits and others from the Latin world of folk Catholicism have carried for centuries.[31]

Mannino escaped harm in the battle and arrived, as expected, at Villa Carolina. Minasola led him in the darkness to Captain Perenze and his *carabinieri*. The killing of Candela was announced, but as befitted the plan, the capture of his comrade was not. To guarantee that no one outside of Luca's immediate confidence would know of how he was taken, Mannino was kept bound hand and foot in the subterranean compartment of a barracks in Calatafimi until after Giuliano's death or, as the prisoner himself reckoned it, for 2640 hours.[32] Giuliano, never learning of what had happened, thought that Mannino must have been killed along with Candela but his body not found.

Three days after Mannino was captured, Antonio Lombardo, the last member of the Labruzzo band of Partinico, was also apprehended. Lombardo had shared leadership of it with two others, the first of whom had been killed in 1948. The other, Giuseppe Labruzzo, disappeared in the following year. The police found his remains in a sack at the bottom of a dry well barely outside of Partinico. The Labruzzo band was one of the island's most feared, having at its pinnacle some four dozen members. Guilty of an almost interminable list of crimes, it was best known for the 1947 slaying of a *carabiniere* colonel in Partinico and the subsequent killing of three more police officers in the town's main plaza. The band was never described as anything other than an association of criminals, although it operated in Giuliano's shadow and sometimes in cooperation with him. Its leaders never enjoyed a popular reputation nor did they attract the attention of journalists or become involved in politics.[33] With the demise of the Labruzzo gang, the only one left of the rural bands that had arisen in the destitution and disorganization of postwar Sicily was Giuliano's.

Now, in mid-March, time was pressing in on Colonel Luca, who in slightly more than two months would reach the statutory age limit for promotion to general. To achieve his goal, he put strong pressure on his subordinate officers to find Giuliano. Lo Bianco told Minasola that he wanted to meet personally with Ignazio and Nino. When Ignazio rejected the request, the officer angrily threatened to send them both off to confinement. The former sheepherder told him that he had better exercise caution, that Nino had once made plans to kill him and might still do so. Lo Bianco took the threat seriously and did not move against the two.

Ignazio Miceli had cooperated indirectly to a point, but turning over a lesser bandit or two was one thing, while consigning Giuliano to Luca—if he had that power—was another. Miceli's main loyalty was to the Verdiani project, not because he cared for Giuliano but almost certainly because he had been promised a substantial financial reward. It is difficult to believe anything other than that a large part of the 80 million lire or more Verdiani had at his disposal to execute his plan was for purchasing Ignazio's cooperation.

Lo Bianco still had Netto Minasola, who could be intimidated much more easily. On April 12, the sheepman gave him two more bandits. After sending word to Nunzio Badalamenti and Castrense Madonia that Giuliano wanted to see them, he picked them up in his truck and, surrounding them with baskets of tomatoes, drove them straight into a police garage in Calatafimi, where they too were hidden away underground.

Pressured still further, Minasola agreed to work with the police in a plot to try to bring Giuliano out of hiding. He got word to the bandit that an extortion demand should be made on a certain landlord down in the direction of Castelvetrano. But the man, who was a part of the plot, agreed to ignore the request, a strategy that it was thought might draw out the bandit himself, since he had so few men left. The police waited at the estate for days without result, until finally a stranger arrived who asked to see the custodian. He was promptly arrested. He turned out to be Giuseppe Marotta, whom Giuliano had sent to inquire about the money. Although he was questioned at length, even by Luca, he soon was let go.[34] The police apparently did not know how close they were to their prey.

April was passing fast and neither Luca nor any of his men still had any sure knowledge of the bandit's whereabouts. Nor did Minasola, who, even though he had dealt directly with Giuliano's men, had to go through Miceli or maybe Albano to reach their chief. For that matter, Miceli did not have direct contact with him either. To locate him or send a message to him he had to go by way of the Castelvetrano Mafia.

If, at the moment, Luca's campaign was faltering, Verdiani's seems to have been moving along at a satisfactory pace. And its essential outlines were coming into relief. The first provision of the basic bargain, the release of Giuliano's mother, had been accomplished; other members of the family were also being freed. In early April, officials of justice in Palermo announced that the original sentence of the bandit's father to five years of confinement had been reduced to twenty months. As he had served almost that much, his release was only a few weeks away. Similarly, as the result of another drastic reduction of sentence, the bandit's brother Giuseppe would be able to return home at about the same time.[35] His sister Giuseppina, who had also been in confinement, was home already. Only Mariannina's case was unpromising. Still accused of participation in the abduction attempt, she would remain in jail for several months more. Even so, the accomplishments of Verdiani, working behind the scenes, had been substantial.

The major task left was the expatriation of Giuliano, or so it might have seemed. Actually, it was now evident that another issue had been raised and that heretofore concealed interested parties were lurking in the shadows. The matter that brought them into view, if only barely, was the impending trial of the bandits for the massacre at Portella della Ginestra, which was scheduled to begin in midyear at latest. Those who already were in custody would be tried in person; the ones still in fugitive status would be tried in absentia. The Italian left was eagerly looking forward to this trial like none other in the immediate postwar years. Less interested in the bandits than in the men who had stood behind them, they hoped that the trail of guilt would lead to the highest levels of the conservative parties, or it would be revealed that the government under the ruling Christian Democratic Party had engaged in a criminal attempt to conceal the truth about Portella della Ginestra.

The left was by no means wholly wrong; there were worried politicians, both inside and outside of the government. Italian court proceedings were notoriously free wheeling, and no one knew what secrets might be revealed before the one at Viterbo would end. Moreover, Giuliano had stated more than once that at the proper moment the real story of the May Day tragedy would be known. It was for these reasons that somewhere within the confines of the Verdiani conspiracy the decision was made to demand from Giuliano a letter in his own handwriting in which he would assume sole responsibility for the attack.

Giuliano was reluctant to give away his trump card. What he knew, what he could tell others, might save him in the end. Prudently, he did not accede to the former inspector when in February he sent him a statement and asked him to copy it and sign it, making it appear to be his own. The text stated that the signer alone knew the truth about the massacre and assumed full responsibility for it. On its margins Verdiani wrote: "This letter is intelligent and good. Write it to me and don't have doubts." [36]

The failure of Giuliano to agree to Verdiani's condition produced further negotiations in March and April, urgent enough that Ignazio Miceli, Nino, and Albano made at least two trips to Rome by air to see the police official. The result was a lengthy "Memoir on Portella della Ginestra" written by Giuliano under the date of April 23. In it, he wrote that he wanted to refute the "slanderous version" that emanated from the "orbit of red imperialism." He then attributed the causes of the attack to his own hatred of communism and the left's opposition to him. And, as he always did, he declared that the killings were the product of a sad error.[37] But no where in it did he affirm flatly that the original inspiration, planning, and execution of the event were exclusively the work of himself and his bandits. This memoir was unsatisfactory to at least some of those within the conspiracy, and another would be demanded of him.

So April went by, as did May, and with it Luca's hope for promotion to general, except by special action. When he submitted his May progress report to his superiors, he had nothing of note to say. It had been a quiet month. His command, he added, was directing its efforts more than ever to intelligence work, "seeking in that way to establish the place and time most propitious for the conclusive action." [38] In plain language, he did not know Giuliano's whereabouts.

Around Montelepre, others also wondered what had happened to him and his men. Persons with whom Mannino, Badalamenti, and Madonia had been in contact heard no more from them. Yet, there was no news of battles or the discovery of bodies. The silence was disturbing.

Maria Lombardo, back at home since February, had hoped to see her son again upon her release, but there was little chance of that. Two *carabinieri* watched her house around the clock, and she was permitted to leave the confines of the town only with permission and under escort. She knew that Giuliano was alive, since messages from him reached her now and then, though few of them said more than that he was well. Those in which he did add something were not heartening. In one, he told her that if she did not hear from him again she should go to Borgetto to see Domenico Albano, whom she had never heard of before. In another, he asked her not to go with the authorities to identify his body in the event that he was killed. And about ten days before he died, she received an anonymous letter that told her he should be wary of those who surrounded him.[39]

Among the larger Italian public, rumors abounded that Giuliano had emigrated already or that he would do so soon. When a member of Montelepre's Badalamenti family was arrested in Brooklyn in June, *Giornale di Sicilia*'s New York correspondent averred that the man was in America to help arrange the bandit's expatriation. He speculated that Giuliano would go by way of Havana to the unguarded coast of Louisiana. His ultimate destination, the reporter believed, might be Detroit, where there was a heavy concentration of Sicilians from Partinico, Alcamo, and Montelepre.[40]

CHAPTER TEN

Castelvetrano–July 5, 1950

Pisciotta's Betrayal

Giuliano had told Jacopo Rizza that Luca would never get him except by way of a traitor. In early June 1950, he learned how close his adversary was to him and that indeed he had been betrayed. Already by the beginning of the previous month, he was worried by his inability to get in touch with his men. He left De Maria's house in May, not to return until late June. In Monreale, in early June, he learned that something was badly wrong when an uncle of Castrense Madonia asked him for news of his nephew. He had heard nothing from Madonia in weeks, Giuliano replied. That was strange, the uncle protested, for Benedetto Minasola had said that Castrense was with Giuliano.[1]

The bandit sensed a betrayal immediately and, with only Pisciotta, boldly abducted Nino Miceli and an associate of his. Tied to trees in an olive grove, the pair was forced to tell Giuliano how his men had been captured. The traitor, they said, was Minasola. Giuliano quickly seized Minasola and took him to the abandoned house where the others were being held. He then sent a message to Luca proposing an exchange of prisoners.

Meanwhile, the authorities were searching for the captives, especially Minasola, upon whose dead body they expected to stumble at any turn. In fact, Minasola was quite alive. Giuliano was in a predicament. Killing his betrayers would satisfy his thirst for vengeance, but they might be worth more to him alive, if, indeed, the authorities should be willing to bargain. He just might get his men back to take with him into exile, a move that he believed was fast approaching. Yet, he did not know how far the conspiracy against him reached, and it was vital that he find out. So, aware that it was unsafe for him to remain with the others, and having much else to do anyway, he departed, leaving the prisoners under Pisciotta's guard. As he left, he angrily threatened to round up Ignazio Miceli, Albano, Marotta, and Castelvetrano's Piccione and, together with the three he had captured already, execute them all under the cover of night in Monreale's main square.

No sooner had Giuliano gone than the shrewd Minasola began to try to convince Gaspare that his chief was lost, that he should save himself by cooperating with the police. A deal could be arranged readily, Minasola assured him. Pisciotta was an easy target, especially as he already doubted that Giuliano's plans for exile would work out— if they were going to leave, they should have left long ago. It took Minasola only the night to persuade him. The men were free by morning, and when they left Minasola had with him Pisciotta's written offer to work with Luca. By the time Giuliano returned to Monreale about two days later, he had heard already of the escape. He demanded an explanation from Pisciotta. Giuliano had stayed away too long, he pleaded, and when he fell asleep the men managed to untie themselves and flee. The bandit chief finally accepted the story and departed for Castelvetrano to try to determine if the conspiracy against him reached there, too. Pisciotta remained in the Monreale area to await his call. The date was approximately June 15.

The newly freed Minasola knocked on Lo Bianco's door at dawn, surprising the police officer, who thought him already dead. He told his story. Pisciotta was acting in good faith, Minasola argued. Lo Bianco should meet with him immediately. Even though the police officer suspected that Giuliano might be plotting to kill him, he knew that he had to take the matter to Luca anyway. The commander shared Lo Bianco's suspicions and counselled him not to go. In contrast, Colonel Giacinto Paolantonio, a long-time associate of Lo Bianco, was less sure that the effort would be futile. In the end, he decided to go through with it. The arrangements, made through Minasola, specified that each come armed with only a pistol—no machine guns.

The meeting, held on the edge of Monreale, came off without mishap but ended indecisively. While Pisciotta agreed to turn over Giuliano, he insisted on a guarantee of his own safety and freedom from prosecution in return. Lo Bianco replied that he could not make such a promise. He suggested instead that Pisciotta might be assisted in emigrating, to which the bandit retorted that he could be killed more easily abroad than at home. He asked to talk personally with Luca.

Luca at first would not consent to meet the bandit, sure that he would be murdered or abducted, but he relented when Paolantonio shamed him into acceptance by threatening to go in his place, pretending to be him.

The meeting between Colonel Luca and Giuliano's best friend took place on June 19 in a house on the outskirts of Monreale. Luca brought Lo Bianco, Paolantonio, and Perenze with him, but he and the outlaw talked alone in a room on the house's third floor. Later in court, Luca testified that Pisciotta had called his chief a "mad criminal" and agreed to turn him in for scarcely more than a promise of protection. Two more meetings were held with Pisciotta in the following days. One of them was attended by a Roman lawyer whom Luca had acquired to represent his newly won collaborator in the trial at Viterbo, then just underway, where he was one of the fugitive defendants. By the end of the second meeting, Luca had given the turncoat bandit a pass stating that as a police confidant he was not to be arrested nor his activities interfered with in any way. The colonel forged Minister of Interior Scelba's signature on it.

Turridu and Aspanu

The pact of late June between Pisciotta and the police sealed Giuliano's fate. Outside of his mother and Mariannina, he really trusted no one except "Aspanu," the familiar name by which he knew Pisciotta. His feeling for him was personal, based on a deep emotional attachment. It was not one that rested mainly on his qualities as a bandit, which, while not inconsiderable, never approached those of a Ferreri, a Cucinella, or a Terranova.

The two had not been boyhood friends, although they had known each other. Contrary to an oft-repeated error, they were not cousins. Pisciotta, unlike Giuliano, went off to war, ultimately fighting against the Germans, and was taken prisoner. Released in June 1945, he returned to Montelepre to be caught up in Giuliano's separatist campaign. By its end, he was known as the bandit chief's lieutenant and personal favorite. Maybe the bond between them was strengthened in the summer of 1946 when Giuliano went out of his way to try to help his friend, who suffered from tuberculosis. No sooner did he learn of a new drug that was said to be effective against the disease than he used important contacts to obtain a large shipment of it from the

United States by air express. That the act eventually may have meant more to the giver than the receiver accords well enough with common wisdom.

Giuliano adopted Pisciotta as his inseparable companion, often permitting only him of all his men to spend the night where he did. Time and again, he showed his loyalty to him. To protect him in the aftermath of Portella della Ginestra, he persuaded a Monreale physician to swear falsely that Pisciotta was in his office for treatment on the day of the attack. Both Stern and Rizza saw the closeness of the two men. Rizza was particularly struck by Giuliano's statement that he and his comrade were as one, although the reporter, like others, was not much impressed by Pisciotta. But friendship is mainly a matter of the heart and not the intellect and, for better or worse, Giuliano was drawn to Aspanu. About ten days before he died, he wrote to his mother that he and his friend had made a pact of loyalty to each other, signed in blood. In those last days, he desperately needed someone around him of trust, and his lieutenant seemed to be the only choice. Luca, he suspected, might have all the others in his pocket. He did not know that Aspanu was in it as well.[2]

During the ten days that followed his departure from Monreale in mid-June, Giuliano seemingly concluded that the conspiracy against him did not extend to the Castelvetrano Mafia. Also during that time, he made a return trip to Monreale to look for Pisciotta, but, upon not finding him, left word that he would call again in a few days. Actually, Pisciotta was in Montelepre under police protection. Mama Giuliano thought that Pisciotta's mother was acting strangely but did not know why. On the night of June 25, a worried and tired Giuliano reappeared at De Maria's house. He had made the trip back to Castelvetrano on foot, De Maria thought.

Near the End

During those last days of June, while Giuliano was frantically trying to protect himself, both Luca's and Verdiani's conspiracies entered their final stages. To arrive at some crucial decisions with respect to Luca's, a high level meeting was held in Palermo, attended by the general commander of the *carabinieri,* the prefect of Palermo province, the provincial police chief, and Palermo prosecutor general Emanuele Pili, in addition to Luca and others. It was decided that credit for the conclusion of the campaign would be divided between the public security police and the *carabinieri,* who had fought and died side by side, though not always harmoniously, for seven years toward that end. It was also agreed that Giuliano should be dead before any public announcement of the successful conclusion of the effort was made. The professed reason for planning the murder of the legendary outlaw was to ensure the secrecy of those who had betrayed him. It scarcely needed saying that there were other reasons for sealing his lips forever. As to how to best guarantee that the public would never learn of the murder, the proposal of one participant met with general approval. The bandit's body would be left at a certain place in the countryside, and the next day the police, alleging that they had exchanged fire with unknown parties during the night, would come upon it as they searched the area. The exact details would be left to Colonel Luca.[3]

Meanwhile, on Verdiani's front, one major concession remained to be exacted from Giuliano before he could be told that his expatriation had been arranged. He had yet to affirm unequivocally that only he and his men, and absolutely no one else, had been involved in any phase of the Portella della Ginestra attack. The long wait since his previous (and unsatisfactory) memoir of April 23 suggests that it was a concession he had resisted stoutly; now, hard pressed, he consented. The document, dated June 28, was delivered in typed form for him to put into his own handwriting and sign. Written in a lawyer's language—the terse covering letter, dated July 2, also sounded nothing like the bandit—the statement met fully the conditions that Verdiani demanded. Interior Minister Scelba was in no way involved with Giuliano, either before or after Ginestra, and, as to specifically the case then being tried at Viterbo, "I vehemently protest there were no principals and others responsible outside of myself."[4] Finally, in desperation, Giuliano had given away his trump card.

In Castelvetrano at De Maria's house, Giuliano expectantly awaited his promised expatriation. He had bought new clothing for the trip and had his bags packed. He sent a message to Pisciotta telling him that on a second notice he should come immediately. The bandit believed that he and Pisciotta would be flown to Tunisia from an abandoned airport near Castelvetrano. The documents for their journey were to be delivered by Verdiani's son, he had been told.

Verdiani almost certainly had something else in mind for Giuliano: the delivery of his dead body to the authorities. Giuliano knew too much about the conservative establishment politicians with whom

Verdiani was associated to be permitted to live. They wanted to guarantee that his most recent memoir would also be his last. As for Verdiani personally, most of all, he likely wanted to deny Ugo Luca the credit for bringing the long campaign to a victorious close.

Verdiani learned of Luca's plan to trap and murder the bandit, Pisciotta's part in it, and other details, not much more than hours before its execution was set to commence.[5] He learned of it easily, since some of the participants in the Palermo summit meeting that approved it were his own partisans. He then sent two messages to Giuliano in Castelvetrano, knowing that either one or both might not be delivered, to alert him to the betrayal—Verdiani, too, did not know whom to trust. One of them, which was intercepted and shown to Luca, read: "Dearest friend, be warned that Pisciotta has passed to Luca's side. Protect yourself immediately." The other, with the same message, reached Giuliano, brought to him at De Maria's house by Marotta late on July 4.

After reading the note, Giuliano despondently told its bearer that everyone wanted to betray him, even Aspanu. Still, he could hardly believe that his friend was doing it. De Maria returned from a movie around 11:00 P.M. to find Marotta and Giuliano in agitated discussion. The bandit should go away with him, to get away from Gaspare, Marotta was telling him, to which he angrily retorted: "If I have to doubt Gaspare, I have to doubt you too! You are all a bunch of cowards and traitors."[6]

By the night of July 4, 1950, almost everyone around Giuliano knew that his end was drawing near. The bandit knew enough to realize that he was in great danger, and most persons in such a situation would have sought to flee. But he had no safe place to go. Anyhow, so far as he knew, the Castelvetrano Mafia was still loyal to him. He also had a hard time believing that Pisciotta had betrayed him. There was the possibility that the whole thing was a plot to flush him out of hiding. Giuliano decided to remain where he was for the time being.

Earlier that same evening, on the northern side of the island, another discussion was carried on for the professed purpose of agreeing on the last minute details of Giuliano's elimination. Luca, Paolantonio, Lo Bianco, and Pisciotta attended. The decisive action was set for the next evening. The participants left around 9:00 P.M., ostensibly to return to their homes, but when Lo Bianco saw Luca head unexpectedly toward the south he was suspicious. He and Paolantonio followed for a ways in their own vehicle but were soon outdistanced not only by Luca's car but also by two others that passed them at high speeds. They turned back, almost certain that they were being excluded from the campaign's final scene.[7]

Colonel Luca was indeed headed toward Castelvetrano, although he stopped short of there, at Camporeale, to await developments. The two other cars drove on. In one, a Fiat 1100, rode Pisciotta, who was let out at the edge of Castelvetrano to go the rest of the way on foot. In the other car, Captain Perenze and his three *carabinieri* took another route.

The hour was a little past midnight. July 5 had arrived. The lights were out and all was quiet in the house on Via Serafino Mannone when a knocking on the front door brought De Maria out of his half-asleep state. Looking down from an upstairs window, he saw that it was Pisciotta. He alerted Giuliano, then went down to open the door. Pisciotta politely inquired after De Maria and his mother's health as they ascended the stairs. He said that he had ridden in on horseback, but De Maria noticed that he was elegantly dressed in a gray suit and silk shirt and, contrary to his usual practice, carried no long arms.

Giuliano confronted his comrade belligerently, striking him and shouting "Bastard! Traitor!" Later, as Pisciotta argued that he had not betrayed him, Giuliano settled down and they talked at length. Finally, Pisciotta convinced him that what he had been told was a lie. Or at least that was Gaspare's version of the conversation, but then it is also the only one.[8] Maybe what he said was correct. Giuliano doubtless wanted to believe that his closest friend was still loyal. Sometime, considerably past midnight, the pair retired, lying side by side in the same bed, as they had done many times before.

A little later, around 3:00 A.M. on that hot night, two bakers were sitting out on the sidewalk only a few steps away from De Maria's house waiting for their bread to rise when they were approached by a pair of *carabinieri* who decisively ordered them to go inside and close the door.

The Announcement of Giuliano's Death

That same morning, about 5:00 A.M., Lo Bianco's telephone rang. On the other end, Colonel Paolantonio matter-of-factly asked: "Do you want to hear some news?" The warrant officer knew what it was even before he heard it. Luca, he was told, had called to report that Giuliano was dead, killed in a running gun battle in Castelvetrano.

Not long after that, Mamma Giuliano answered the knock on the door that she had feared for seven years. The *carabinieri* were there. They told her that if she wanted to see her son she should go with them to Castelvetrano. She asked them for no details. Quietly, and with sinking heart, she sensed what had happened. The family doctor offered to drive her, so that she would not have to ride with the police. Mariannina received the dreaded notice in her Palermo prison cell.

All over Italy, and many other places, too, the death of the renowned Sicilian bandit was announced in bold headlines and special editions. The later stories reported that Prime Minister Alcide De Gasperi, following an extraordinary meeting of the cabinet in Rome, had announced Colonel Ugo Luca's imminent promotion to brigadier general for exceptional merit.

Earlier that morning, Giuliano's half-dressed, bloodstained body lay face down in the enclosed courtyard at the house of De Maria. Half of the men and boys of Castelvetrano, it seemed, were gathered in the street outside, each one struggling to get close enough to be boosted up by a friend so as to look over the wall to see it. Some journalists were already there, while others were racing from locations throughout the nation to get to the small city on Sicily's southern coast as quickly as possible.

Mamma Giuliano arrived in the afternoon. Taken to the morgue, where the body then rested, she look at it and fainted away. Her doctor was concerned for her health, since she suffered from heart trouble, but after regaining consciousness, she insisted upon being taken to the place where her son had died. There, with cameras clicking, the 60-year-old mother, her head covered with a black shawl, knelt to kiss the bloodstain on the pavement of the courtyard where the body had lain.

Captain Perenze gave the official account of how Giuliano had died. The key to locating the bandit, he related, was a police confidant who had to remain unidentified. He had told the police of Giuliano's decision to leave Italy, and they expected him to depart from somewhere in the Castelvetrano area. They were particularly watching an abandoned airport near there. In coordination with their informer, the decisive action was set for the night of July 4. Colonel Luca ordered a small operation, involving only four *carabinieri*. To protect the collaborator, the local police were not told of it. The plan called for their

informer to go to the house (unidentified in the account) where Giuliano was staying and accompany him to another residence (also unidentified), where they were to meet other bandits and supporters to
make their final plans for leaving. When the pair left the first location,
Giuliano would be seized alive. They had strict orders to use firearms
only in "absolute necessity."

About 3:15 A.M., the captain continued, the informer came out, his
shoes in his hand, followed seconds later by two others who were
armed. Before anything else could happen, the pair saw the *carabiniere* nearest to them and fired, thereby setting off a 45-minute battle.
During it, the police recognized one of the armed men as Giuliano
when he passed under a street light. A search located him when the
firing ended, badly wounded in a courtyard, his submachine gun and
pistol by his side. In response to the dying man's plea, Perenze went
into the house to get him some water and left another *carabiniere* on
guard. When he returned the famous outlaw had expired. His accom-
plice had gotten away. The informer also had disappeared.[9]

Had Giuliano Really Died That Way?

The deaths of famous people, especially those by violence, lend themselves to controversy, and Giuliano's fit the pattern from the beginning. Hardly had the ink dried on the first newspapers, when
questions began to be asked. Even the staunchly progovernment *Giornale di Sicilia* reported on July 7 that the accounts coming from Castelvetrano contained contradictions. In Viterbo, Giuliano's men stated
that they did not believe the story at all. In no way, some of them said,
would the chief have let himself be driven into a courtyard with only
one exit. In Castelvetrano itself, reporters swarmed everywhere, asking questions of everyone and gathering every fact and rumor.

The results, if hastily acquired, were fascinating to talk and write
about. The more people thought about them, the more questions they
asked. A good many men had gotten into De Maria's courtyard to see
the body, through their friendship with local police. As they thought
about what they had seen, they realized that things had not looked
right. The body was clad only in an undershirt, trousers, and shoes,
and, when it was stripped at the morgue, amidst a crowd of male
onlookers, it was found that Giuliano had been wearing no under-
shorts. His belt had been put through only two loops; his large, gold

watch was not on his wrist; he carried no money. He simply was not dressed like a man who was on his way to an important meeting. And the bandit chief was known to be a man who cared for his looks.

But, as they thought about it, what struck them as most strange was the pattern of bloodstains. The body, rather badly shot up, was lying face down. Yet, from appearances, the blood from the wounds had strangely run upward. Some also noticed that Giuliano's back was dusty and that there were scratches on his arms and shoulders, all suggesting that the body had been dragged.

The residents of Via Mannone talked to each other, and sometimes guardedly to reporters. One had heard a shot or two, like pistol fire, and later a short burst from what sounded like an automatic weapon. No one had heard the 45-minute battle that the *carabinieri* had reported, certainly not the firing of the 191 rounds of ammunition that Perenze claimed had been expended by the police alone. Along another nearby street where, according to the *carabinieri*, hostile contact had first been made, residents had heard nothing. Then, there were the bakers only a few steps up the street. They had seen only a lone man run from De Maria's house. Nedda, De Maria's servant girl, it was now remembered, had told neighbors that her employer had a relative staying with him whom she was not allowed to see. And so it went.

The True Story

One of the northern reporters in town, Tommaso Besozzi, representing the weekly *L'Europeo* of Milan, had worked on Sicilian topics before. He heard these rumors and more, too, talked confidentially to a good many people, and came up with his own version of the bandit's death. In a real scoop in *L'Europeo*'s July 16 and 24 issues, he quite accurately sketched Minasola's betrayal of the bandit (using fictitious initials in place of the Monreale sheepman's name), Pisciotta's betrayal of his chief, and Giuliano's presence in Castelvetrano at the house of Gregorio De Maria. Pisciotta, he wrote, had shot and killed a sleeping Giuliano, and then been whisked away by the *carabinieri* to disappear from public view. The police had taken the body down to the courtyard and fired on it with an automatic weapon, so as to create the appearance that the bandit had perished in battle. The fabrication, he concluded , was for the protection of the police informers.[10]

Some days later in the Chamber of Deputies, Interior Minister Scelba, angrily rebutting one of Pietro Nenni's socialists, called Besozzi's version and other variants of it, "the fantasy of journalists."[11] In fact, the story told by Perenze on July 5 remained the official account of how Giuliano died; even after Perenze himself disavowed it.

Actually, the Milan reporter had uncovered the true story surprisingly quickly, or at least one that was close to the truth, for his version was substantially corroborated later by three of the major participants, De Maria, Pisciotta, and Perenze. A composite of the most believable testimony about the event indicates that Perenze had instructed Pisciotta to lure Giuliano out so he could be killed in another location. But Verdiani's warning note to Giuliano threw that plan awry. When Pisciotta arrived at De Maria's house, Giuliano confronted him angrily, easily gaining the upper hand, and if Pisciotta even broached the subject of their going out, he flatly refused. The two finally went to bed. Outside Perenze worried and wondered, unaware of what was causing the delay. The first rays of dawn would soon appear, and with them the early risers, perhaps a peasant on his way to a distant field. The captain was almost ready to call off the mission.

Inside, Giuliano wearily went to sleep at last, more or less convinced that Pisciotta was still loyal to him. Beside him, Pisciotta feigned sleep, wide awake, beset by doubts, excited, all kinds of thoughts racing through his mind. With things going so badly, he must have pondered, what if Luca's plot failed and Giuliano learned beyond any doubt of his own role in the conspiracy? What would his life be worth then? Moving stealthily, he retrieved his pistol and shot his long-time comrade twice at close range.

Perenze heard the shots, as did De Maria, suddenly awakened by them. The first thought that crossed his mind was of a police assault. Pisciotta rushed into his room and out, saying there had been shots. De Maria expected Giuliano to follow, but when he did not, he went timidly into the room to find him dead, still in bed, lying on his back, his eyes and lips closed as if he were in a deep sleep. Crazy with fright, De Maria rushed down to bar the door that Pisciotta had left open. He then dressed, tried to calm his terror-stricken mother, and jumped out the bathroom window into the garden, intending to run to Marotta's house. A *carabiniere* who heard him hit the ground grabbed him. Pisciotta had told the captain what he had done and been rushed out of town to go into hiding.

Perenze told De Maria and his mother to say nothing ever about what had happened there; that, if they did, they would be arrested for harboring a criminal. He told them to clean up the blood and dispose of all signs of it; neighbors later saw a bloodstained sheet that Nedda indiscretely left in view. Assisted by De Maria and the other *carabinieri*, the captain hurriedly dressed Giuliano's body, dragged it down to the courtyard, placed the bandit's firearms and knapsack by its side, and told De Maria to go into the house and close all doors and windows. He then shot the dead body with his submachine gun. Luca, who was called on police radio, arrived from Camporeale as soon as possible, but not before a crowd of townspeople had gathered, alerted by De Maria's neighbors. A false story of what had happened had to be concocted hurriedly, and the other *carabinieri* told it. It was all too fast, and before the day was over, the story had begun to unravel.[12]

Laid to Rest

In the days that followed, the body of the bandit was Castelvetrano's main attraction. Hundreds of men and boys went to the morgue to see it, lying on a slab, strangely vulnerable in its nakedness. They stood around it, marvelled at it, commented on its various features, and inspected closely the two sets of bullet holes, adding their own ideas of how they had gotten there. Although the *carabinieri* were upset by the ease with which so many could get in to see the body, as they had been by those who had gotten in to De Maria's courtyard when Giuliano's body was there, they could do little about it. Castelvetrano was a small city, and too many, it appeared, had a friend who worked in the morgue.

In Montelepre, at Via Castrense di Bello, 135, a simple band of black graced the door; below it, on a small white card: "For the death of my son." Giuliano's family prepared for the funeral. Mamma Giuliano asked the monsignor to permit the body to lay in state in the church, but the *carabinieri* quickly ruled that out. There was a long delay in releasing the body; all that came out of Castelvetrano were statements that the necessary papers had not yet been issued. It was supposed that the authorities did not want it inspected by others, as if that had not happened already. Finally, the family was told that the remains would be brought to Montelepre on July 19 before dawn, the odd hour dictated by the authorities' fears of demonstrations.

On that day, the police had the cemetery under guard by 3:00 A.M. At 4:17, *Giornale di Sicilia*'s reporter noted precisely, the family arrived in two cars. A funeral van accompanied them, bringing flowers and wreaths, together with the other decorative effects of a Sicilian funeral. Meanwhile, in Castelvetrano, legal wrangling over the body unexpectedly continued; only at 5:25, hours behind schedule, was it finally released. Then the car carrying it, together with two escort vehicles, made the long, mountainous trip by way of Salemi, Alcamo, and Partinico—a route Giuliano had known well in better times— coming to the cemetery by a circuitous route that avoided the town of Montelepre. It was a late 11:35 A.M. when they arrived.

In the town's small cemetery, graced like other Italian burial grounds by stately cypresses, the most famous bandit of all Sicily, and Italy, was laid to rest. No bells were ringing; there were no crowds. Only the immediate family and the police were there; others were forbidden. The elder Giuliano, still on Ustica, could not come, nor could Mariannina, in prison in Palermo. There was no priest to say a few kind words. The police had forbidden that, too. No tears were shed. Mamma Giuliano looked only depressed, tired, worn out. It was well into early afternoon before the police and the tiny group of seven mourners left the stillness of the cemetery behind them. The small marble slab that had been put in place read simply: "Salvatore Giuliano, 1922–1950." On that quiet noonday, there at the foot of Giuliano's mountain, an epoch of Sicilian history had ended.[13]

CHAPTER ELEVEN

Viterbo

THE TRIAL OF THE THIRTY-SIX DEFENDANTS charged with the attack at Portella della Ginestra began in Viterbo, north of Rome, on June 12, 1950, in the old Church of the Discalced Carmelites, by then converted into a court building. The proceedings were to be difficult and long, to end only in May 1953. Hardly had the trial gotten underway before, in early July, it was interrupted by a long recess. However, the cause was not the death of the star defendant, who was being tried in absentia anyway, but rather by the belated announcement that the police had been secretly holding three of the accused while the court was in session. By the time the trial got underway again in a sustained fashion, in the next year, Gaspare Pisciotta had been arrested. He became the star defendant.

Pisciotta, following his flight from De Maria's house in the early morning of July 5, was initially under Captain Perenze's care. He was a problem for Luca and his command; for while they were protecting him, the public security police were avidly looking for him, if only to embarrass their rivals. Luca, in sum, did not know what to do with him. Pisciotta did not want to go into exile. What he wanted—complete amnesty in recognition of his services—Luca did not have the power to grant.

In actuality, after being briefly sheltered in Perenze's apartment, Pisciotta took refuge in his own home, where he remained until his capture. His house, like so many others in Montelepre of those years, had a hidden compartment, in this instance a quite small one between the ceiling of one room and the floor of his mother's bedroom above it. The police had searched the house many times, both before and after the death of Giuliano, without discovering the hiding place.

Maybe, as the weeks and months passed, the fugitive became too bold and someone saw him and informed the authorities. In any event, the provincial chief of police sent a force of 200 men to Montelepre on the night of December 4 to place the Pisciotta home and the rest of the town, too, under constant watch. One contingent was in the house itself, and Pisciotta, unable to bear his cramped quarters any longer, surrendered late the next afternoon. Sweaty and dishevelled, he received permission from his captors to clean up and change clothing before being taken to Palermo. He was in chains but superbly clad by the time he faced the public and the press. While his capture did not compensate the public security police for Luca's outsmarting of them exactly five months to the day earlier, it was immensely gratifying nonetheless.[1]

The trial at Viterbo was the nation's most interesting in many a year. Its anticipated sensational revelations equally were feared by some and hoped for by others. At the least, the public expected to be entertained. Sooner or later, almost everyone believed, somebody was going to "empty the sack"—a phrase that became one of the reporters' favorites. It would likely be Pisciotta, many thought, who would do so.

The proceedings dealt only with the thirty-six men who were charged specifically with the crimes at Ginestra. The state tried hard to restrict questioning and testimony to what the thirty-six allegedly had done there, especially striving to stay away from charges of the complicity of politicians in the attack, as well as from the subject of Giuliano's death. Many of the lawyers, on the other hand, hoping to damage the conservative government, wanted to focus on those two matters. In the end, neither happened to either side's satisfaction.

The three dozen defendants, Pisciotta apart, provided little of interest at Viterbo, other than a chance for the spectators to get a firsthand look at the famed Sicilian bandits. Giuliano's main henchmen, Terranova, Mannino, Cucinella, and eight others, all claimed that they had been nowhere near the scene of the crime on May Day 1947 and knew nothing of what had occurred there. Most of the others, the so-called lesser group, Giuliano's temporary help, said not even that much. By the time the trial started, they had withdrawn the confessions they had made earlier, claiming they had been subjected to extreme physical abuse or outright torture. It was generally believed that their confessions had been obtained under duress, since in Sicily, while in one's right mind, one did not willingly confess to crimes that also implicated others. Torture was about the only way to secure a confession, and it was widely used.[2]

Typical of the lesser group was a young Montelepre native by the name of Rizzitelli, who by then had been in jail for two years awaiting trial. Asked what he was charged with, he answered, looking at the floor, that he did not know. Asked if he knew what the others were charged with, his response was again in the negative. That he was from Montelepre was his only admission, and he was still looking at the floor when he made it.[3] Things, however, would look up for young Rizzitelli at trial's end, for he would be acquitted.

The only defendant who talked much at Viterbo was Pisciotta, who talked too much. He was likely to say anything in his frequent emotional outbursts. If he had thought of it, he would have accused the pope of hatching the Ginestra attack, someone said. He did lay the responsibility for it on the monarchists and Mattarella and, in addition, accused Minister of Interior Scelba of it, too. Defense lawyers encouraged him and the others to make such accusations, since a part of their strategy was the attempt to make it appear that if the defendants had committed any crimes they had done so on orders from high government officials.[4]

Pisciotta's most sensational revelation came on April 11, 1951, when he admitted that he had killed Giuliano—he had never before made that admission in public. Five days later, rising to say that he wanted to make a statement of international importance, he added that he had killed Giuliano on Scelba's orders. On another occasion, he charged that Verdiani had tried to kill Luca; and, on still another, to the merriment of spectators, that the bandits, the Mafia, and the public security police were as inseparable as the Holy Trinity.

Pisciotta gave few details when questioned on his charges, and even when he did the details usually were confused. By the time the trial ended, it could only be wondered if he knew very much. Maybe, that was exactly what he wanted people to believe. His revelations came mostly in emotional outbursts. After he regained his composure, he was likely to repudiate all or part of what he had just said, or to so confuse it with contradictions as to render it useless as testimony. Clearly, he was a frightened man, unwilling to reveal all that he knew and unwilling to identify those whom he feared.

Still, Gaspare was a handsome fellow who tried to present an appearance of confidence and elegance. His elaborate wardrobe of the most advanced styles impressed and entertained reporters and spectators to no end. He could arrive one day in a velvet sport coat, silk shirt, trousers of the latest cut, and shoes fashioned from the skin of some exotic beast, all of it set off by a showy tie and flashy pair of stockings, to then come back the following day in an equally arresting, and totally new, attire.

Try as it did to confine testimony to the actions of the accused, the court at times went well beyond those bounds. Before the trial ended, dozens of persons who had nothing to do with the May Day attack had been brought before it, among them General Luca, Major Perenze, Verdiani, Ignazio Miceli, Marotta, Marotta's wife, Albano, and De Maria. What brought them to Viterbo was the trial's most interesting matter, the one that caused it to last so long, and potentially its most explosive. The matter was Giuliano's personal papers and what had happened to them after his death.

Both the lawyers for the defense and those representing the victims explored and exploited this issue to the fullest, and it was of utmost importance. Pisciotta testified that Giuliano had a memoir of some twenty pages which, among much else, named those who had ordered the May Day attack. That the bandit had the story of his career in writing had long been known, and it was assumed that multiple copies of it existed as a safeguard. Pasquale Sciortino supposedly took one with him to America in 1947. In the fall of 1949, further allegations had a by then more complete account making its way to a bank in France, taken there via Tunisia by a Sicilian-American who later took up residence in New Orleans. Finally, it was believed that Giuliano kept a copy in his possession. He carried at all times a brown leather folder, which, in addition to a photograph of Pisciotta, contained various papers, including, it seemed likely, a copy of his memoirs.[5]

There was more than one person who had been in a position to get Giuliano's papers on the night of his death. De Maria was a suspect, as were Marotta, Pisciotta, and Perenze; so was Luca, even if he did arrive late. Pisciotta asserted that he once had the memoir in his possession but had given it to Perenze. Perenze answered that Pisciotta had promised to give him the document but never delivered it.

Subsequent testimony indicated that Perenze was correct. Both he and Luca testified that Pisciotta, then claiming that someone else had the document, set up a rendezvous at which it was supposed to be given to them. On Luca's instructions, the captain went in civilian clothes to Kilometer 5 along the Castelvetrano–Mazara del Vallo highway, where he stopped his vehicle and raised the hood as a signal. A man whom he identified as a stranger approached, and after they exchanged the agreed upon code word, the man told him that he no longer had the documents, that he had burned them out of fear. This testimony led to a further complication when a letter was revealed that Perenze wrote to Pisciotta in explanation of the mission's failure. In it, he referred to the man whom he had met at Kilometer 5 as the *avvocaticchio,* an approximate Italian equivalent of "jackleg lawyer." In fact, that was the term both Pisciotta and Perenze commonly used when referring to De Maria. Thus, fingers pointed toward him as the one who burned Giuliano's memoirs. De Maria was quickly called— he had been arrested for harboring Giuliano and was already in Viterbo.

De Maria strenuously denied that he had ever seen the memoirs or met Perenze at Kilometer 5. Pisciotta refused to name the mysterious person, warning that if he did the man's family would be "exterminated" within 24 hours. At this point, a surprise witness was called, Serafino Di Peri, a former mayor of Bolognetta, who, while serving a two-year term for being part of a Mafia association, had been with De Maria in jail. A fiery, white-haired old man of 75, he challenged the timid De Maria to tell the court what he had told him, of how he had burned papers and been threatened with death for what he knew.

Finally breaking down under Di Peri's badgering, in a session in which judicial decorum was wholly abandoned, De Maria admitted that he had burned some of Giuliano's things but not any memoirs. Nor had he burned the bandit's folder of papers; instead, he said, it had disappeared. Pressed hard, he pleaded that he could not talk about such things, that threats had been made against both himself and his mother. Asked who had made them, he answered that he could not tell, that he was terrified, that the man who made them was "capable of anything." When the court's president confronted him, he conceded that the threats came from within Castelvetrano, but when asked if the Italian-American Nicola Piccione had made them he brought that line of questioning to a close with a pitiful plea: "No, don't insist. I beg you. Even if it was him, I could not say." Denying to the end that he knew anything about the memoirs, De Maria suggested that Pisciotta must have gotten them, or else Giuliano had given them to Marotta the evening before he died. The possibility that Marotta might have some of Giuliano's papers was a matter the court was investigating already.[6]

Although, a few days earlier, Marotta had denied ever having the memoirs, he admitted to having a letter Giuliano had written. It had been given to him to mail, he said, but he had never done so. The letter was addressed to a newspaper and contained references to Ginestra. Marotta's revelation created a minor sensation, so great was the hunger for anything in Giuliano's handwriting. The police in Sicily were wired instructions to seize it immediately. All they got, however, were a few well soaked and practically illegible fragments. As Maria Vittoria, Marotta's wife, later testified, she saw the police agents approaching and, fearing that the letter might implicate her husband, tore it up and threw the pieces into a tub of wash water. Despite the news that the episode created, it is doubtful that the letter said anything new. Maria Vittoria's description of its contents made it appear to be nothing more than just another of Giuliano's many letters to the press, which it probably was.[7]

Another bizarre trail that also led to Marotta was more promising. Senator Giuseppe Casadei told the court of a strange series of events in which he was involved after a campaign appearance in Castelvetrano in the June 1951 elections. He had been flagged down in his automobile on the highway near the Greek ruins of Selinute by a local lawyer, Salvatore Azzara (like Casadei, a socialist), who told him that he knew a man who had papers of Giuliano's for sale. The man was Pino Marotta, the lawyer told Casadei. The papers consisted of a letter and diary of approximately forty pages. The senator pursued the matter further in the following days but to no avail. Azzara told him that Marotta had become wary because of De Maria's recent arrest, a fate that he feared would also be his. Both the lawyer and Marotta, who admitted to knowing each other well, were questioned on the matter. They admitted the truthfulness of some portions of Casadei's testimony but denied others, especially with respect to the alleged diary, of which they disclaimed any knowledge. The letter, Marotta claimed, was the same one that his wife later threw in the laundry water.[8]

With a pile of denials like these, the search for the truth about Portella della Ginestra was finally called off in the late fall of 1951. After more than 200 sessions and nearly that many witnesses, it had become evident that no one was going to empty the sack. Nor was the court any closer to solving the mystery of Giuliano's alleged memoirs than it had ever been. When the trial ended, the left was still demanding that new witnesses be called and old ones recalled, but there was scant likelihood that its prolongation would have any salutary results. It seemed to have run its course, however profoundly disappointing it had been to many people. Near its end, *L'Ora*'s Enzo Perrone summed up many feelings when he wrote that it was coming to a close in "the drywell of contradictions, drowned in a feast of lies, shipwrecked in a boundless sea without lighthouses."[9]

The three dozen defendants had been all but forgotten by the trial's final session. In May 1952, some six months after the testimony concluded, their verdicts were handed down. Twelve, among them Pisciotta, Sciortino (in absentia), Mannino, and Terranova, were given life sentences; four received lesser penalties; the remaining were acquitted. Many of the defendants, including some of those acquitted, still faced prosecution on other charges. Indeed, the number of trials that involved Giuliano's men was expected to total about eighty. Pisciotta alone was charged in thirty-four separate crimes. Later, however, the crimes of many of the defendants were combined under general charges. One giant trial of 1954 had approximately 100 defendants who were variously charged with having participated in an armed band or in an association of delinquents. Most of them were convicted. Some, however, Albano, Antonino and Ignazio Miceli, Marotta, and De Maria included, were given light enough sentences that they were released then or soon thereafter. Giuliano's sister Mariannina, who was already at liberty, was acquitted, as was Benedetto Minasola.[10]

The Continuing Pursuit of the Truth

After the Viterbo trial, expectations withered that full revelations about Ginestra would ever be made, but they did not die. Many believed that Pisciotta would still let the secrets out. They thought that he might yet substantiate his many accusations and resolve his contradictory statements about them; and he threatened periodically to tell the whole truth. While in prison, in Palermo's Ucciardione Penitentiary, he also was writing his memoirs, allegedly with all the secrets included, in hope that he could sell them to a publisher for a handsome sum.[11]

In early February 1954, Gaspare asked to talk to the prosecutor general, promising that he would tell the truth about various episodes in Giuliano's career, including some that related to his death. The head prosecutor was busy and sent an assistant, Pietro Scaglione, who told Pisciotta to write out what he had told him. He agreed, but asked for several days to focus his thoughts. There did not seem to be much urgency to the task, on either Pisciotta or the official's part. Evidently, nevertheless, some people still feared what Pisciotta might reveal. He had lived in fear of being assassinated ever since Giuliano's death. In prison, he would accept no one but his father, who was being held for trial, too, as a cell mate. He ate and drank only what he himself prepared or what his mother brought to him. He knew that prison officials could not effectively protect him from his fellow inmates; for, within the walls of Palermo's notorious penitentiary, the influence of the Mafia was strong. Indeed, there was hardly a more formidable obstacle to a confession that implicated mafiosi than the knowledge that after you made it you would return to Ucciardione.

On the morning of February 10, 1954, Pisciotta made coffee for himself and his father as usual. A guard on his customary rounds came into the cell, chatted for a few moments, and went on his way. Gaspare drank some of the coffee, as did his father, each one sweetening his own from the same bowl of sugar. Soon, Gaspare, feeling intense pain, cried out that he had been poisoned. His death, coming almost immediately, was caused by his swallowing 20 centigrams of strychnine, enough, one said, to kill forty dogs. The subsequent investigation of his death produced no conclusive results as to who had poisoned him. Both his father and the guard were suspects. Suspicion also fell on a mafioso, a prisoner who worked in the dispensary and had access to the medicine that Pisciotta took. It was also possible, as some of his fellow inmates argued, that he had killed himself, finally realizing that his services to the state were not going to be rewarded.[12]

Assuming that Pisciotta did not take his own life, it is difficult to conclude that it came as the result of anything other than the fears of the Mafia. Maybe there were mafiosi who were afraid of what he might yet say about Ginestra, but more likely, their fears were related to Giuliano's last months and death. Charges against Pisciotta for the slaying of Giuliano were pending. If the trial had been held, the search for evidence would logically have enveloped a network of Mafia associations stretching across Sicily from Palermo to Castelvetrano. The greater wonder is not that they killed Pisciotta but that they let him live so long.

His death punctured a hole in the remaining hopes for new revelations but did not completely deflate them. There were the memoirs that Pisciotta had been writing, for instance; and, within a short time, Gaspare's younger brother Pietro began to try to sell them to the Communist Party. He first talked to leading communists in Bologna, a center of party strength, but they advised him to take his proposition to their Palermo comrades. One of the problems, both in Bologna and initially in Palermo, was Pietro's insistence that the memoirs be read only after the purchase. Finally, in Palermo, he relented, telling Giuseppe Montalbano that he could read them if he would agree to certain conditions as to time and place. Montalbano accepted the offer.

One night, as had been agreed, he was picked up by Pietro and taken blindfolded to a house somewhere in the city. There, while sipping tea and eating cookies, he read the two notebooks that Pisciotta had filled. When he gave his summary to Li Causi and the other party heads, he advised them to pay the several millions that Pietro was asking. They refused, on the grounds that the notebooks contained no new information. After then, Pietro presumably gave up on the effort.[13]

Even after all the disappointments, many people still awaited new revelations, possibly in one or more of the trials that were yet to be conducted. One, in particular, Pasquale Sciortino's appeal of the life sentence that he had received in absentia at Viterbo, seemed to hold promise. Mariannina's long-absent husband returned to Italy in April 1953, after having been arrested in the previous year in San Antonio, Texas, where he was serving in the United States Air Force under an assumed name. By the time of his return, he had been away from Italy for almost six years and had never seen his small son, Giuseppe, whom Mariannina had with her when she went to Palermo to greet him upon his return. Of course, he was in custody, and the couple got scarcely more than a glimpse of each other. As for Giuseppe, his father thought that he looked like any other little boy.

Sciortino's return had been much anticipated. If no one else would tell the truth about Giuliano's violent antileftist campaign of May and June 1947, he might do so. Crucially, he had been in a position to know whose signature was affixed to that famous letter that prompted Giuliano to make his final decision to attack the May Day meeting.

In the trial, held in 1956, Sciortino swore that his only activities in the band were related to the separatist revolt, which was covered by the 1946 amnesty. Subsequent to the revolt's collapse early in that year, he was associated with the Giuliano family only as Mariannina's reluctant husband. He could not have been at Portella della Ginestra, since at the time he was suffering from an appendicitis attack, nor did he have any part in the raids on leftist headquarters in the following month. It quickly became evident that he was pursuing the same strategy that had been adopted by all others in the band. This trial was the last one in which there was a realistic expectation that someone might finally empty the sack, and it did not happen. Sciortino's original life sentence, however, was reduced to twenty-five years.[14]

Mariannina fought hard for her husband in the years that followed, continuing to try to secure his release, even in the face of indications that he had married again while in the United States. She still loved him and wanted him back. He was not insensitive to her feelings, nor to little Giuseppe's. Maintaining, however, that it was not only a forced marriage but also one that had virtually ruined his life, he was not inclined to accept the role of a dutiful husband. During his years in prison, Mariannina came several times with their son to visit him, but when he was let out, many years later, he chose not to return to Sicily to live with Mariannina and Giuseppe.

After the trials ran their course and Pisciotta died, interest in Giuliano began to subside. There was a realization that concrete answers to the remaining questions about him probably would never be found. Some suspicious observers saw a continuing conspiracy to eliminate one by one those who might be capable of telling the truth, or at least parts of it. When Verdiani died in Rome in 1953 in his mid-sixties, there were those who said that he had been poisoned. Many said the same thing when Cusumano Geloso, the intermediary between Giuliano and leading monarchists, died alone in his Palermo apartment while still a young man. There was no doubt that others died by violence: Benedetto Minasola, assassinated in 1960 in mid-afternoon of a market day in front of San Giuseppe Jato's city hall; the mafioso suspected of poisoning Pisciotta, shot and killed in Palermo in 1961; Pietro Scaglione, the justice official who heard Pisciotta's last "confession," murdered in 1971, by which time he had risen to become the prosecutor general in Palermo.

The guilty parties were never identified in any of these cases. And there were also others. None of these deaths, however, could be tied in a specific way to anything having to do with Giuliano. Anyhow, deaths of police, other public officials, and mafiosi—ordinary citizens too, if they witnessed something they were not supposed to see—were common in Sicily, as they have continued to be.

In the late 1960s and early 1970s, a revival of interest in Giuliano resulted from the investigations of a parliamentary anti-Mafia commission. A major portion of its hearings was devoted to going over the ground of Portella della Ginestra one more time. That the event should be looked into so thoroughly at such a late date was explained by the membership on the commission of leading communist parliamentarians, among them Girolamo Li Causi. Li Causi and his fellow leftists had never given up hope of linking the massacre to leading conservative figures and their political parties, and this opportunity, they realized, might well be their last.

The surviving police officers, most of them retired by then, were called to tell their stories again. Ex-bandits were brought in from their prison cells to tell theirs; for the most part, they lied fully as much as they had on previous occasions. Some others who had possible connections, Prince Alliata, for example, also appeared. In sum, the effort disappointed those who hoped for sensational revelations. Other than for Montalbano's revelation of the Ramirez letter, only bits of new information or, more often, verification of old rumors of a minor nature emerged. Nothing new was said about the memoirs, although it was learned that Giuliano's brown leather folder had been taken by Perenze. Paolantonio, who saw it later, said that it then contained nothing of much interest, except for a list of names and addresses. There were no politicians on it, he testified, although quite a number of Mafia figures were, among them a prominent Italian-American. Curiously, no commission member pressed him to divulge the names.[15]

The memoirs of Gaspare Pisciotta were remembered by Li Causi, and Pietro was brought up from Montelepre to tell the commission about them. Gaspare's younger brother denied that the memoirs ever existed and, furthermore, swore that he had never seen Giuseppe Montalbano—to whom he had once tried to sell them. Pietro, however, was not a very convincing liar and broke down under intense questioning to admit that some of the allegations might be true; but he quickly added that he had two children at home who, if he told the commission what he knew, would no longer be there by the time he returned. Pressed even harder, after making that admission, he regained his bearing and flatly denied even that which he had just said. Pietro was permitted to retire.[16] After two decades and more, the year was 1971, the conspiracy of silence that covered the case of Giuliano was holding. It served Pietro well. He died in 1982, quite young, at 54, but of natural causes.

If the living would not tell the story, various members of the commission hoped that government documents would, and they made a thorough search for all of those that they knew about. Although they found many, some of the key ones that they wanted were not forthcoming. Especially, they wanted one prepared by the Palermo prefect in 1948 that reputedly named Sicilian politicians who had given Giuliano their cooperation and protection. Government spokesmen denied that it ever existed; antigovernment commission members were certain that it had either been destroyed or carefully hidden away.

In the end, the major significance of the commission hearings was the demonstration of concern by conservative politicians over possible new revelations of Giuliano's political connections. The conclusion that they believed there was ground that might best be left unturned was inescapable.[17] There was even a fight over the publication of the commission's documentation. It was won by the majority conservative faction, which voted to publish only selected documents from the collection. Predictably, many of the items that reflected unfavorably on the government were left unpublished. Fortunately, the government critics did not accept defeat. The documents were in the public domain, and a leftwing cooperative completed their publication.

The Long-Lost Girlfriend

In Montelepre, the family of Giuliano would long live in his shadow. Journalists and other writers, both domestic and foreign, frequently sought out especially Mamma Giuliano and Mariannina to get their stories. Often, they were visited by the merely curious who just wanted to see them. Some of the episodes that involved them were bizarre in nature, none more so than one that came to a head in 1960–1961.

A story had been around throughout most of the preceding decade that Giuliano had had a girlfriend in Messina province, in far eastern Sicily, to whom he entrusted his memoirs and a fortune in money and jewels. Not much public attention was paid to the matter, which for the most part was attributed to someone's overactive imagination, but in late 1960 it became a front page story. Maddalena Lo Giudice of the mountain town of Antillo, in Messina province, announced that all of the rumors were true. What was more, she asserted, she also had an 11-year-old son, appropriately named Salvatore, whom Giuliano had fathered! The Giuliano family had known of her early—she first wrote them an anonymous letter a few days after Giuliano died—and, after learning her identity, had dealt with her extensively. It was worth the effort, if for no other reason than because the money, jewels, and memoirs could be construed to belong to them. They had never gotten any satisfaction from her, but the story about the alleged son aroused their interest again.

It turned out to be a messy affair, as for the most part it had always been. Lo Giudice, whose age was given as merely over 30, refused to produce the boy, saying only that he was living in Catania. Mariannina and other members of her family again went to the woman's villa, demanding the memoirs and a visit with the boy. While Lo Giudice hedged, especially on the boy, she did produce a quantity of jewelry that she said Giuliano had left with her. Her father said otherwise. According to him some of it had always been in the family, while a portion had been bought recently from Sansone's jewelry store in Messina. Sansone confirmed the latter claim. So it continued for a while, until, before many weeks had passed, the persistent Mariannina was told by the police to stay out of Messina province for no fewer than three years and Lo Giudice, claiming that she was to star in a film on Giuliano's life, was sent away by her father to a Messina convent. It was hard to conclude that the stories of the Antillo spinster were other than the products of a troubled mind.[18]

Nonetheless, a movie was being made of Giuliano's life, directed by Naples-born Francesco Rosi and released in 1961. In the course of the filming in Sicily, the Giuliano family unsuccessfully sought to secure a legal prohibition of the production, alleging that its portrayal was damaging to the bandit's reputation. In 1962, Rosi brought *Salvatore Giuliano* to Montelepre's main plaza for a free showing. If he expected much of a reaction, he was disappointed. The more than 1000 people in attendance sat through it passively. A reporter was surprised that they showed so little emotion, but in reality, the townspeople had learned to hide their feeling from inquisitive strangers a long time earlier. Also, as one resident commented, the film did not picture something that had happened there, to them; it was only a movie.

The reactions of movie goers elsewhere, and critics, too, were often not dissimilar to those displayed in Montelepre. Rosi's production did not tell Giuliano's story in a satisfactory way. Past the initial scene of his dead body in De Maria's courtyard, it reserved major attention for the investigation of his death and the trial of his men at Viterbo. Giuliano appeared only in occasional flashbacks, and the overall impact was of a man under the power of external forces. Although both Rosi and *Salvatore Giuliano* earned firm positions in the history of the

Italian cinema, the film did not appeal much to general audiences. Done in a near documentary style, it had neither plot nor heroes. As *The New York Times*'s film critic said, its technical brilliance was not accompanied by a "simple, sustained emotional pull." [19] *Salvatore Giuliano* was too celluloid, too detached. It did not portray adequately the drama and the passion of its subject's life.

CHAPTER TWELVE

The Meaning of It

AN UNDERLYING ASSUMPTION OF THIS BOOK is that the history of banditry does not lend itself readily to theorizing.[1] Each episode of banditry, certainly each bandit, originated in a conjunction of personality traits, life situations, individual motivations, societal conditions, and casual happenings, that, in its totality, was unique. This makes the construction of an inclusive explanation of the origins of banditry that goes beyond platitudinous generalities to meaningful specifics severely difficult. It suggests that the history of banditry may more realistically be studied in terms of individual rebellions and closely related episodes.

The following discussion of aspects of historical and social science theory in relation to the origins of banditry is confined to the category of criminality that may be described as traditional rural banditry; it is also confined to the Western world. Giuliano fits well enough into the traditional rural bandit mold, although his career occurred after this type of banditry had disappeared from most of the Western world. He may rightly be considered the last notable example of the kind in Italy. He was also something of a transition figure, like the 1930s depression-era robbers of rural and small-town America. No argument is made here that traditional rural banditry deeply differed from its urban counterpart. But, the setting was different and banditry in traditional rural societies, which were disappearing so fast under the onslaught of rapid urbanization, improved communications, and runaway technology in the mid-twentieth century, seems to be a suitable subject for study.

During the 1960s, interest in old fashioned brigands experienced a resurgence among scholars and the informed reading public from the publication of Eric Hobsbawm's *Bandits*.[2] The noted British marxist historian focussed his attention not on common criminals but rather on a select group that he identified as "social bandits," among whom he quite justifiably counted Giuliano. But, going much beyond setting forth a typology of bandits, he sought also to establish a connection between social bandits and revolution and suggested that social banditry was most likely to appear where traditional societies were moving toward modern industrial organization with its accompanying class struggle. His views have become so popular that in scholarly discussions of banditry they almost invariably are brought up, in spite of considerable evidence that their general application is severely limited.

Social bandits, Hobsbawm wrote, were distinguished from ordinary brigands by virtue of being peasant outlaws who, although branded as criminals by the state, enjoyed the admiration and support of their own communities. He divided them into several categories, the sterling example being the "noble robber." The noble robber was driven outside the law by an act of injustice, he righted wrongs, he had the support of the people, he aided them, he yearned to live honestly and honorably, and so on. It will be recognized that the parallels between the noble robber and Giuliano are striking. Born a peasant, remembered as a good boy, his first crime occasioned by the threat of severe punishment for an infraction of the law that the rich committed with impunity, the near solid identification of his fellow townspeople with him, his giving to the poor, a lack of torture and irrationally brutal crimes on his record, and his betrayal by his best friend—all his qualifications for membership in the world's club of noble robbers were impressive. Unlike so many of his fellow members, whom careless writers and popular fancy admitted to that select group on the most fragile of evidence, he qualified.

Affinities between social bandits and revolution were not generally direct and obvious, Hobsbawm freely conceded. He recognized that bandits seldom became revolutionaries. Rather, their links to revolution lay in unconscious motivation; that is, their violence, expecially when against the state or the wealthy, might rightly be interpreted as the unconscious rejection of unjust societies. In the related part of his overall argument, he sought to establish that the masses of peasants also unconsciously supported revolution. He saw this, he thought, in their interests in tales of bandits and the tendency to sometimes accept them as heroes. He interpreted this to mean that, for the peasants, bandits were symbols of opposition to class oppression and unjust rulers.

The argument from folklore is not a major concern of ours here, but, perhaps, it should be noted in passing that it is not totally inapplicable to Giuliano. Many people did see him as an enemy of unjust authority, at least before May 1947. But, in general, the roots of the support that his area gave him, which we noted early in the book, were more obvious and direct than those Hobsbawm sought to establish.[3] Moreover, the support persisted after his links to the privileged classes and state authority became known. Whether Hobsbawm's contention has much general validity may be debated. Suffice it to say here that popular interest in stories of crime and the occasional heroization of criminals has never been confined to the oppressed. Nor is there evidence that the stories of noble robbers—the alleged symbols of opposition to injustice—originated among the peasantry. They were much more likely to be born in the minds of clever storytellers who recognized their almost universal appeal.[4]

For his overall argument, as regards both folklore and real bandits, Hobsbawm has been criticized as well as frequently imitated. The criticism ranges from allegations that his connecting links were tenuous to suggestions that he knew little of the outlaws on whom he based his arguments. In fact, his data were taken more often from legends, ballads, popular verse, books for the masses, and other highly imaginative accounts than from the hard stuff of history. Such sources, as has often been pointed out, served well his interests in folklore, but they hardly were fitting support for his conclusions about real bandits.

Of course, in the real world, traditional brigands were drawn into armed struggles of various kinds on occasion, as was Giuliano, either because the breakdown of order allowed them freer movement or because they were recruited for their expert use of violence. Whether they then became leftist revolutionaries, defenders of the old order, power and property usurpers in their own behalf, or whatever depended on many things. Most who distinguished themselves from common criminals by joining a cause joined the defenders of the traditional order, like Giuliano. As an anticommunist and opponent of the Sicilian left, he was true to form, as he was when instead of urging the landless to rebel against the landed he demanded that the landlords treat peasants fairly. In adhering to the independence movement, too, he was acting in a predictable manner, for bandits were most likely to be enlisted in causes of that nature. Hobsbawm duly noted all of this and provided numerous and wide-ranging illustrations of it, but at the cost of considerable damage to his larger argument. In the end, he was left with little to support firsthand links between bandits and revolution other than the highly elusive argument of unconscious motivation, which alone does not go far.

Hobsbawm's claim of generalized affinity between the appearance of social bandits and the transition of a society toward capitalism does not seem to have application to the direct origins of Giuliano's initial revolt. The causes of his first crime were not so obscure. They lay rather in the deprivation and disorder left by the war in Sicily. In 1943, the shortage of foodstuffs, together with the existence of the black market and the resultant crackdown ordered by the Allied Military Government, were the obvious external causes of young Giuliano's fall into banditry. Other than for these, the blame lay on him, for his impetuous and violent reaction to being caught trafficking in the black market.

Beyond Giuliano's first crime, a broad interpretation of Hobsbawm's contention seems at first glance to be valid. Sicilian rural society was undergoing severe tensions in the immediate postwar years, as the agrarians and the Mafia sought to defend their archaic order against the peasants and the left. The time of his banditry thus fits comfortably enough into the mold. But, crucially, does this time parallel link him in a significant way to revolutionary aspirations, conscious or unconscious? The answer to this question seems clear. The evidence that would link Giuliano to revolutionary aspirations is weak; the evidence to the contrary is overwhelming. One simply cannot ignore his attack on peasants and the left at Portella della Ginestra on May Day 1947, nor his longstanding, intimate, and far-reaching ties to the Mafia, the agrarians, and the conservative politicians, the mainstays of the old order. He was, above all else, an outlaw who accommodated himself to the existing structure of power. Against such firm evidence, the convoluted argument that he was at heart, or unconsciously, a revolutionary is not particularly relevant. It has more the air of romanticism than reality.

Yet, had Giuliano pursued the unlikely course of breaking out of the old order and joining the left—if he had championed Girolamo Li Causi rather than trying to abduct him—he would have been as near perfect an example of Hobsbawm's social bandit as historians are likely to find. After all, he was an unusually intelligent, attractive, and likeable brigand. Although the roll call of his crimes was indefensibly long by any civilized standard, he was not, within the context of the commonly sordid outlaw world, an exceptionally bad man. He was never completely brutalized by his life outside the law, like many others who plied his trade. His record was clean on torture and casual killings, acts that so often disgrace bandits. What might have happened to him if he had not been caught up in the political currents that were sweeping over Sicily is difficult to say, but maybe, he was saved from extreme degredation by his early association with the separatist movement, in that it gave him a heroic image to value and protect. Likely, too, his youthfulness and early death saved him from a worse record. He was spared the additional years of desperation and increasing hardness that almost irresistably degrade men who, still struggling for freedom and survival, grow into middle age as outlaws. Beyond that, one can attribute Giuliano's relative uprightness to strength of character and the unmistakable concern that he had for his place in history.

Another strand of inquiry into the world of peasants emphasizes the rationality of their responses to alterations in the structural circumstances of their lives.[5] Rather than being bound by tradition and striking out violently in the face of change, they realistically maneuver to take advantage of it in order to advance their interests. They are mentally flexible people, ever on the lookout for opportunities, much like the time-honored images of shrewd peasants in folklore. They distinctly are not Hobsbawm's peasants-turned-brigands, robbing and murdering in alleged moral rage.

When applied to bandits, and to Giuliano in particular, the theory of the rational peasant is not without some apparent validity. Of course, it fits mafiosi much better. They were prime examples of calculating shrewdness and the acquisitive urge. Even so, these are characteristics that successful brigands also shared. In many ways, Giuliano—his mother, too—exemplified the astute peasant. His enterprising activity as a youth in the olive oil business might be recalled and also the arrangement that the family tried to force on the bakers who wanted to go into business in Montelepre. The latter effort was calculated to help build the family fortune in a manner which, on the surface, was legitimate; it was typical Mafia behavior. The amount of wealth that Giuliano's well developed acquisitive urge brought him during his bandit career needs no further comment, except to add that it provided him with so little real profit. This last, discordant note suggests, as the reader may already have decided, that serious problems accompany the effort to equate Giuliano's bandit life to the life of a clever peasant entrepreneur, whatever evidence there is to the contrary.

The rational peasant hypothesis assumes that the actor will act rationally; that he or she will pursue life strategies in which the probable end results are worth reaching. A rational peasant would not choose a course of action that might very well lead to death or a long-term loss of freedom. It is in this sense that the rational peasant idea begins to break down when applied generally to bandits. It would be hard to argue that traditional rural banditry, full-time outlawry, in modern Western society was ever in the main a manifestation of rational behavior. The risks were too great, as they clearly were in Giuliano's time.

Additionally, a perusal of the lives of well-known bandit chiefs suggests that fairly few deliberately chose outlaw careers. The word *fall* often has been used instructively to mark the passing of a person from lawful society to outlawry. It suggests that conditions or circumstances almost irresistibly pushed the person outside the law or that the person acted with little forethought. The application of the first meaning to Giuliano's case might be debated, but the second clearly applies. His fall into outlawry was the consequence of a momentary, foolhardy, desperate, dangerous act of youthful bravado motivated by fear. The element of reasoned judgment, a careful weighing of the act of murdering a *carabiniere* against the probable costs, was missing. To be sure, his shrewdness led him to exploit his outlaw status to the fullest, more than sufficiently to bring him fame and fabulous quantities of loot; but, realistically, there never was much doubt, as he knew, that his early and violent death might be, even most probably would be, the final cost.

None of this is intended as criticism of the rational peasant thesis, or of its exponent, Samuel Popkin. His successful application of it was to Vietnamese peasants not bandits. In the search for a theoretical setting for bandits, however, suggestions have been made that Popkin's ideas might be profitably employed in this area of study, too. Something similar was done by historian Paul Vanderwood, who posited the idea that the Mexican bandits he surveyed were motivated chiefly by the desire for financial gain.[6] The contention cannot be discounted, since being a bandit, by definition, suggests the acquisition of wealth. In his sweeping survey, however, Vanderwood did not provide the detailed histories that would tie the origins of the bandit careers of these men to the profit motive. The fact that they engaged in robbery and extortion, after they were bandits, does not establish that they became bandits specifically for the purpose of enriching themselves. Giuliano's story, as we have seen, would not support such a supposition.

If the foregoing theories do not explain with any precision why Giuliano became an outlaw, neither do other currently fashionable ideas. The social science theories of relative deprivation and frustration-aggression might possibly be applied to him, but being so general in nature, they are more effectively applied to collective criminal or violent behavior. They enlighten us little about why individuals react in different ways when subjected to the same or similar influences, or why, under equally trying circumstances, some become criminals and others do not. Similarly, current attempts to identify psychological traits that may incline individuals toward criminal behavior suffer from a similar defect, in that, too often, the same traits are found in many others who do not become criminals.[7]

It might be wondered if successful and renowned brigand chiefs like Giuliano were really typical of bandits. Might not the more ordinary men who formed the ranks in their bands have fitted better into the theoretical models? In the case of Giuliano's men, some of them already were criminals when they joined his band. They were products of various conjunctions of postwar circumstances similar to the one that produced him. Others were village toughs or Mafia-prone types who were attracted to his ranks, once he demonstrated power and success. Still many others, in contrast, especially his temporary recruits, apparently were men and youths of no particular exception, other than their willingness to confront danger and take very serious risks. They joined Giuliano because he was admired and trusted locally, he was nearby, and he wanted them. More than that, however, the times were extremely hard, and Giuliano offered them employment at good pay. Most of these men, it may be assumed, would not have been attracted to him if better work had been available to them. But, then, the same may be said about Giuliano, too, as well as about many of the regulars in his band. If he had been gainfully employed in legitimate commerce he likely would not have engaged in the illegitimate commerce that led to the fateful confrontation with the police at Quattro Molini.

The point of this discussion seems to be, quite simply, that bad economic conditions made men more likely to become bandits. This lends general support to the social bandit theory, which rests heavily upon the effects that economic deprivation sometimes have on people. It does nothing, on the other hand, to corroborate the rational peasant thesis as applied to banditry. Resorting to banditry could not have been considered a rational act, for, again, the risks were too great. It is true that Giuliano for long protected the core of his band with remarkable success, but even then, many of those who had earlier served in it or on its periphery, as well as their families and friends, were being arrested, tortured, sent off to confinement, and held in prison without trial. Overall, the actions of neither the bandits nor their protectors are adequately explained by a theory that centers on the pursuit of rational self-interest. Nor does it explain the general loyalty of the people of Montelepre to Giuliano. Had rational self-interest been their main motivation, they would have betrayed him to the authorities not long after they began to be subjected to massive police repression.

Despite both scholarly and popular interest in traditional rural bandits, it might be suggested here, in candor, that not too much should be made of their collective existence. For all their renown, they were not very numerous. There were more of them in some times than others, but in Giuliano's time, only some three dozen bands existed in all Sicily, most of them small and short lived. Most Sicilians went untouched in any way by them. This suggests that their presence in immediate postwar Sicily was not broadly significant. It suggests also that, in the main, the histories of these bandits reveal more of significance when they are dealt with as individuals, or as small groups, in their specific settings, than when they are treated as a collective whole.

Our conclusion on the origins of Giuliano's rebellion proposes no new theories. Existing ones that work along the lines where individuals and societies intersect appear to do the job well enough. Too often, theoreticians seem to think that their kite is the only one that will fly. Our conclusion rests on no such assumption. The matters with which it deals are too basic to the complex nature of the human condition to be treated with such confidence. In short, Giuliano possessed personality traits, among them impetuosity, rebelliousness, extreme individualism and self-conceit, as well as bravery and courage, that help to explain his reactions to adversity. As well, he was decidedly romantic and, in his youthful adventuresomeness, dangerously willing to test life's limits. Within the mindset of the society there existed characteristics, such as a perverted sense of individual honor and a preference for settling affairs in extralegal ways, that encouraged criminal behavior. His society was passing through severe tensions, brought on by deprivation, unemployment, and disorders. These were on a scale sufficiently high to draw forth unlawful or abnormal behavior among at least some of those individuals whose psychological configurations and situations in life predisposed them toward it. Lastly, the organs of state authority in the immediate postwar period were too weak to enforce lawful behavior. Yet, none of this predestined Giuliano to the life of an outlaw. Chance, that illusive factor in history, danced through his life, as for good or ill, it seemingly does through the lives of us all. If a circumstance or two, or a happening or two, had been other than they were, Giuliano might have had a very different and much longer life. He might have had the opportunity to grow into old age, a respected citizen of Montelepre or Palermo—or, as he sometimes seemed to want, of a far-off place like New York, Detroit, or Kansas City.

On July 6, 1980, only one day past the thirtieth anniversary of Giuliano's death, Mariannina, her son Giuseppe, and a few representatives of one of the island's small bands of surviving separatists gathered in Montelepre. They came to dedicate a modest little monument to the Sicilian independence movement and to remember Giuliano's services to it. Although the event was public, with speeches and a rosary, and all were welcome, not more than two dozen people participated, dignitaries and spectators combined. The tiny parade that made its way under the separatist banner from the town to the cemetery starkly contrasted to those times of old when firebrand MIS orators, Mariannina by their side, drew throngs to the town's main square. Now, under very different and much subdued circumstances, this anachronistic little gathering pronounced its judgments on Giuliano. Some pretentious words were spoken, but when Mariannina was asked to speak, hers were brief and from the heart. Matronly, in her late fifties, still vivacious and attractive, she said about her brother: "He was good and honest. Turridu did what he did only from fear and out of poverty." [8]

Few would agree that Mariannina had satisfactorily summed up Giuliano's life. There were sides to it left unmentioned, some of them very dark ones. But, even so, that so few came to remember him seemed not altogether fitting. He was Montelepre's most famous son and an integral part of its not-so-distant past. Probably, more than many of its older natives would have wanted to admit, he had reflected their attitudes toward life; otherwise, they would not have borne the heavy cost of protecting him so fully for so long. True, by 1980, he was to many people in Montelepre only a part of a world that used to be. Among the older ones, some still spoke of him guardedly and others with sadness. Many of their memories of that decade were not good ones, and few would have wanted to relive them. But, perhaps, now and then, someone there recalled those years and, momentarily setting aside the bitter memories, echoed what Saverio, a Montelepre native, once told Tommaso Besozzi, "What times those were, eh? When Giuliano was king of the mountain, and made the world tremble." [9]

Appendix

Value of Italian Lire in U.S. Dollars, 1943–1950

Converting Italian currency into dollar equivalents during Giuliano's time is complicated by several factors, including fixed versus black market rates, a multiple-exchange system, and at times, wild fluctuations. What follows is only an attempt to give the reader some indication of how much Giuliano's ransoms were worth.

The Allied Military Government, upon its establishment in 1943, set the exchange rate at 100 lire to the dollar. The first official devaluation occurred in early 1946, when the rate was fixed at 225. In 1946, however, the legal free rate rose to 600; then in 1947 it exceeded 900 at one point before settling back to around 600. During 1948, 1949, and 1950, it was in the 575–625 lire range.

Sources: U.S. Department of Commerce, *World Trade Developments, 1948* (Washington: U.S. Government Printing Office, 1949), pp. 80–81; Shepard B. Clough, *The Economic History of Modern Italy* (New York: Columbia University Press, 1964), pp. 293–96.

Notes

Chapter One

1. "Il memoriale di Frank Mannino," edited by Milziade Torelli, *Vita*, Feb. 2, 1961.

2. The most useful books that treat Giuliano extensively are Tommaso Besozzi, *La vera storia del bandito Giuliano* (Milan: Vitagliano, 1959); Filippo Gaja, *L'esercito della lupara* (Milan: Area, 1962); Gavin Maxwell, *Bandit* (New York: Harper, 1956), the only book on Giuliano in English prior to this one; Salvatore Nicolosi, *La leggenda di Giuliano: Vita di un fuorilegge* (Naples: "Il Tripode," 1977); Vito Sansone and Gastone Ingrascì, *Sei anni di banditismo in Sicilia* (Milan: Le Edizioni Sociali, 1950); Aristide Spanò, *Faccia a faccia con la mafia* (Milan: Mondadori, 1978).

3. Very informative on Sicily at this time is Salvo Di Matteo, *Cronache di un quinquennio: Anni roventi, la Sicilia dal 1943 al 1947* (Palermo: G. Denaro, 1967).

4. The most reliable information on Giuliano's family background was given to me by his sister, Mariannina Giuliano Sciortino, and her son, Giuseppe Sciortino.

5. The principal sources on Giuliano's youth and fall into banditry are Mariannina Giuliano, "Il memoriale di Mariannina Giuliano," *Epoca*, Nov. 3, 1951; Jacopo Rizza, "Un giorno con Giuliano," *Oggi*, Dec. 29, 1949; Salvatore Giuliano, "Il diario di Salvatore Giuliano," *Epoca*, Jan. 29, 1961. The first is by Giuliano's sister, the second by a journalist to whom Giuliano told his story, the third a sketchy diary, confined to 1944–1945, attributed (rightly, it appears) to Giuliano.

6. *Giornale di Sicilia,* July 25, 1947.

7. M. Giuliano, "Il memoriale"; Rizza, "Un giorno"; S. Giuliano, "Il diario."

8. S. Giuliano, "Il diario"; M. Giuliano, "Il memoriale."

9. Gaja, *L'esercito,* pp. 140–41; Sansone & Ingrascì, *Sei anni,* p. 55; *Giornale di Sicilia,* Aug. 25, 1946; Besozzi, *La vera storia,* p. 36.

10. On the image of Sicilian bandits, see Leopoldo Franchetti, *La Sicilia nel*

1876: Condizioni politiche e amministrative, 2d ed. (Florence: Vallecchi, 1925), pp. 27–35, 144–150. Vittorio Consoli, *Briganti siciliani tra storia e leggenda* (Catania: Giuseppe Bonanno, 1968) summarizes the history of banditry in Sicily. A standard work on the period of unification is Franco Molfese, *Storia del brigantaggio dopo l'Unita,* 4th ed. (Milan: Feltrinelli, 1976).

11. S. Giuliano, "Il diario."
12. S. Giuliano, "Il diario." Feb. 19, 1961.
13. Rizza, "Un giorno"; testimony of Giovanni Lo Bianco, in *Testo integrale della relazione della Commissione Parlamentare d'inchiesta sul fenomeno della mafia,* vol. 2 (Rome: Cooperativa Scrittori, 1973), pp. 1632–33, hereinafter cited as *Testo integrale.*
14. Besozzi, *La vera storia,* p. 79. On the value of the lira, see Appendix.
15. Mario Rossani, *Vita segreta del "Sire di Montelepre,"* (Rome: A Chicca, 1955), pp. 35–40; Michael Stern, *No Innocence Abroad* (New York: Random House, 1953), p. 72.
16. S. Giuliano, "Diario"; "Chi è il bandito Giuliano?" *Sicilia del Popolo* (Palermo), Jan. 23, 1946.
17. Ibid., "Chi è il bandito."
18. Ibid.; S. Giuliano, "Il Diario."
19. *Sicilia del Popolo,* Jan. 23, 1946.
20. Giuseppe Calandra, "Memoriale," *ABC,* Jan. 29, 1961; Giuseppe Calandra's testimony, *Testo Integrale,* pp. 1447, 1450, 1681.
21. For example, Calandra, "Memoriale."
22. Rizza, "Un giorno," Jan. 5, 1950.
23. *Sicilia del Popolo,* July 6, 1950.
24. S. Giuliano, "Diario."
25. Bianco's testimony, *Testo integrale,* p. 1633.
26. Maria Lombardo Giuliano, "Mio figlio Giuliano," *L'Europeo,* Nov. 27, 1960, Giuliano's mother's recollections of him.
27. *Sicilia del Popolo,* Sept. 6, 1945.

Chapter Two

1. On Italy, see Denis Mack Smith, *Italy: A Modern History* (Ann Arbor: University of Michigan Press, 1969), and Martin Clark, *Modern Italy, 1871–1982* (London: Longman, 1984); on Sicily, Denis Mack Smith, *A History of Sicily: Modern Sicily after 1713* (New York: Viking, 1968), and M. I. Finley, Denis Mack Smith, and Christopher Duggan, *A History of Sicily* (New York: Viking, 1987).
2. On this movement and conditions in Sicily at the time, see Giuseppe Carlo Marino, *Storia del separatismo siciliano 1943–47* (Rome: Riuniti, 1979); Salvatore Nicolosi, *Sicilia contro Italia: Il separatismo siciliano*

(Catania: Carmelo Tringale, 1981), and for the most complete account, Monte S. Finkelstein, "The Sicilian Separatist Movement: 1943–1946" (Ph.D. disser., Florida State University, 1981). Also, Francesco Paternò Castello di Carcaci, *Il movimento per l'indipendenza della Sicilia, memorie del Duca di Carcaci* (Palermo: S. F. Flaccovio, 1977); Mario Centorrino and Emanuele Sgroi, *Economia e classi sociali in Sicilia, la stagione delle scelte 1943–1947* (Palermo: Vittorietti, 1979); Gaetano Cingari, Francesco Brancato, and Massimo Ganci, *La Sicilia contemporanea* (Naples: Società editrice Storia di Napoli e della Sicilia, 1979); Di Matteo, *Cronache;* Gaja, *L'esercito;* Michele Jacoviello, *La Sicilia dalle lotte per l'indipendenza dall'Italia all'autonomia regionale: 1943–1948*(Naples: Simone, 1978); Santi Correnti, *Storia di Sicilia come storia del popolo italiano* (Milan: Longanesi, 1972), pp. 265–70; Alfredo Li Vecchi, "Autonomismo e separatismo," in *Storia della Sicilia*, vol. 9 (Palermo: Società editrice Storia di Napoli e della Sicilia, 1979), pp. 277–95; Jack E. Reece, "Fascism, the Mafia, and the Emergence of Sicilian Separatism (1919–1943)," *Journal of Modern History* 45 (June 1973): 261–76. Two recent works cover well the overall political and international situation of Italy in the 1940s but pay little attention to Sicily: David W. Ellwood, *Italy 1943–1945* (New York: Holmes and Meier, 1986), and James Edward Miller, *The United States and Italy, 1940–1950* (Chapel Hill: University of North Carolina Press, 1986).

3. Salvo Barbagallo's *Una rivoluzione mancata* (Catania: Bonanno, 1974) is about Canepa. Also see Finkelstein, "The Sicilian Separatist Movement," pp. 16–18, 54–57.

4. Andrea Finocchiaro Aprile, *Il movimento indipendentista siciliana* (Palermo: Libri Siciliani, 1966) is mainly a collection of the separatist leader's speeches and writings, but in his introduction, Massimo Ganci gives an insightful appraisal of the movement and Finocchiaro Aprile's place in it. Also see Finkelstein, "The Sicilian Separatist Movement," pp. 57–67; and Nicolosi, *Sicilia contro Italia*, pp. 25–27, 66–67, and passim.

5. Ganci, in Cingari et al., *La Sicilia contemporanea*, pp. 347–63, delineates Allied interests as they impinged on separatist aims.

6. Gaja, *L'esercito*, pp. 146–54, especially Montalbano's letter to Gaja, pp. 153–54. On Montalbano, see p. 101.

7. A police report placed actual party membership at near 32,000 but noted that authoritative estimates of total support (both members and sympathizers) stood just short of 500,000, out of a total population of approximately 4 million (Report dated Nov. 1, 1944, in PCM, 8/2 1092, 1944–46). See bibliographical note, p. 247, on this source.

8. Cingari et al., *La Sicilia contemporanea*, pp. 348–350; Franco Grasso, ed., *Girolamo Li Causi e la sua azione politica per la Sicilia* (Palermo: Libri Siciliani, 1966); Emanuele Macaluso, *I comunisti e la Sicilia* (Rome: Riuniti, 1970). On Li Causi, also see pp. 44–45.

9. *Sicilia del Popolo,* Mar. 14, 1948, lauds Mattarella's contributions to the party. On the charges, see chapter 6, especially p. 132.

10. Gaja, *L'esercito,* pp. 160–80; Finkelstein, "Sicilian Separatist Movement," pp. 407–409.

11. Marino, *Storia del separatismo,* pp. 105–106.

12. This section provides the nonspecialist a brief overview of the nature and development of the Sicilian Mafia, which formed a vital part of the milieu of Giuliano's life and death. No attempt is made to present in depth the theoretical and historical issues that Mafia specialists raise. From the many studies in the field, I have relied especially on the following. Among the older books, Franchetti, *La Sicilia nel 1876;* Napoleone Colajanni, *Nel regno della mafia* (Rome: La Rivista Popolare, 1900); G. Alongi, *La Mafia* (Bologna: Arnaldo Forni, 1977), a reprint of an 1887 work. Two oft-cited surveys, Michele Pantaleone, *Mafia e politica* 5th ed. (Turin: Einaudi, 1978); and Salvatore Francesco Romano, *Storia della mafia* (Milan: Mondadori, 1966). Other works, some of greater theoretical orientation, that collectively present the Mafia's complexity and variety are Anton Blok, *The Mafia of a Sicilian Village, 1860–1960* (New York: Harper and Row, 1974); Henner Hess, *Mafia and Mafiosi: The Structure of Power,* translated by Ewald Osers (Lexington, Mass.: D. C. Heath, 1970); Filippo Sabetti, *Political Authority in a Sicilian Village* (New Brunswick, N.J.: Rutgers University Press, 1984); Jane Schneider and Peter Schneider, *Culture and Political Economy in Western Sicily* (New York: Academic Press, 1976), pp. 173–201 and passim; Francesco Renda, *Socialisti e cattolici in Sicilia 1900–1904: le lotte agraria* (Caltanissetta-Rome: Sciascia, 1972), with a full chapter devoted to the Mafia, pp. 377–419. Also, the portions that pertain to the Mafia in Finley, et al., *A History of Sicily,* especially pp. 157–58, 180–84, 208–209, 213–14, 225–29, reflect the newer scholarship.

13. Sabetti, in his *Political Authority in a Sicilian Village,* pp. 138–39 and passim persuasively makes this point for the commune that he studied.

14. Ibid., pp. 32–42; Blok, *The Mafia of a Sicilian Village,* pp. 182–89; Enzo D'Alessandro, *Brigantaggio e mafia in Sicilia* (Florence: G. D'Anna, 1959), pp. 109–17 and passim.

15. Pantaleone, *Mafia e politica,* pp. 26–29. On mobster Lucky Luciano's alleged cooperation with U.S. invasion forces, Estes Kefauver's *Crime in America* (New York: Greenwood Press, 1968), concludes that testimony on the charge was contradictory; Rodney Campbell, *The Luciano Project* (New York: McGraw-Hill, 1977), argues that the allegation was true. Finkelstein, "The Sicilian Separatist Movement," pp. 23–25, accepts this latter view.

16. Pantaleone, ibid., pp. 42–43; Cingari et al., *La Sicilia contemporanea,* p. 349.

17. Pantaleone, ibid., pp. 74–75 and passim; the quotation from the police document appeared in *La Voce Socialista* (Palermo), May 14, 1944.

18. Cingari et al., *La Sicilia contemporanea*, p. 349.
19. *Voce Socialista*, Oct. 14, 1944; Pantaleone, *Mafia e politica*, p. 200.
20. The following summary of the history of Sicily's land tenure system is based generally on Denis Mack Smith, "The Latifundia in Modern Sicilian History," in *Proceedings of the British Academy*, vol. 51 (London: Oxford University Press, 1965), pp. 85–124; Enzo Nocifora, *Dal latifondo all'assistenza* (Milan: A. Giuffrè, 1981); Finley et al., *A History of Sicily*, pp. 139–41 and passim; and Sabetti, *Political Authority in a Sicilian Village*, a substantial case history that includes much on this topic.
21. Finley et al., ibid., p. 166.
22. A telling analysis of the contracts and the status of peasants in the "Vallone," a vast area of landed estates in the deep interior to the southeast of Palermo, is found in Luigi Lumia, "La questione agraria nella zona del 'Vallone' in rapporto alle inchieste del 1875," *Nuovi Quaderni del Meridione* 13 (1975): 83–117.
23. On the *Fasci*, see Peter Schneider, "Rural Artisans and Peasant Mobilisation in the Socialist International: The *Fasci Siciliani*," *The Journal of Peasant Studies* 13 (April 1986): 63–81; and, for a much longer treatment, Salvatore Francesco Romano, *Storia dei Fasci Siciliani* (Bari: Laterza, 1959).
24. Renda, *Socialisti e cattolici in Sicilia*; Sabetti, *Political Authority in a Sicilian Village*, pp. 96–104.
25. Finley et al., *A History of Sicily*, p. 202.
26. The foregoing survey of the 1917–1922 period is based on Luisa Accati, "Lotta rivoluzionaria dei contadini siciliani e pugliese nel 1919–1920," *Il Ponte* 26 (October 1970): 1263–93; Giuseppe Carlo Marino, *Partiti e lotta di classe in Sicilia: da Orlando a Mussolini* (Bari: De Donato, 1976); Sabetti, *Political Authority in a Sicilian Village*, pp. 119–32.
27. Franco Ferrarotti, *Rapporto sulla mafia* (Naples: Liguori, 1978), pp. 269–70; Di Matteo, *Cronache*, pp. 248–49.
28. *Voce Socialista*, July 8, 1944; *Voce Communista* (Palermo), July 22, 1944; Gaja, *L'esercito*, pp. 215–20.
29. Macaluso, *I communisti*, p. 27.
30. Antonio Sorgi, in "Quindici anni di lotte contadine," *Il Ponte* 15 (1959): 620–35, refers to aspects of this situation.
31. On Li Causi, see Grasso, *Girolamo Li Causi*; Jacoviello, *La Sicilia*, pp. 62–72.
32. Li Causi's speech was reported in *Voce Comunista*, Sept. 9, 1944; Togliatti's on September 16, 1944. Sidney Tarrow discusses the Communist Party's shift toward a more moderate stance in *Peasant Communism in Southern Italy* (New Haven, Conn.: Yale University Press, 1967), pp. 279–91.
33. Exactly what happened that day at Villalba has been hotly disputed. The account here is based mainly on *Voce Comunista*, Sept. 20, 1944; *Voce della Sicilia*, Aug. 6, 1947; and an official report, Prefect of Caltanissetta

to Minister of Interior, Sept. 24, 1944, in MI Gab., f. 3448, b. 43, 1944. Carcaci, *Il movimento*, pp. 105–106, and *Indipendente*, a clandestine separatist journal without date or place of publication (a copy is in MI Gab., f. 559, b. 8, 1945), dispute the left's account. On the judicial proceedings, see Jocoviello, *La Sicilia*, pp. 76–77, and Emanuele Macaluso, *La mafia e lo stato* (Rome: Riuniti, 1971), pp. 72–73.

34. On the Gullo decrees, Sara Gentile, "Mafia e gabelloti in Sicilia, il PCI dai decreti Gullo al lato di De Gaspari, " *Archivio Storico per la Sicilia Orientale* 69, no. 3 (1973): 491–508; Salvatore La Rosa, "Transformazioni fondiarie, cooperazione, patti agrari," in *Storia della Sicilia*, vol. 9 (Palermo: Società Editrice, Storia di Napoli e della Sicilia, 1970), pp. 126–39.

Chapter Three

1. Text found in MI Gab., f. 11, 315, b. 129, 1945. See bibliography, p. 247, on this source. The translation from the Italian, in this instance as elsewhere, is my own.

2. Carcaci, *Il movimento*, pp. 168–70; S. Giuliano, "Diario," Feb. 5, 12, 1961.

3. Gaja, *L'esercito*, pp. 199–206.

4. *Giornale di Sicilia*, June 20 and 21, 1945, contains the official version of the incident. For a summary of doubts about it and Varvaro's comments, see Salvo Barbagallo, *Randazzo, 17 Giugno 1945: Anatomia di una strage* (Catania: Nuovo Mundo, 1976), pp. 20–22 and passim, and by the same author, *Una rivoluzione mancata*, pp. 119–132. For more information and variant versions, see: Gaja, *L'esercito*, pp. 209, 229–32; Nicolosi, *Sicilia contro Italia*, pp. 291–329; Finkelstein, "The Sicilian Separatist Movement," pp. 500–507.

5. Marino, *Storia del separatismo*, p. 165; Nicolosi, ibid., pp. 330–31.

6. Giuseppe Montalbano, "Memoria illustrativa," in Camera dei Deputati, VII Legislatura, *Documentazione allegata alla Relazione conclusiva della Commissione Parlamentare d'inchiesta sul fenomeno della mafia in Sicilia*, vol. 4, Part 1 (Rome: Senato, 1978), pp. 790–91 (this volume is cited hereafter as *Documentazione*); Gaja, *L'esercito*, pp. 233–35.

7. On the Sagana meeting, see Carcaci, *Il movimento*, pp. 212–25; the recollections of some of the participants, in Marcello Cimino, "L'uragano separatista," *L'Ora* (Palermo), Mar. 24, 1966; testimony of Pasquale Sciortino, in *Testo integrale*, pp. 1550–52.

8. The quotations are from Cimino, "L'uragano separatista," Mar. 24, 1966.

9. On the authorities' knowledge of illegal separatist activities, see High Commissioner Aldisio's report, dated Apr. 15, 1945, in MI Gab., f. 11, 435, b. 35, 1950/52; report of July 15, 1945, by Commanding Officer, "Sabauda Division," in MI Gab., f. 559, b. 8, 1945. Carlo Levi's *Cristo*

si è fermato a Eboli (Turin: Einaudi, 1945) gives a good picture of what confinement was like.

10. The text of Giuliano's proclamation is in Montalbano, "Memoria illustrativa," *Documentazione,* p. 795. On female bandits during the 1860s, see Molfese, *Storia del brigantaggio,* pp. 133–34.

11. "Il memoriale di Mannino."

12. Francesco Barone, *Una vita per Giuliano* (Genoa: Immordino, 1968), pp. 15–19 and passim.

13. "Il memoriale di Mannino."

14. Barone, *Una vita,* p. 26; Giuseppe Montalbano, "Contributo all'inchiesta sulla mafia—Responsabilità (per associazione a delinquere) dei promotori, degli organizzatori e dei capi della banda Giuliano," *Montecitorio* 17 (May 1963): 76–77, containing the text of the police interrogation of Pietro Gaglio of Giuliano's army.

15. *Sicilia del Popolo,* Feb. 23, 1947; testimony of Sciortino, in *Testo integrale,* p. 1555.

16. Giuliano's abductions are described more fully in Chapter V.

17. Transcription of Frank Mannino's court testimony in Felice Chilanti, *Da Montelepre a Viterbo* (Rome: Croce, 1952), p. 142 (a volume hereafter cited as Chilanti); Barone, *Una vita,* p. 53; testimony of Giuseppe Cardella, the Custonaci resident, as reported in *L'Ora,* Oct. 8, 1952.

18. Giuliano, "Diario," Feb. 12, 1961; Nicolosi, *Sicilia contro Italia,* pp. 430–46; testimony of Sciortino, *Testo integrale,* pp. 1552–53. Brunelli's detailed report, dated Dec. 12, is in MI Gab., f. 11, 435, b. 35, 1950/52.

19. Barone, *Una vita,* pp. 23–25.

20. S. Giuliano, "Diario," Feb. 12, 1961.

21. *Voce della Sicilia,* Dec. 28, 1945; S. Giuliano, "Diario," Feb. 12, 1961; Calandra, "Memoriale," Feb. 12, 1961; "Il memoriale di Mannino," Feb. 2, 1961.

22. *Giornale di Sicilia,* Dec. 31, 1945; *Voce della Sicilia,* Dec. 31, 1945.

23. *La Sicilia* (Catania), Jan. 20, 1946; Cimino, "L'uragano separatista," Apr. 1, 1966; report on Gallo's trial, *Giornale di Sicilia,* July 13, 1950; Finkelstein, "The Sicilian Separatist Movement," pp. 555–57.

24. Sansone and Ingrascì, *Sei anni,* pp. 95–96; Nicolosi, *La leggenda,* p. 30.

25. *La Sicilia,* Jan. 5, 1946; *Voce della Sicilia,* Jan. 8, 1946; Barone, *Una vita,* pp. 29–31.

26. See Giuliano's reaction in his "Diario," Feb. 12, 1961.

27. "Il memoriale di Mannino," Feb. 2, 1961.

28. Ibid.; Calandra, "Memoriale," Feb. 12, 1961; *Sicilia del Popolo,* Jan. 9, 1946; *Voce della Sicilia,* Jan. 9, 1946; *La Sicilia,* Jan. 9, 1946, has the estimate of rebel strength.

29. S. Giuliano, "Diario," Feb. 12, 1961; Calandra, "Memoriale," Feb. 12, 1961; *Sicilia del Popolo,* Jan. 9, 1946; *Voce della Sicilia,* Jan. 9, 1946; *La Sicilia,* Jan. 9, 1946.

30. S. Giuliano, "Diario," Feb. 12, 1961; *Sicilia del Popolo,* Jan. 10, 1946.

31. On Montelepre under siege, see *Sicilia del Popolo,* Jan. 20, 1946; Stefano Mannino, *Mitra e poltrone* (Palermo: G. Denaro, 1964), pp. 26–34, written by the town mayor of the time; *La Sicilia,* Feb. 10, 12, 14, 1946; *Voce della Sicilia,* Jan. 16 and 17, 1946; Di Matteo, *Cronache,* p. 442; Nicolosi, *La leggenda,* pp. 37–38; Besozzi, *La vera storia,* p. 47.
32. *Voce della Sicilia,* Jan. 25, 1946.
33. *Voce della Sicilia,* Jan. 17, 1946.
34. *Voce della Sicilia,* Jan. 19, 1946.
35. Prefect, Palermo, to Minister of the Interior, Jan. 27, 1946, in MI Gab., f. 21, 195, b. 192, 1946–47; Sciortino's testimony, *Testo integrale,* pp. 1557–58; *Voce della Sicilia,* Jan. 27, 29, 1946; *La Sicilia,* Jan. 26, 1946.
36. Giuseppe Romita, *Dalla monarchia alla republica* 2d ed. (Milan: Mursia, 1966), pp. 64–65; *Voce della Sicilia,* Feb. 16, 1946.

Chapter Four

1. S. Giuliano, "Diario," Feb. 12, 1961.
2. Barone, *Una vita,* pp. 54–58.
3. S. Giuliano, "Diario," Feb. 19, 1961; General Command, Carabinieri, to Minister of the Interior, Apr. 25, 1946, in PCM, 22692-25/1.6.4., 1944–1947.
4. Report of the High Commission of Sicily to Minister of the Interior, July 8, 1946, in MI Gab., f. 11, 435, b. 35, 1950/52.
5. *La Sicilia,* Feb. 7, 1946.
6. Sciortino's testimony, *Testo integrale,* pp. 1556–57.
7. Marino, *Storia del separatismo,* pp. 224–25; Gaja, *L'esercito,* p. 319.
8. Report of the High Commission of Sicily to Minister of the Interior, July 8, 1946; Marino, *Storia del separatismo,* pp. 210–20.
9. Nicolosi, *Sicilia contro Italia,* pp. 473–80.
10. Maxwell, *Bandit,* p. 86.
11. Mannino, *Mitra e poltrone,* pp. 46–47.
12. Sciortino's testimony, *Testo integrale,* p. 1558; M. Giuliano, "Memoriale," Nov. 10, 1951.
13. Ibid.; Jacopo Rizza interview with Mariannina Giuliano, *Corriere Lombardo,* Oct. 15–16, 1951; Daniele Nello Enriquez, "Turridu, anima mia!," *Domenica del Giornale di Sicilia,* Aug. 10, 1947.
14. Cingari et al., *La Sicilia contemporanea,* pp. 387–95; Roberto La Rosa, "Nel 37–anniversario dell'autonomia," *Sicilia Indipendente,* May 1983, a bitter, pro-separatist view.
15. Marino, *Storia del separatismo,* pp. 210–213; interview with Antonino Varvaro, in *Chiarezza* (Palermo), Apr. 7, 1946.
16. Presidenza della Regione Siciliana, *Le elezioni in Sicilia, 1946–1956* (Milan: A. Giuffrè, 1956), pp. 421–49.

17. Sansone and Ingrascì, *Sei anni*, p. 116.
18. *La Sicilia*, June 6, 1946.
19. Report of High Commission of Sicily to Minister of Interior, July 8, 1946.
20. Giovanni Lo Bianco, "Memoriale del Maresciallo Lo Bianco," *L'Ora*, Dec. 11–12, 1961; Nicolosi, *La leggenda*, pp. 46–48.
21. S. Giuliano, "Diario," Feb. 19, 1961; Calandra, "Memoriale," Feb. 19, 1961; *Voce della Sicilia*, Apr. 2, 1946.
22. Calandra's "Memoriale," Feb. 19, 1961, and his testimony in *Testo integrale*, pp. 1690–91.
23. *Giornale di Sicilia*, Oct. 31, 1946; *L'Ora*, Oct. 31, 1946.
24. Frank Mannino's testimony, as recorded in Chilanti, pp. 143–44.
25. Giuliano's bitterness toward MIS leaders is reported in a document dated July 15, 1946, in *Documentazione*, pp. 171–72.
26. Maxwell, *Bandit*, pp. 101–105.
27. Antonio Terranova's testimony, *Testo integrale*, p. 1599.
28. Barone, *Una vita*, pp. 92–158.
29. *Voce della Sicilia*, July 2, 1946; *Giornale di Sicilia*, July 14, 1946.
30. *Giornale di Sicilia*, Aug. 31, 1946; M. Giuliano, "Il memoriale," Nov. 10, 1951.
31. The three abductions, especially Agnello's, were reported widely in the press. Most notably, see *Voce della Sicilia*, June 18, 1946; *L'Ora*, July 30, Aug. 1, 1946, Dec. 6, 1950; *La Sicilia*, June 26, 1946; *Sicilia del Popolo*, Aug. 1, 1946. Also see Mannino's testimony, in Chilanti, p. 146.
32. Testimony of Mannino at Trapani trial, reported in *Giornale di Sicilia*, Oct. 20, 1950.
33. Tito Parlatore, *L'eccidio di Portella di Ginestra* (Rome: n.p., 1954), p. 39, the text of the prosecution's summary at the Viterbo trial.
34. Testimony of Mannino at Trapani trial, in *Giornale di Sicilia*, Oct. 20, 1950.
35. Calandra, "Memoriale", Feb. 19, 1961; Tommaso Besozzi, "Nuove rivelazioni sul bandito di Montelepre," *Il Giorno* (Milan), Nov. 22, 1957.
36. *Sicilia del Popolo*, Mar. 31, 1950; Besozzi, *La vera storia*, pp. 117–18.
37. Besozzi, ibid., p. 157; *L'Ora*, Feb. 26, 1953; "Il memoriale di Mannino," Feb. 16, 1961.
38. Besozzi, *La vera storia*, p. 170.
39. Testimony of Giovanni Lo Bianco, *Testo integrale*, p. 1639.
40. Terranova's testimony, *Testo integrale*, pp. 1598, 1618, and at the Viterbo trial, as reported in *Sicilia del Popolo*, Feb. 11, 1950.
41. S. Giuliano, "Il diario," Feb. 19, 1961.
42. Nicolò Colicchia's testimony, given at the trial of his abductors, reported in *L'Ora*, Feb. 25, 1953.
43. *L'Ora*, Feb. 14, 1953, Mar. 9, 1957.
44. Besozzi, *La vera storia*, pp. 157–59.

Chapter Five

1. *L'Ora,* Aug. 11, 1946.
2. On dissension in the MIS and the formation of the MIS–DR, see High Commissioner of Sicily to Minister of the Interior, July 8, 1946, in MI Gab., f. 11, 435, b. 35, 1950/52; Prefect of Messina to Minister of the Interior, Feb. 5, 1947, in MI Gab., f. 53, b. 3, 1947, and on Mar. 28, 1947, in f. 11, 435, b. 35, 1950/52; Carcaci, *Movimento,* pp. 344–45; Augusto Leca, "Metamorfosi nel MIS in quattro anni di vita," *Voce della Sicilia,* Jan. 12, Feb. 1 and 2, Mar. 4, 1947; Nicolosi, *Sicilia contro Italia,* pp. 527–32.
3. Carcaci, ibid., p. 351.
4. Giuseppe Quatriglio, "Turi Giuliano Sanfedista," *Domenica del Giornale di Sicilia,* June 29, 1947; testimony of Varvaro, *Testo integrale,* p. 1725.
5. *Elezioni in Sicilia,* pp. 451–72.
6. Nicolosi, *Sicilia contro Italia,* pp. 575–76.
7. M. Giuliano, "Il memoriale." Nov. 10, 1951.
8. Di Matteo, *Cronache,* pp. 483–84; MI Gab., b. 100, 1947, contains numerous police reports of land invasions.
9. *Il Mattino di Sicilia* (Palermo), Apr. 20, 1947. After only a few years, the latifundia system on the old scale was shattered, much of the change brought about by a 1950 law that limited holdings to 200 hectares and obligated owners to improve and use their land under penalty of expropriation. Pantaleone, *Mafia e politica,* p. 167; Francesco Renda, *Movimento de massa e democrazia nella Sicilia del dopoguerra* (Bari: De Donato, 1979), pp. 54–55.
10. A sympathetic characterization of Giuliano as a socialist in sentiment is provided by Oscar Bardi, "Io difendo Giuliano (Intervista con l'avv. Giuseppe Savagnone)," *Domenica del Giornale di Sicilia,* July 13, 1947.
11. The text of the letter is found in Gavin Maxwell, *Dagli amici mi guardi Iddio: Vita e morte di Salvatore Giuliano* (Milan: Feltrinelli, 1957), pp. 11–12. This is the translation into Italian of Maxwell's *Bandit.*
12. *Testo integrale,* pp. 1023, 1701; *L'Ora,* Nov. 26, 1960.
13. The account here is based mainly on Stern's *No Innocence Abroad,* pp. 64–65, 82–92, 100; also see *Sicilia del Popolo,* Feb. 13, 1948, and Maxwell, *Bandit,* pp. 116–19.
14. Nicolosi, *La leggenda,* p. 60; *Sicilia del Popolo,* May 1, 1947.
15. *Chiarezza,* Feb. 2, 1947.
16. *Elezioni in Sicilia,* pp. 451–72.
17. See the deposition of Giovanni Genovese, a Montelepre mafioso who was present, in *Documentazione,* pp. 515–16.
18. Terranova's testimony, *Testo integrale,* pp. 1599–1600.
19. Report of Gen. F. di Giorgis, *Documentazione,* p. 492; recollections of a participant, in Lino Jannuzzi, "Riscostruiamo venti anni dopo la vera

storia della strage di Portella della Ginestra," *L'Espresso,* May 7, 14, 1967.

20. *Voce della Sicilia,* May 2, 1947; report of Bentenino Roselli, Inspector General of Public Security, *Documentazione,* p. 362.

21. Testimony of Ettore Messana, reproduced in Jannuzzi, "Riscostruiamo." For more on Ferreri and his link to Messana, see pp. 123–24.

22. See Li Causi's statement, *Testo integrale,* pp. 1593–94. Also, Terranova's testimony, reported in *Giornale di Sicilia,* June 22, 1950; Tommaso Besozzi, "Nuove rivelazioni sul bandito di Montelepre," *Il Giorno,* Nov. 26, 1957; Nicolosi, *La leggenda,* p. 59; Giuseppe Scianò, "Ricordando Portella della Ginestra," *Sicilia Indipendente,* May 1983.

23. Testimony of one of the hunters, in Chilanti, p. 301; Roselli report, *Documentazione,* pp. 363–64.

24. *Voce della Sicilia,* May 2, 1947; *Sicilia del Popolo,* May 11, 1947.

25. Testimony by Ragusa, in Chilanti, pp. 39–40.

26. Report by Di Giorgis, *Documentazione,* pp. 492–93.

27. M. Giuliano, "Il memoriale," Oct. 16, 1951, containing recollections of a conversation among Giuliano, his sister, and Sciortino; Giuliano's written statement dated July 2, 1950, parts of which appear in *Giornale di Sicilia,* July 6, 1950.

28. Gregorio De Maria's testimony on a conversation with Giuliano, reported in *L'Ora,* Oct. 16, 1951; Nicolosi, *La leggenda,* p. 59.

29. Maxwell, *Bandit,* p. 127.

30. Terranova's testimony, *Testo integrale,* pp. 1599–1600; *Giornale di Sicilia,* July 6, 1950.

31. Excerpt from Giuliano's written statement of May 4, 1950, in Grasso, *Girolamo Li Causi,* p. 175.

32. See, for instance, *Voce della Sicilia* (Sicily's communist organ), May 2, 1947.

33. Scelba's statement on May 2, in Assemblea Costituente, *Atti della Assemblea Costituente, Discussioni dal 16 Aprile al 19 Maggio 1947,* (Rome: Camera dei Deputati, n.d.), pp. 3436–37; *Voce della Sicilia,* May 3, 1947.

34. Ragusa's testimony, in Chilanti, p. 40.

35. *Voce della Sicilia,* May 2, 1947; testimony of Giovanni Lo Bianco, *Testo integrale,* pp. 1629–30; Roselli report, *Documentazione,* p. 351.

36. *Voce della Sicilia,* May 3, 1947; *L'Unità,* June 27, 1950.

37. *Voce della Sicilia,* May 2 and 3, 1947; Lo Bianco's testimony, *Testo integrale,* p. 1630.

38. Pantaleone, *Mafia e politica,* pp. 74–75.

39. Roselli report, *Documentazione,* pp. 350–51.

40. Roselli report, pp. 363–64, and Messana to Chief of Police, June (day illegible), 1947, p. 489, both in ibid.; testimony of a police official, in Chilanti, pp. 39–44; Lo Bianco's testimony, *Testo integrale,* p. 1636.

41. *Giornale di Sicilia,* June 22, 1947.
42. Di Giorgis report, *Documentazione,* pp. 493–94; report by the Palermo *carabinieri,* June 23, 1947, in MI Gab., f. 827, b. 19, 1947; *L'Ora,* June 24, 1947.
43. A photographic reproduction of the actual manifesto is in *Giornale di Sicilia,* June 24, 1947.
44. *Giornale di Sicilia,* June 24, 1947.
45. *L'Ora,* July 13, 1951.
46. The leftist charges are found, among other places, in *Sei anni,* by Sansone and Ingrascì, two of the defendants in Stern's suit. On the trial, see *L'Ora,* June 26, 1952.
47. On Montalbano, *Documentazione,* pp. 684–86; Chilanti, p. 393.
48. Pisciotta's testimony, in Chilanti, pp. 154–64.
49. Ibid., pp. 371–72.
50. *L'Ora,* Dec. 23, 1953.
51. *Testo integrale,* pp. 1461–63.
52. Ibid., pp. 1481–96.
53. Rizza's testimony, in Chilanti, pp. 372–75; *L'Ora,* Aug. 31, Sept. 8, 1951, and *Sicilia del Popolo,* Aug. 31, 1961. Also on the Rizza interview, see pp. 171–73.
54. See p. 132.

Chapter Six

1. Paolantonio's testimony, in Chilanti, pp. 298–301.
2. M. L. Giuliano, "Mio figlio," Nov. 13, 1960.
3. Paolantonio's testimony, *Testo integrale,* p. 1711.
4. The official version of Ferreri's killing appeared in *L'Ora,* June 29, 1947. For additional information and other versions, see Nicolosi, *La leggenda,* pp. 76–78; Centro Siciliano di Documentazione, *1947–1977, Portella della Ginestra: una strage per il centrismo* (Palermo: Centrofiori, 1977), pp. 43–44, 47, 91–92; Giuseppe Loteta, "Riapriamo il dossier su Portella della Ginestra," *L'astrolabio,* Mar. 22, 1970. On the rivalry between the public security police and the *carabinieri,* see pp. 165–66.
5. Scelba to Commander, Carabinieri, Rome, July 29, 1947, in MI Gab., f. 827, b. 19, 1947.
6. *Sicilia del Popolo,* July 2, 1947.
7. *Sicilia del Popolo,* July 10, 13, 1947.
8. Sciortino's testimony, *Testo integrale,* pp. 1559–64, 1571–81; M. Giuliano, "Il memoriale," Oct. 27 and Nov. 10, 1951; Father Di Bella's testimony, in Chilanti, pp. 12–14; Mannino, *Mitra e poltrone,* pp. 127–63.
9. *Giornale di Sicilia,* Nov. 22, 1947.
10. *L'Ora,* Jan. 9, 1948.
11. M. Giuliano, "Il memoriale," Oct. 27 and Nov. 10, 1951; *Giornale di Sicilia,* Jan. 24, 1950; Calandra, "Memoriale," Feb. 26, 1961.

12. Court testimony in *L'Ora,* May 16, 18, 1951, in Chilanti, pp. 147–48, and in Jannuzzi, "Ricostruiamo"; quotations are from letters of Giuliano, in Grasso, *Girolamo Li Causi,* pp. 174–75. One of those who sought to prove the charges against Mattarella was the social activist and scholar Danilo Dolci. His evidence, as well as the legal problems that its public release brought him, are presented in his book, *The Man Who Plays Alone,* trans. Antonia Cowan (New York: Pantheon, 1968), especially pp. 223–24, 338–39, 353–54.

13. Morina's report, in Sansone and Ingrascì, *Sei anni,* pp. 163–64.

14. Testimony of Mannino and Terranova, in Chilanti, pp. 145, 149–50.

15. For Giuliano's letters, see *Giornale di Sicilia,* Apr. 15 and 18, 1948; Terranova's testimony on the planned radio broadcast is found in Chilanti, p. 150.

16. *Elezioni in Sicilia,* pp. 473–99.

17. Pisciotta's testimony, in Chilanti, p. 156; *L'Ora,* Sept. 8, 1951; Pantaleone, *Mafia e politica,* pp. 131–32.

18. July 18, 1948.

19. *L'Ora,* Feb. 3, 1955.

20. Rizza, "Un giorno," Jan. 5, 1950.

21. Helpful in elucidating the meaning of the killing of Santo Fleres and Giuliano's relations with the Mafia in this period are Michele Pantaleone, "La mafia e il potere," *L'Espresso,* Dec. 21, 1958; Spanò, *Faccia a faccia,* p. 136; Nicolosi, *La leggenda,* pp. 80–82; Jacopo Rizza, "Così trovai Giuliano," *Epoca,* Aug. 25, 1951; Sansone and Ingrascì, *Sei anni,* pp. 167–68; Maxwell, *Bandit,* pp. 141–43.

22. Quoted in Spanò, *Faccia a faccia,* p. 136.

Chapter Seven

1. Ugo Luca report, dated Feb. 1, 1950, in *Documentazione,* p. 81.

2. M. L. Giuliano, "Mio figlio Giuliano," Nov. 13, 1960.

3. Spanò, *Faccia a faccia,* pp. 139–42.

4. *L'Ora,* Sept. 15, 1948.

5. The letter is quoted in *Giornale di Sicilia,* Dec. 16, 1948.

6. *Giornale di Sicilia,* May 7, 1948; *L'Ora,* May 1, 1954.

7. *Sicilia del Popolo,* Aug. 5, 1948; *L'Ora,* May 25, 1960.

8. *Giornale di Sicilia,* Aug. 28, 1948.

9. *Sicilia del Popolo,* Oct. 17, 1948.

10. *Giornale di Sicilia,* Nov. 25, 1948; *Sicilia del Popolo,* Nov. 25, 1948; "Il memoriale di Mannino," Feb. 16, 1961.

11. *Sicilia del Popolo,* Dec. 1, 1948.

12. *L'Ora,* Dec. 17, 1948; *Giornale di Sicilia,* Dec. 24 and 25, 1948.

13. *Sicilia del Popolo,* Nov. 9, 1948.

14. This description of Montelepre in late 1948 is based on Carlo Soresi, in

Sicilia del Popolo, Oct. 19, Nov. 9, Dec. 25, 1948, and Enzo Perrone, *L'Ora,* Dec. 29, 1948.

15. M. L. Giuliano, "Mio figlio," Nov. 13, 1960.
16. "Il memoriale di Mannino," Feb. 23, 1961; Terranova's testimony, *Testo integrale,* p. 1618.
17. Mannino's testimony, in Chilanti, pp. 140–41; *Giornale di Sicilia,* Sept. 22, 1949.
18. Mannino's testimony, *Testo integrale,* pp. 1530–31; *L'Ora,* Feb. 19, 1949; *Giornale di Sicilia,* May 24, Sept. 22, 1949.
19. "Il memoriale di Mannino," Feb. 23, 1961.
20. M. L. Giuliano, "Mio figlio," Nov. 13, 1960; "Il memoriale di Mannino," Feb. 2 and 9, 1961; General Inspectorate to Chief of Police, Oct. 1, 1947, in *Documentazione,* p. 499.
21. Besozzi, in *La vera storia,* p. 142, uses the quoted phrase. The following is based mainly on Cyliakus' own account, "Voi parlate con Giuliano," *Oggi,* Jan. 23 and 27, Feb. 3 and 10, 1949. Other sources are noted.
22. *Giornale di Sicilia,* Mar. 15, 16, 19, 23, 25, 27, 1949; Inspector General Verdiani to Minister of the Interior, Mar. 13, 1949, in PCM, 15.2, n. 36697, 1949.
23. "Il memoriale di Mannino," Feb. 16, 1961.
24. *L'Ora,* Mar. 15, 1949.
25. Spanò, *Faccia a faccia,* p. 145.
26. M. Giuliano, "Memoriale," Nov. 3, 1951; "Il memoriale di Mannino," Feb. 16, 1961.
27. Besozzi, *La vera storia,* pp. 141–42; Maxwell, *Bandit,* p. 96.
28. See pp. 171–73.

Chapter Eight

1. *Sicilia del Popolo,* Feb. 18, 1949.
2. *L'Ora,* Feb. 19, 1949.
3. *Giornale di Sicilia,* July 6, 1947; *L'Ora,* July 19, 1951, Mar. 11, 1953.
4. *Giornale di Sicilia,* Jan. 27, 1949; *L'Ora,* Jan. 27, 1949.
5. *Giornale di Sicilia,* Apr. 8, 1949; *L'Ora,* Apr. 9, 1949; Sansone and Ingrascì, *Sei anni,* pp. 180–82.
6. *Giornale di Sicilia,* Apr. 20, 1949.
7. Verdiani's report is in *Documentazione,* pp. 290–94.
8. Ibid.; *L'Ora,* May 7, 1949.
9. *L'Ora,* May 4 and 8, 1949.
10. *Giornale di Sicilia,* May 20, 1949.
11. *L'Ora,* June 2, 28, 1949; *Sicilia del Popolo,* June 7, 1949; *Giornale di Sicilia,* June 8, 1949.
12. *Sicilia del Popolo,* June 26, 1949.
13. *Giornale di Sicilia,* July 3 and 5, 1949.

14. *Sicilia del Popolo,* July 10 and 12, Aug. 12, 1949; *L'Ora,* Aug. 31, 1954, Sept. 23, 1955, Nov. 13, 1958; Pantaleone, "La mafia e il potere"; Felice Chilanti, Mario Farinella, Enzo Lucchi, and Enzo Perrone, "Tutto sulla mafia," *L'Ora,* Nov. 13, 1958.
15. Paolantonio's testimony, *Testo integrale,* p. 1450.
16. *Giornale di Sicilia,* July 23, 1949.
17. Testimony by Verdiani, in Chilanti, pp. 272–73, and by Miceli, pp. 344, 356; Spanò, *Faccia a faccia,* pp. 167–68.
18. The most complete story of the attempted abduction of Mattarella near Alcamo is found in Pantaleone, "La mafia e il potere," Dec. 21, 1958. On it and the other attempts, also see *Sicilia del Popolo,* Aug. 9, 1949; letter by Mattarella, in *L'Espresso,* Jan. 11, 1959, denying that the attempt ever occurred; Terranova's testimony, in Chilanti, p. 148; Cyliakus, "Voi parlate con Giuliano," Feb. 3, 1949.
19. Pantaleone, "La mafia e il potere," Dec. 21, 1958.
20. Reports by Verdiani on Aug. 20 and 31, and by Colonel Lo Denti on Aug. 20, in MI Gab., f. 1489/12, b. 19, 1949. The Palermo press reported the incident extensively.
21. *Documentazione,* pp. 199–211.
22. Testimony by Luca, in Chilanti, p. 292.
23. Luca's testimony, ibid., pp. 287, 291.

Chapter Nine

1. On Luca, Spanò, *Faccia a faccia,* p. 174, and Maxwell, *Bandit,* p. 152; on Perenze, Maxwell, pp. 152–53.
2. Luca's plans are outlined in his report dated Oct. 8, 1949, *Documentazione,* pp. 19–23; also see Perenze's testimony, *Testo integrale,* pp. 1437–38.
3. Among other such statements, see Nicolosi, *La leggenda,* p. 46.
4. For Luca's brief remarks to the press, see *Giornale di Sicilia,* Sept. 16, Oct. 27, 1949.
5. *Sicilia del Popolo,* Sept. 7, 1949.
6. *Giornale di Sicilia,* Sept. 8, 1949; Palermo Prefect to Minister of the Interior, in MI Gab., f. 1489/1, b. 18, 1949.
7. Luca summarized the events and results of the entire campaign in his report dated July 31, 1950, in *Documentazione,* pp. 139–50.
8. Rizza, "Un giorno," Jan. 5, 1950.
9. Ibid.; *Giornale di Sicilia,* Oct. 14 and 15, 1949.
10. Luca's summary report, *Documentazione,* pp. 139–50.
11. Pisciotta's testimony, in Chilanti, p. 163; Nicolosi, *La leggenda,* p. 50.
12. *Giornale di Sicilia,* Dec. 22, 1949, Jan. 27, 29, 1950.
13. *Documentazione,* pp. 61–62.

14. Marotta's testimony, in Chilanti, pp. 347–48, and De Maria's memoir, ibid., pp. 68–72.
15. Testimony of Marotta, Miceli, Albano, and Pisciotta, in ibid., pp. 346–52; Spanò, *Faccia a faccia,* pp. 196–98.
16. Report of Verdiani's testimony, *L'Ora,* July 25, 1951.
17. Lo Bianco, "Memoriale," Dec. 21 and 22, 1961.
18. Extract from the Viterbo sentence, in Gaja, *L'esercito,* pp. 357–62.
19. *Giornale di Sicilia,* Jan. 4, 22, 1950; *L'Unità,* Jan. 22, 1950.
20. *Giornale di Sicilia,* Jan. 27, 1950.
21. In Chilanti, pp. 193–94.
22. Lo Bianco's testimony, *Testo integrale,* p. 1659.
23. De Maria's memoir, in Chilanti, pp. 68–74.
24. Francesco Bresàola, *La giovinezza di Emilio Salgari* (Verona: "I.C.A.," 1963).
25. *L'Ora,* Sept. 15, 1948.
26. Article by Enzo Perrone (who saw the notebook), *L'Ora,* Oct. 16, 1952.
27. Chilanti, p. 359.
28. Paolantonio's testimony, *Testo integrale,* p. 1707.
29. Lo Bianco's story of this period is found in his "Memoriale" and in *Testo integrale,* pp. 1648–56. Calandra's "Memoriale," covers much the same ground but is less valuable.
30. *Giornale di Sicilia,* Mar. 14, 1950; *Sicilia del Popolo,* May 14, 1950.
31. For other examples of this practice, see Sanna-Salaris, *Una centuria di delinquenti sardi* (Turin: Bocca, 1902), pp. 98–109; and Billy Jaynes Chandler, *The Bandit King: Lampião of Brazil* (College Station: Texas A&M University Press, 1978), pp. 207–208.
32. Mannino's testimony, in Chilanti, pp. 142–46.
33. *Sicilia del Popolo,* Jan. 20, 1950.
34. Lo Bianco's testimony, *Testo integrale,* p. 1651.
35. *Giornale di Sicilia,* Apr. 11, 1950.
36. The text of the letter is in *L'Ora,* May 31, 1951.
37. The text is in Gaja, *L'esercito,* pp. 382–90.
38. In *Documentazione,* pp. 121–23.
39. M. Giuliano, "Il memoriale," Nov. 24, 1951; M. L. Giuliano, "Mio figlio," Nov. 20, 1960.
40. *Giornale di Sicilia,* June 26, 1950.

Chapter Ten

1. The best account of the betrayal of Giuliano is Lo Bianco's "Memoriale," especially the Dec. 22 and 29 installments, and his testimony, in *Testo integrale,* pp. 1648–56; also see Luca's testimony, in Chilanti, pp. 291–94, and Nicolosi, *La leggenda,* pp. 104–10.
2. On the relationship of the two men, see especially M. Giuliano, "Il memoriale," Nov. 17 and 24, 1951.

3. Spanò, *Faccia a faccia*, pp. 185–86. Spanò, the son of one of the heads of the antibandit campaign, was privy to "inside" Public Security Police information.

4. *Giornale di Sicilia*, July 6, 1950; *L'Ora*, June 5, 1951; *Giornale d'Italia* (Rome), May 13, 1952.

5. Spanò, *Faccia a faccia*, p. 200.

6. Luca's and Marotta's testimony, in Chilanti, pp. 296, 369–70.

7. Lo Bianco, *Testo integrale*, p. 1654.

8. Perenze's testimony on what Pisciotta told him, *Testo integrale*, pp. 1432–37; De Maria's memoir, in Chilanti, pp. 72–74.

9. Perenze's report, *Documentazione*, pp. 157–63.

10. In addition to Besozzi's articles, entitled "Un segreto sulla fine di Giuliano," see his *La vera storia*, pp. 212–23.

11. *Giornale di Sicilia*, July 27, 1950.

12. Perenze's testimony, *Testo integrale*, pp. 1432–39; De Maria's memoir, in Chilanti, pp. 72–74; Pisciotta's admissions came at the Viterbo trial, although without details; also see Lo Bianco's "Memoriale," Jan. 2–3, 1962, and an article (author's name not given), "Come Pisciotta uccise Giuliano," *Oggi*, Apr. 26, 1951. The text of the "in house" investigation of Luca's conduct by a commission of three generals is in *Testo integrale*, pp. 1379–81.

Controversy over the circumstances of Giuliano's death continued for several years. New theories were advanced as to the authorship of the action and the place of its occurrence. It was said, variously, that not Pisciotta but the police, probably Perenze, had killed him; that he was killed in Monreale or as he was transported bound hand and foot from Monreale to Castelvetrano; that the Monreale Mafia killed him and sold his body to the police; and that an American mafioso was hired to eliminate him. No "hard" evidence supported any of these theories. On them, see Tommaso Besozzi, "Riapriamo il caso Giuliano," *L'Europeo*, Nov. 26, Dec. 3, 1950, and, by the same author, "Nuove rivelazioni," *Il Giorno*, Nov. 22, 23, 26, 27, 1957; *L'Ora*, Aug. 22, Sept. 22, 1951; Giuseppe Montalbano, *L'autonomia della Regione Siciliana e alcune questioni di diritto processuale penale* (Palermo: G. Mori, 1952), pp. 104–105.

13. *Giornale di Sicilia*, July 8, 9, 19, 20, 1950.

Chapter Eleven

1. Perenze's testimony, in Chilanti, pp. 321–22; *Giornale di Sicilia*, Dec. 6, 1950; Tommaso Besozzi, "La verità sulla morte di Giuliano," *L'Europeo*, Dec. 17, 1950.

2. See, for example, the report in *Giornale d'Italia*, Feb. 9, 1952.

3. Chilanti, p. 97

4. Introduction to *Testo integrale*, pp. 1007–1008, 1021.

5. Pantaleone, *Mafia e politica,* p. 129; *Giornale di Sicilia,* Sept. 20, 1949. Sciortino denied the charge, but said that he believed the memoir existed (*Testo integrale,* pp. 1587–88).
6. On the memoirs, see testimony in Chilanti, especially pp. 158–59, 260, 288–90, 320, 322, 424–25; also *Giornale d'Italia,* May 16, 1951, and *L'Ora,* Oct. 20, 1951.
7. Testimony in Chilanti, pp. 400, 412; *L'Ora,* Oct. 12, 17, 18, 1951.
8. Testimony in Chilanti, pp. 423–34; *L'Ora,* Oct. 26 and 30, 1951.
9. *L'Ora,* Oct. 18, 1951.
10. *Giornale d'Italia,* May 6, 1952; *L'Ora,* May 14, 1954.
11. Maxwell, *Bandit,* pp. 207–68.
12. *L'Ora,* Feb. 10–12, 16, 17, Mar. 2, 3, 29, 1954, Feb. 11, 1955, Aug. 7, 1956; testimony in *Testo integrale,* pp. 1521–22, 1609–11, 1735.
13. Montalbano's testimony, *Documentazione,* pp. 712–13, and *Testo integrale,* pp. 1741–45.
14. *L'Ora,* Apr. 22, 1953, Mar. 29, Aug. 12, 1956; Sciortino's testimony, *Testo integrale,* pp. 1561–62, 1580–84.
15. Sciortino's testimony, ibid., pp. 1436, 1452–53.
16. Ibid., pp. 1729–32.
17. Giuseppe Loteta, "Riapriamo," Mar. 15, 1970.
18. *L'Ora,* Apr. 21, 1953, Nov. 28, Dec. 2, 3, 6, 1960, Jan. 25, 26, 1961; Renzo Trionfera, "Il figlio di Giuliano," *L'Europeo,* Dec. 18, 1960.
19. *L'Ora,* June 20, 1961, Mar. 8, 1962. On the film, see R. T. Witcombe, *The New Italian Cinema: Studies in Dance and Despair* (New York: Oxford University Press, 1982), pp. 159–60, and Mira Liehm, *Passion and Defiance: Films in Italy from 1942 to the Present* (Berkeley: University of California Press, 1984), pp. 212–13; Howard Thompson's review appeared in *The New York Times,* Sept. 8, 1964.

Chapter Twelve

1. On some of the difficulties in theorizing about the causes of banditry, see Dretha M. Phillips, "Latin American Banditry and Criminological Theory," in Richard W. Slatta, ed., *Bandidos: The Varieties of Latin American Banditry* (New York: Greenwood Press, 1987), pp. 181–90.
2. Hobsbawm's early ideas on bandits were presented in *Primitive Rebels* (New York: Norton, 1965), pp. 13–29 and passim, a book originally published in 1959. *Bandits* first appeared in 1969, but the revised edition (New York: Pantheon Books, 1981) is recommended instead. In it, the author refers to various critiques of his ideas and adds his own later thoughts on the subject. I have discussed the social bandit theory more fully in *The Bandit King,* pp. 240–47, and "Brazilian *Cangaceiros* as Social Bandits," in *Bandidos,* pp. 97–112.
3. See pp. 19–21.

4. Chandler, "Brazilian *Cangaceiros*," pp. 103–105.

5. The rational peasant thesis is set forth in Samuel L. Popkin, *The Rational Peasant: The Political Economy of Rural Society in Vietnam* (Berkeley: University of California Press, 1979), especially pp. 1–31, 243–267.

6. Paul J. Vanderwood, "Nineteenth-Century Mexico's Profiteering Bandits," in *Bandidos*, pp. 11–31, and the same author's *Disorder and Progress: Bandits, Police and Mexican Development* (Lincoln: University of Nebraska Press, 1981).

7. The social science and psychological literature on these subjects is extensive. On the former, a good place to start is Ted Robert Gurr, *Why Men Rebel* (Princeton, N.J.: Princeton University Press, 1970), whereas Stanton E. Samenow, *Inside the Criminal Mind* (New York: Times Books, 1984) is an interesting example of the latter.

8. *Gazzetta del Sud* (Palermo), July 7, 1980; *Il Diario di Palermo*, July 8, 1980.

9. Quoted in Besozzi, *La vera storia*, p. 48.

Bibliography

Documents

The Archivio Centrale dello Stato in Rome contains valuable documents for the study of Giuliano and his times. The papers that I used were from the following governmental bodies, especially the second (which has responsibility for internal security): Presidenza del Consiglio dei Ministri (cited herein as PCM); and Ministro dell'Interno (MI Gab.)

My search for documents was made easier by the parliamentary commission that, in the late 1960s and early 1970s, engaged in a far-reaching investigation of the Mafia and its links. It accumulated an impressive array of documentation and testimony, a portion of which it ordered published. The volume that contains the material dealing with Giuliano is Camera dei Deputati, VII Legislatura, *Documentazione allegata alla Relazione conclusiva della Commissione Parlamentare d'inchiesta sul fenomeno della mafia in Sicilia,* vol. 4, Part 1 (Rome: Typografia del Senato, 1978); it is cited here as *Documentazione.*

Out of a desire to protect conservative interests, the majority on the commission voted to publish only a selected portion of the accumulated documents. The documents were now in the public domain, however, and a leftist group published the rest in three immense volumes, the following of which, in addition to much else, contains over 700 pages of documents and testimony on Giuliano in a section entitled "Relazione sui rapporti tra mafia e banditismo in Sicilia." It is *Testo integrale della relazione della Commissione Parlamentare d'inchiesta sul fenomeno della mafia.* vol. 2 (Rome: Cooperativa Scrittori, 1973); it is cited here as *Testo integrale.*

Some of the documents pertaining to the 1943–1950 period are not yet accessible to researchers. This is true of any that may someday come to the Archivio di Stato in Palermo. It is also true of the official records of trial proceedings. Of course, the trials themselves are public and, fortunately, the press carries extensive reports of popular ones. Also, nothing prevents interested individuals from making their own transcripts of the testimony. Documents introduced as evidence also find their way to the public, mostly through lawyers who "leak" them or openly distribute them to reporters. The following volume, compiled by a well-known writer-journalist, largely substitutes for the unavailability of the official record in the important Viterbo trial. It contains over 400 pages of trial testimony, in addition to some of the documents introduced into the proceedings and, occasionally, the compiler's comments. It is Chilanti, Felice. *Da Montelepre a Viterbo* (Rome: Croce, 1952); it is cited here as Chilanti.

In addition, many of the items listed under "Works Cited" are also primary sources, either because they contain firsthand recollections or because they, too, reprint documents.

Newspapers

Chiarezza (Palermo)
Corriere Lombardo (Turin)
Il Diario di Palermo
Gazzetta del Sud (Palermo)
Il Giornale d'Italia (Rome)
Giornale di Sicilia (Palermo)
L'Ora (Palermo)
Il Mattino di Sicilia (Palermo)
La Sicilia (Catania)
Sicilia del Popolo (Palermo)
L'Unità (Rome)
La Voce Comunista (Palermo)
La Voce della Sicilia (Palermo)
La Voce Socialista (Palermo)

Works Cited

Accati, Luisa. "Lotta rivoluzionaria dei contadini siciliani e pugliesi nel 1919–1920." *Il Ponte* 26 (October 1970): 1263–93.

Alongi, G. *La mafia.* Turin: Bocca, 1887; reprint ed., Bologna: Arnaldo Forni, 1977.

Assemblea Costituente. *Atti della Assemblea Costituente, Discussioni dal 16 Aprile al 19 Maggio 1947.* Rome: Camera dei Deputati, n.d.

Barbagallo, Salvo. *Randazzo, 17 Giugno 1945: Anatomia di una strage.* Catania: Nuovo Mondo, 1976.

———. *Una rivoluzione mancata.* Catania: Bonanno, 1974.

Bardi, Oscar. "Io difendo Giuliano (Intervista con l'avv. Giuseppe Savagnone)." *Domenica del Giornale di Sicilia,* July 13, 1947.

Barone, Francesco. *Una vita per Giuliano*. Genoa: Immordino, 1968.
Besozzi, Tommaso. "Nuove rivelazioni sul bandito di Montelepre." *Il Giorno*, November 22, 23, 26, 27, 1957.
———. "Un segreto sulla fine di Giuliano." *L'Europeo*, July 16 and 23, 1950.
———. "Riapriamo il caso Giuliano." *L'Europeo*, November 26, December 3, 1950.
———. *La vera storia del bandito Giuliano*. Milan: Vitagliano, 1959.
———. "La verità sulla morte di Giuliano." *L'Europeo*, December 17, 1950.
Blok, Anton. *The Mafia of a Sicilian Village, 1860–1960*. New York: Harper and Row (Harper Torchbook), 1975.
Bresàola, Francesco. *La giovinezza di Emilio Salgari*. Verona: "I.C.A.," 1963.
Calandra, Giuseppe. "Memoriale." *ABC*, January 29, February 5, 12, 19, 26, March 5, 1961.
Campbell, Rodney. *The Luciano Project*. New York: McGraw-Hill, 1977.
Carcaci, Francesco Castello di Paternò. *Il movimento per l'indipendenza della Sicilia: Memorie del Duca di Carcaci*. Palermo: S. F. Flaccovio, 1977.
Centorrino, Mario, and Emanuele Sgroi. *Economia e classi sociali in Sicilia: La stagione delle scelte (1943–47)*. Palermo: Vittorietti, 1979.
Centro Siciliano di Documentazione. *1947–1977, Portella della Ginestra: Una strage per il centrismo*. Palermo: Centrofiori, 1977.
Chandler, Billy J. *The Bandit King: Lampião of Brazil*. College Station: Texas A&M University Press, 1978.
———. "Brazilian *Cangaceiros* as Social Bandits: A Critical Appraisal." In *Bandidos: The Varieties of Latin American Banditry*, edited by Richard W. Slatta, pp. 97–112. New York: Greenwood Press, 1987.
"Chi è il bandito Giuliano." *Sicilia del Popolo*, January 23, 1946.
Chilanti, Felice, Mario Farinella, Enzo Lucchi, and Enzo Perrone. "Tutto sulla mafia." *L'Ora*, November 13 and 14, 1958.
Cimino, Marcello. "L'uragano separatista." *L'Ora*, March 6, 9, 11, 13, 16, 17, 22, 24, 30, April 1, 1966.
Cingari, Gaetano, Francesco Brancato, and Massimo Ganci. *La Sicilia contemporanea*. Naples: Società editrice Storia di Napoli e della Sicilia, 1979.
Clark, Martin. *Modern Italy, 1871–1982*. London: Longman, 1984.
Colajanni, Napoleone. *Nel regno della mafia*. Rome: La Rivista Popolare, 1900.
"Come Pisciotta uccise Giuliano." *Oggi*, April 26, 1951.
Consoli, Vittorio. *Amori e tromboni: Briganti siciliani tra storia e leggenda*. Catania: Giuseppe Bonanno, 1968.
Correnti, Santi. *Storia di Sicilia come storia del popolo italiano*. Milan: Longanesi, 1972.
Cyliakus, Maria. "Voi parlate con Giuliano." *Oggi*, January 23 and 27, February 3 and 10, 1949.

D'Alessandro, Enzo. *Brigantaggio e mafia in Sicilia*. Florence: G. D'Anna, 1959.

Di Matteo, Salvo. *Cronache de un quinquennio: Anni roventi, la Sicilia dal 1943 al 1947*. Palermo: G. Denaro, 1967.

Dolci, Danilo. *The Man Who Plays Alone*. Translated by Antonia Cowan. New York: Pantheon, 1968.

Ellwood, David W. *Italy 1943–1945*. New York: Holmes and Meier, 1986.

Enriquez, Daniele N. "Turridu, anima mia!" *Domenica del Giornale di Sicilia*, August 10, 1947.

Ferrarotti, Franco. *Rapporto sulla mafia*. Naples: Liguori, 1978.

Finkelstein, Monte S. "The Sicilian Separatist Movement." Ph.D. dissertation, Florida State University, 1981.

Finley, M. I., Denis Mack Smith, and Christopher Duggan. *A History of Sicily*. New York: Viking, 1987.

Finocchiaro Aprile, Andrea. *Il movimento indipendentista siciliano*. Edited by Massimo Ganci. Palermo: Libri Siciliani, 1966.

Franchetti, Leopoldo. *La Sicilia nel 1876: Condizioni politiche e amministrative*, 2d ed. Florence: Vallecchi, 1925.

Gaja, Filippo. *L'esercito della lupara*. Milan: Area, 1962.

Gentile, Sara. "Mafia e gabelloti in Sicilia: Il PCI dai decreti Gullo al lato di De Gasperi." *Archivio Storico per la Sicilia Orientale* 69, no. 3 (1973): 491–508.

Giuliano, Maria Lombardo. "Mio figlio Giuliano." *L'Europeo*, November 13, 20 and 27, 1960.

Giuliano, Mariannina. "Il memoriale di Mariannina Giuliano." *Epoca*, October 27, November 3, 10, 17, 24, 1951.

Giuliano, Salvatore. "Il diario di Salvatore Giuliano." *Epoca*, January 29, February 5, 12, 19, 1961.

Grasso, Franco, ed. *Girolamo Li Causi e la sua azione politica per la Sicilia*. Palermo: Libri Siciliani, 1966.

Gurr, Ted Robert. *Why Men Rebel*. Princeton, N.J.: Princeton University Press, 1970.

Hess, Henner. *Mafia and Mafiosi: The Structure of Power*. Translated by Ewald Osers. Lexington, Mass.: D. C. Heath, 1970.

Hobsbawm, Eric J. *Bandits*, rev. ed. New York: Pantheon, 1981.

———. *Primitive Rebels*. New York: Norton, 1965.

Jacoviello, Michele. *La Sicilia dalle lotte per l'indipendenza dall'Italia all'autonomia regionale: 1943–1948*. Naples: Simone, 1978.

Jannuzzi, Lino. "Ricostruiamo venti anni dopo la vera storia della strage di Portella della Ginestra." *L'Espresso*, May 7 and 14, 1967.

Kefauver, Estes. *Crime in America*. Garden City, N.Y.: Doubleday, 1951; reprint ed., New York: Greenwood Press, 1968.

La Rosa, Roberto. "Nel 37° anniversario dell'autonomia." *Sicilia Indipendente*, May 1983.

La Rosa, Salvatore. "Trasformazioni fondiarie, cooperazione, patti agrari." In *Storia della Sicilia*, vol. 9, pp. 111–47. Palermo: Società editrice Storia di Napoli e della Sicilia, 1979.

Leca, Augusto. "Metamorfosi nel MIS in quattro anni di vita." *La Voce della Sicilia*, January 12, February 1 and 2, March 4, 1947.

Levi, Carlo. *Cristo si è fermato a Eboli*. Turin: Einaudi, 1945.

Liehm, Mira. *Passion and Defiance: Films in Italy from 1942 to the Present*. Berkeley: University of California Press, 1984.

Li Vecchi, Alfredo. "Autonomismo e separatismo." In *Storia della Sicilia*, vol. 9, pp. 277–95. Palermo: Società editrice Storia di Napoli e della Sicilia, 1979.

Lo Bianco, Giovanni. "Memoriale del Maresciallo Lo Bianco." *L'Ora*, December 9–30, 1961.

Loteta, Giuseppe. "Riapriamo il dossier su Portella della Ginestra." *L'Astrolabio*, March 15, 22, 29, 1970.

Lumia, Luigi. "La questione agraria nella zona del 'Vallone' in rapporto alle inchieste del 1875." *Nuovi Quaderni del Meridione* 13 (1975): 83–117.

Macaluso, Emanuele. *I comunisti e la Sicilia*. Rome: Riuniti, 1970.

———. *La mafia e lo stato*. Rome: Riuniti, 1971.

Mack Smith, Denis. *A History of Sicily: Modern Sicily after 1713*. New York: Viking, 1968.

———. *Italy: A Modern History*. Ann Arbor: University of Michigan Press, 1969.

———. "The Latifundia in Modern Sicilian History." In *Proceedings of the British Academy*, vol. 51, pp. 85–124. London: Oxford University Press, 1965.

Mannino, Frank. "Il Memoriale di Frank Mannino." Edited by Milziade Torelli. *Vita*, January 26–March 2, 1961.

Mannino, Stefano. *Mitra e poltrone*. Palermo: G. Denaro, 1964.

Marino, Giuseppe Carlo. *Partiti e lotta di classe in Sicilia: da Orlando a Mussolini*. Bari: De Donato, 1976.

———. *Storia del separatismo siciliano, 1943–1947*. Rome: Riuniti, 1979.

Maxwell, Gavin. *Bandit*. New York: Harper, 1956.

———. *Dagli amici mi guardi Iddio: Vita e morte di Salvatore Giuliano*. Milan: Feltrinelli, 1957.

Miller, James Edward. *The United States and Italy, 1940–1950*. Chapel Hill: University of North Carolina Press, 1986.

Molfese, Franco. *Storia del brigantaggio dopo l'Unita*, 4th ed. Milan: Feltrinelli, 1976.

Montalbano, Giuseppe. "Contributo all'inchiesta sulla mafia—Responsabilità (per associazione a delinquere) dei promotori, degli organizzatori e dei capi della banda Giuliano." *Montecitorio* 17 (May 1963): 75–79.

———. *L'autonomia della Regione Siciliana e alcune questioni di diritto processuale penale*. Palermo: G. Mori, 1952.

Nicolosi, Salvatore. *La leggenda di Giuliano: Vita di un fuorilegge.* Naples: "Il Tripode," 1977.

———. *Sicilia contro Italia: Il separatismo siciliano.* Catania: Carmelo Tringale, 1981.

Nocifora, Enzo. *Dal latifondo all'assistenza.* Milan: A. Giuffrè, 1981.

Pantaleone, Michele. *Mafia e politica,* 5th ed. Turin: Einaudi, 1978.

———. "La mafia e il potere." *L'Espresso,* November 30–December 21, 1958.

Parlatore, Tito. *L'eccidio di Portella della Ginestra: Requisitoria pronunciata al processo celebrato a Viterbo dinanzi alla Corte d'Assise dall'aprile 1951 al maggio 1952.* Rome: n.p., 1954.

Phillips, Dretha M. "Latin American Banditry and Criminological Theory." In *Bandidos: The Varieties of Latin American Banditry,* edited by Richard W. Slatta pp. 181–90. New York: Greenwood Press, 1987.

Popkin, Samuel L. *The Rational Peasant: The Political Economy of Rural Society in Vietnam.* Berkeley: University of California Press, 1979.

Presidenza della Regione Siciliana. *Le elezioni in Sicilia, 1946–1956.* Milan: A. Giuffrè, 1956.

Quatriglio, Giuseppe. "Turi Giuliano Sanfedista?" *Domenica del Giornale di Sicilia,* June 29, 1947.

Reece, Jack E. "Fascism, the Mafia, and the Emergence of Sicilian Separatism (1919–1943)." *Journal of Modern History* 45 (June 1973): 261–76.

Renda, Francesco. *Movimento di massa e democrazia nella Sicilia del dopoguerra.* Bari: De Donato, 1979.

———. *Socialisti e cattolici in Sicilia 1900–1904: Le lotte agrarie.* Caltanissetta-Rome: Sciascia, 1972.

Rizza, Jacopo. "Così trovai Giuliano." *Epoca,* August 25, 1951.

———. "Un giorno con Giuliano." *Oggi,* December 22 and 29, 1949, January 5, 1951.

Romano, Salvatore Francesco. *Storia dei Fasci Siciliani.* Bari: Laterza, 1959.

———. *Storia della mafia.* Milan: Mondadori, 1966.

Romita, Giuseppe. *Dalla Monarchia alla Republica,* 2d ed. Milan: Mursia, 1966.

Rossani, Mario. *Vita segreta del "Sire di Montelepre."* Rome: A. Chicca, 1955.

Sabetti, Filippo. *Political Authority in a Sicilian Village.* New Brunswick, N.J.: Rutgers University Press, 1984.

Samenow, Stanton E. *Inside the Criminal Mind.* New York: Times Books, 1984.

Sanna-Salaris. *Una centuria di delinquenti sardi.* Turin: Bocca, 1902.

Sansone, Vito, and Gastone Ingrascì. *Sei anni di banditismo in Sicilia.* Milan: Le Edizioni Sociale, 1950.

Schneider, Jane, and Peter Schneider. *Culture and Political Economy in Western Sicily.* New York: Academic Press, 1976.

Schneider, Peter. "Rural Artisans and Peasant Mobilisation in the Socialist International: The *Fasci Siciliani*." *The Journal of Peasant Studies* 13 (April 1986): 63–81.

Scianò, Giuseppe. "Ricordando Portella della Ginestra." *Sicilia Indipendente*, May 1983.

Sorgi, Antonino. "Quindici anni di lotte contadine." *Il Ponte* 15 (1959): 620–35.

Spanò, Aristide. *Faccia a faccia con la mafia*. Milan: Mondadori, 1978.

Stern, Michael. *No Innocence Abroad*. New York: Random House, 1953.

Tarrow, Sidney G. *Peasant Communism in Southern Italy*. New Haven, Conn.: Yale University Press, 1967.

Trionfera, Renzo. "Il figlio di Giuliano." *L'Europeo*, Dec. 18, 1960.

Vanderwood, Paul J. *Disorder and Progress: Bandits, Police and Mexican Development*. Lincoln: University of Nebraska Press, 1981.

———. "Nineteenth-Century Mexico's Profiteering Bandits." In *Bandidos: The Varieties of Latin American Banditry*, edited by Richard W. Slatta, pp. 11–31. New York: Greenwood Press, 1987.

Witcombe, R. T. *The New Italian Cinema: Studies in Dance and Despair*. New York: Oxford University Press, 1982.

Index